Impossible Things

An Adult Memoir

L. Renae Spann

©2025 L. Renae Spann All rights reserved.

No part of this publication may be reproduced, distributed, or transmitted in any form or by any means, including photocopying, recording, or other electronic or mechanical methods, without the prior written permission of the publisher, Parker Publishers, except in the case of brief quotations embodied in critical reviews and certain other non-commercial uses permitted by copyright law.

For permission requests, write to the author, addressed to:

L. Renae Spann

Dedicated to Seymour Metters III. My one true love and biggest supporter in my best years of life. He has accepted me for who I am and encourages me to be all that I can be. Never doubted that I could write this memoir and have trust in me. I thank him for bringing out the best in me. There is no one I would rather spend the rest of my life with.

About The Book

Although the advice and information in the book is believed to be true and accurate at the time of publication, neither the author nor the publisher can accept legal responsibility for any errors or omissions that may be made. The publisher makes no warranty, express or implied, about the material contained in this document.

This book reflects the author's present recollections of experiences over time. Some names and characteristics have been changed, some events have been compressed, and some dialogue has been recreated.

Table of Contents

Preface Acknowledging my Earthly Angels 1
Introduction 8
Chapter 1 Our Family 13
Chapter 2 My Childhood 24
Chapter 3 Growing Up Too Fast 43
Chapter 4 We're in The Army Now 61
Chapter 5 The Doctor 78
Chapter 6 College and Beyond 111
Chapter 7 Marriage No. 2 139
Chapter 8 Moving on Without My Mom 159
Chapter 9 Just Michelle and Me 196
Chapter 10 The Real Prince Charming 219
Chapter 11 Happily, Ever After 249
Chapter 12 My Unconventional Path to Success 265
About the Author 283
Gallery 285

Preface
Acknowledging my Earthly Angels

On my life's journey, God placed many phenomenal people along my path to assist in ordering my footsteps. I call these special people my Earthly Angels. Reminiscing, I realize that they were each placed in my life at specific times and for specific reasons. It was never by chance. I know each one was a divine intervention. I list them here by the order in which they came into my life, not necessarily by order of importance. They were all critical factors and willing participants in the mission of guiding me on my journey and directing me to my destiny. There were also Earthy Angels whose names I never knew. They only appeared briefly along my path to support and encourage me in my lowest times. I acknowledge and thank them for their positive effect on my journey.

My mother, Helena Spann, saw who I was and who I could be early on. She kept true to that positive image of me being someone special. The sacrifices she made not just for me but for our family have not gone unnoticed. She not only had the determination to give me what was necessary to survive a sometimes cruel world, but she was an example of how to press on in the face of adversity. She deposited the seed of faith in me and was obedient to raise me in the way I should go so that in

L. Renae Spann

her absence, I would know to look to God. Helena's sharing of God's love through the Bible and staying in constant prayer for me were the major components of my survival and success. Only now do I understand what she did for me. And I acknowledge my mother, Helena Spann, as my first Earthy Angel.

I had many co-workers in my young adult life, but there is one in particular who made an impact with her faith walk and belief in Jesus. She helped water the seeds that my mother planted in me. My fellow Jersey girl, Debbie Vaughn, is someone I met when I was a single mother working at a company in East Brunswick, NJ. I was a temporary secretary, and Debbie was a computer analyst. We met at the right time in our lives. My mother died months before and I was trying to fill my mother's shoes by helping my disabled younger sister while raising my teenage daughter. Debbie was extremely intelligent about many things and had wisdom that she was willing to share. She was a good role model for me because she was raising two children at that time. It made my life a little easier knowing that I had a new friend whom I could confide in and get advice on just about anything. Our friendship extends over 30 years now and she was called by God to assist me with this book that was prophesied to me over 26 years ago. I was able to share the good, bad, and ugly with Debbie and she did not judge me or waiver as my friend and Christian sister. She enthusiastically took on the challenge of listening to my life stories and comforted me whenever the pain of bad memories came up. I appreciate her diligent patience, persistence, and caring spirit when taking on the job of compiling my memoirs. Debbie Vaughn is designated as my second Earthly Angel.

My favorite cousin, Jean Griffin, was a vital woman of God in my life and she operated on powerful spiritual gifts. We called each other often when I lived in Baltimore. It wasn't until I started a personal relationship with the Lord that I noticed Jean's extraordinary gifts. She was never ashamed to praise the Lord in public as the spirit would move her. She had great knowledge of the Bible and read it constantly. I am thankful that she would pray for me and with me whenever I needed it. Jean and my mother always understood each other. My mother knew who Jean was and about her spiritual gifts. I greatly miss Jean. My third Earthly Angel, Jean Griffin, went home to be with the Lord in October 2024.

I find my dear friend, Cathy Talbert, to be the most fascinating of all my Earthly Angels. She came into my life at a time when I was homeless and in despair. Her cheerful and joyous manner instantly lifted my spirits when we met. I was searching for work at Lockheed Electrics in Norcross, GA. I did not know that Cathy would be my friend, Christian sister, and prayer partner for the rest of my life. Our sisterly bond is like no other. The level of trust and respect I have for her is unprecedented. Cathy has the gift of prophecy and, like all true prophets, what Cathy says, comes to pass. It was as though the Lord used her to order my footsteps out of my despair and give me the hope I needed to press on. With her gentle spirit, she gives strength, and encouragement, and makes me want to get closer to the Lord daily. Cathy nourished my faith walk and taught me even more about the Bible. She helped make me fearless in my life journey as I know now I have the power of Christ by my side. I am glad she is still in my life. May she continue to bless others as she has blessed me. Cathy Talbert is my fourth Earthly Angel.

I met Annette Pullman at Macy's at Norcross Mall in GA where I worked as a Sales Associate. She came in as a customer needing my assistance with bedding and we immediately clicked. I felt like I had known her for a long time because she was so easy to talk to. Annette played a major part in my life when, after only knowing her for three weeks, she lent me the money I needed to make my mortgage payment. I did not know anyone who would have that amount of money to help me or would freely lend it to me, but Annette did. She lifted the stress off of me so that I could better focus on looking for full-time work and helping my daughter through a crisis. God's timing was impeccable. I am thankful that Annette was obedient and led by the Spirit to lend me that money. In less than one month, I was able to pay her back. It was a faith walk for both of us. She has been an inspiration and encouragement for both my daughter and me to this day. Annette Pullman is my fifth Earthly Angel.

When I met Gladys Dark she was also a single, working mom like me. I had just changed jobs and was looking for work at a temp agency where she was a recruiter. At that time, I was in a family crisis with my daughter and I needed a job with a more flexible schedule. I also had to make enough money to keep my mortgage payment current. After telling Gladys of my situation with my daughter, she was instrumental in assisting me. She not only found me a temporary assignment, but she also facilitated the sale of my house a few months later. She was a licensed realtor and at one point, owned a house cleaning business. Because she helped with the quick sale of my house, I was able to move to Arlington, VA where I soon met my husband, Seymour Metters III. Gladys' extraordinary faith in God really impressed me and made me feel that everything would work out for my good. Gladys is a woman of many talents. She has moved from glory to glory as she helps others with her missionary work and several businesses. She uses her talents and creativity to reinvent herself and to do the will of God. Thank you, Jesus, for allowing me to cross paths with Dr. Gladys Dark, my sixth Earthly Angel.

Ruth Wilson came into my life when I was preparing for my wedding to Seymour Metters III in Arlington, VA. Ruth's husband at the time, Pastor Rick Hudock, counseled and married us. Pastor Hudock felt it was not appropriate for me to move in with Seymour while we prepared for the wedding. So, he and his wife, Ruth, offered to let me stay with them until the wedding. In those two months of staying at their home, I really got to know Ruth's genuine heart and dedicated spirit. She planned my wedding without charging me. Ruth was careful with every detail of the wedding as she knew it was ordained by God. Ruth and Pastor Rick Hudock had 4 beautiful girls that both Seymour and I still treat as our goddaughters to this day. I will always love and appreciate them for all they did at that precious time in my life. Ruth Wilson is my kind and sweet Earthly Angel number seven.

I thank God for using these and other extraordinary people to guide me along my path as He ordered my steps.

Arleen Wilson, Business Coach & Sr. Consultant

Arleen Wilson served as a mentor during my transition to CEO of Symtech Corporation. Although Seymour Metters III was my lead in navigating government contracting and day-to-day operations, it was Arleen who guided me in understanding the expectations and challenges of leadership as a Black woman in this industry. She helped me move from worker bee to Chief Executive Officer in a relatively short time, and her direction and support made that shift much easier.

Impossible Things

Arleen's knowledge of the government contracting world was matched by her wisdom and grace. She had been with Symtech long before I joined, working in the Human Resources Department. What gave her tremendous credibility in my eyes was how much she reminded me of my own mother — her unwavering dedication and her quiet strength.

Even while on dialysis for her kidneys, Arleen never missed work or complained. After her kidney transplant, she returned to work without hesitation or excuse. Like my mother, she had a strong constitution and an incredible threshold for pain. Her faith and positive attitude shone through, and I watched her manage everything from proposals and HR manuals to employee issues and secret security clearances — all while keeping the office harmonious.

Watching Arleen's example motivated me to work harder and absorb all I could to succeed as a CEO. A special kudos to my dear friend and colleague, Arleen A. Wilson, for going above and beyond to ensure my success. Much love, always.

L. Renae Spann

Introduction

When I was a little girl growing up on West 3rd Street in Plainfield, New Jersey in the 1960s and 1970s, one of my favorite movies was Rodgers and Hammerstein's Cinderella – the one that was made for television by CBS in 1965 and aired annually thereafter on channel 2. Back then, most people I knew had a black and white TV that only received seven channels and that was if you had a good roof antenna. There were no cable channels, no VCRs or DVDs. You had to buy the weekly TV guide magazine and study the broadcast schedule to know when to be in front of the television to see your favorite programs. If you missed something, you had to wait until the next time it was aired. So, for my favorite movie, Rodgers and Hammerstein's Cinderella, that wait could be a whole year before I would have the chance to watch it again.

Even so, I managed to watch it every time it aired. I was glued to the television set. I knew the dialog and the lyrics to every beautiful song dramatizing the story of a poor little girl who meets a charming prince, marries him, and lives happily ever after. There was not one Black character in that movie, but that didn't matter to me. There weren't many black characters on television and in movies at that time. I was used to watching shows where no one looked like me. I identified with Marsha Brady from the Brady Bunch, I wanted a house like theirs, and I was also Cinderella.

Impossible Things

I was a black girl growing up in an 80-year-old, 1,600 square foot house with 3 small bedrooms, one bathroom, living room, formal dining room, large kitchen with an old-fashioned pantry that had doors that entered from the kitchen and could then swing out to the dining room. The square footage did not include the unfinished attic and basement that showed its age. Those areas were kept only for storage. This little house on West Third Street was a source of pride for my parents as other family members and friends rented their homes. My parents were homeowners.

Even so, what people didn't know was that I was really a princess. I could see a different life. Someday, my prince would find me and it would be love at first sight. Then we would get married and live happily ever after. I knew it would happen. As the song says, "Impossible things are happening every day."

We were a family of six, my parents, Helena and Harmon, my older brother, Harmon Jr., my younger sisters, Darlene and Marlene, and me, Lucerchia Renae Spann, but everybody called me Renae. When we were just babies and toddlers, our family lived on the East end of Plainfield in a small apartment that had mice. This is all our parents could afford at the time, but my mother was determined to get us into better conditions. After a few years there, she found a vacancy in a 4-family house on West 3rd street in Plainfield where we lived in an upstairs, 3-bedroom apartment. This was so much better and we lived there until I was around 11 years of age. My father was a janitor at a Veterans Hospital, in Lyons, NJ. My mother worked the night shift at a factory down the street making rubber products. She worked the graveyard shift and saved for a down-payment on the house. Finally, we moved across the street to the small, two story, 3-bedroom house with a big backyard. That was the place we called home into our adulthood. We had a secure family life in Plainfield. Our financial resources were limited like most working-class Black families of that time, but we were well cared for. We had two hard working parents who loved us and, like other families, there were also challenges, secrets, and dysfunctions to be dealt with.

That was my reality, but I was a starry-eyed little girl with fantastic dreams. I dreamed of the day my prince would find me and of living in a house like the Brady Bunch. Believe it or not, I eventually got everything I wanted, even the prince! But it didn't come without many missteps and storms. I was naïve and had no idea how much harm existed in the world. I eventually found out that the world can be a dangerous and cruel place with many wolves in sheep's clothing, lurking in the shadows and in the broad daylight.

I have suffered traumas, cruelty, and abuse. I have been alone and terrified. But the one thing that got me through it all was my relationship with God. I have experienced so many miracles in my life, sometimes I can hardly believe my own story. My life has taught me that no matter what I am going through, God is always there guiding me. He has sent many angels my way when I needed help and He has ordered my steps through the most difficult situations. As you read my story, I want you to remember that there are no coincidences. I believe everything happens for a reason and all things can work together for your good. It has been my experience that God, with the help of His angels, will see you through the most difficult and devastating circumstances if you let Him. If you just ask, you can experience miracles.

As I was writing this book, a few people asked me what would make my book so interesting to read. What is the purpose and goal of writing my story? My chief reason is to break free from the chains that bound me for so many years. Because of the traumas in my life, guilt, shame, and fear became a part of my existence. These feelings attached themselves to me and made me feel damaged. I felt like I should hide and not let anyone know what I have been through. But I learned that there is no freedom in hiding. There is no healing in shame. I wanted to completely heal from the past and live my best life. So, I looked to God.

By focusing my attention on God, I started to see how He had been with me all along through every situation. He inspired me to write my story, but every time I tried, I realized it was too much for me to bear. It was too painful to relive the past and share what I had been through. Those memories brought up shame, fear, disappointment, and humiliation. How could I tell the world about all of my missteps and mistakes? What would people think of me?

Then my healing began. God taught me that forgiveness is essential for total freedom and complete healing. I had to be true to myself and bear all as I became aware of just how much trauma and disappointment I had experienced in my life. He slowly and gently walked me through all of the painful events of my past and healed them one by one, guiding me to first forgive myself. Then teaching me how to forgive others who hurt me. God helped me press past all the brokenness and receive the life that He has ordained for me. What a beautiful life it is!

The experiences I share in this book have caused discomfort and grief for me while writing but therein lies my freedom. There are no more secrets because my healing is in the sharing. Everything has finally been dealt with and is out in the open. The past no longer has power over me. I don't fear embarrassment or judgement from anyone because God is my judge. Truth be told, I know many people crave this level of freedom, healing, and courage to tell all in their lives and not worry about what others will think. I want you to know you absolutely can do it too.

This is the purpose and goal of sharing my story. I pray that this book will bless, encourage, and empower you to break free from the past that torments you. I want you to be inspired to look to God to find your total freedom and complete healing, to get everything that is coming to you, to tap into your heavenly account, and to get all your heart desires. I pray that you ultimately find and live your best life!

Chapter 1
Our Family

    Helena Fulton was an extraordinary and remarkable woman of color but often mistaken for a white woman. My mother, Helena, was born in Baltimore, Maryland on April 10, 1932 to Alice (Williams) Fulton, a caramel skinned, African American woman of 5' 7" and Pat Garrett Fulton, a fair skinned, mulatto man who stood a gigantic 7 feet tall. Helena was born a beautiful light skinned Black baby with jet black, straight hair. She was born on an Easter Sunday morning. They said she was born with a veil over her face, which is a medical anomaly, occurring in less than one out of 80,000 live births. It is an incredibly rare event where the baby is born encased in their amniotic sac. In much of the Black culture, it is said that babies born with a veil possess rare spiritual gifts which made Helena special from the very beginning. She was the oldest of 5 other siblings and was looked upon to lead the way and to be an example. I believe Helena did very well considering the rough time she had growing up.

    Helena's father, Pat Garrett, was an alcoholic and also a bootlegger. He made and sold liquor during the time of prohibition. Her mother, Alice, was a strict Seventh Day Adventist who always wore white nurse-type dresses when she went to church and work. At home, she wore an old house dress with large pockets where she kept a brown, paper bag of money. Alice was the submissive wife allowing Pat to take full charge of all family decisions.

My mother, Helena, grew up having to avoid sexual predators in her family and suffered abuse with beatings for no legitimate reason. Helena had to grow up fast. She had to work at an early age to help with family expenses. After finishing school, she worked two jobs and gave one of the paychecks to her mother. Going to school in Baltimore, she faced jealous or hostile kids who wanted to fight her because of her beautiful hair and fair skin. So, she became a brutal fighter to defend herself. Later, Helena desired to become a Baltimore police officer but failed the physical due to a heart murmur.

Helena had a high tolerance for pain as she suffered health issues all her life. Among her illnesses were Rheumatic Fever at 15 years of age, painful varicose veins, a slipped disc, colon cancer, rheumatoid arthritis, stomach ulcers, migraine headaches and a stroke that left her temporarily paralyzed on one side of her body. She also had an operation on a nerve in her neck, where she died and had a near death experience (NDE) while on the operating table. This is what made my mother an extraordinary and remarkable woman of God. She always kept the faith, bounced back and kept moving. I miss her so, if I can be half the woman she was, I will be a superwoman. She was my "shero."

When my mother saw her opportunity to leave Baltimore and venture into a better life, she jumped on it. She took a bus to

Impossible Things

New York where she worked as a cook for wealthy Jewish families. Although she never misled or tried to pass as white, she allowed employers to assume she was white and received a higher wage than she would have if they knew she was Black. Once, when my mother got hurt on the job when the elevator door trapped her foot and caused a broken ankle, she had to take time off from her job. My grandmother Alice, who had chestnut brown skin color, went to the house where my mom worked and picked up her check while Helena was on sick leave. When the employer saw that Helena's mother was black, she told my grandmother, Alice, that Helena could not come back to work there. From that time until my mother, Helena, died she worked in a factory, did office cleaning, cared for elderly people and was a seamstress. These various jobs allowed her to express herself creatively, making use of her many talents, and most importantly, she could be closer to home for us.

My father, Harmon Spann, was originally from Sumter, South Carolina and he was born on November 23, 1927. The year is not confirmed as a birth certificate was never generated. His mother was a 16-year-old unwed albino girl named Peg who gave him away to a neighboring family named Spann. There was no formal adoption. Harmon's life was even worse than Helena's as he literally picked cotton in the hot fields. He was given a tin plate, spoon and fork, designated for him exclusively. He ate his meals outhe back porch because the family believed that since his mom was albino, other kids could catch something from him. He had to pick cotton at an early age with his pockets sewn shut so he would keep working. That Spann family really treated him like a slave. He had to cater to them and do their bidding even as an adult. He was at their disposal. Harmon did not make it past the 5th grade and he was functionally illiterate with no major trade to make a decent living. Surprisingly, he was musically gifted and learned to play the guitar and organ without being able to read music. When Harmon got an opportunity to leave, he took it and migrated north to New York to make a better life for himself.

My parents met each other at a dance hall in Harlem. My mother was taken by how well my father danced and how he resembled the actor, Sidney Poitier. He was an extremely handsome man, about 5 '11, cocoa-brown skin, and had a suave and humble manner. My mother thought he was just what she dreamed of in a spouse. The week after they met, my mother thought it would be a good idea for him to come over so they could get to know each other better. Harmon came by and sat on the front steps with her and they shared some of their life experiences and became friendly. My father was never interested in my mother physically as a partner even though she had a beautiful face and gorgeous long, black, and wavy hair. Harmon was not attracted to full-figured, light skinned women. He knew that white women were taboo for Black men in the south. He felt Helena looked too white and would cause problems for him when they were seen together in public. My mother, however, was determined to get together with Harmon. She gave him $20 to go to the corner store. He was supposed to get some liquor for them to drink and a pack of Raleigh cigarettes.

Impossible Things

Harmon left and was gone for a few hours. Helena was concerned but continued to wait for him. Around 10:00 that night, a man named John Linen came and told her that Harmon asked him to bring back the bottle of liquor and a pack of Raleigh cigarettes to this address and a beautiful woman will be there waiting. Needless to say, Helena was hurt but she had to face the reality – Harmon did not feel the same about her. She decided to have a few drinks with John. They dated and within several months were married.

This marriage, of course, did not work as it was not built on love and they were not evenly yoked. John would stay out late at night and sometimes not come home at all until a few days later. With this type of conduct, Helena did not want to sleep with him as she was concerned about contracting a sexually transmitted disease. One night, John came home late and drunk and put a gun to Helena's head because she refused to have sex with him. When she got out of that situation, she left. Later, she met up again with Harmon and told him everything.

This time when Helena saw Harmon, she had a figure like a Coca-Cola bottle as she would say. She was just stunning and Harmon saw her differently. He also felt so bad that he sent John to meet her that night. They started dating even though my mother was still legally married to John. Several months later, Helena officially got divorced and married my father Harmon. It was not until all of us kids were grown did we figure it out. After counting down from their marriage date, we realized that my brother Harmon, Jr. had actually been conceived while

Helena was still married to John Lynnon. We thank God we all are from the same mother and father.

Ever since I can remember we have always called our mother by her first name, Helena and called our father 'My Daddy.' Helena said we girls called her Mommy until my brother, Harmon Jr., came back from living with our grandparents. Harmon Jr. once lived with our grandparents in Baltimore for many months after Helena had a stroke. He lived with our grandparents while Helena recuperated and regained her strength. When Harmon Jr. returned home to the family, he noticed that we were calling our mother Mommy. He immediately said, "That's not mommy, that's Helena." We knew most children did not call their mother by her name like that. It was considered disrespectful. But until this day, the name, Helena, is a term of endearment to us. It is an expression of our love and respect.

Our family life on West 3rd street was good. We were well loved and cared for. Helena was a dedicated wife and mother. She would come home from her factory job early in the morning and wake us up. She would get us ready for school, fix our lunches and make us walk over 2 miles to Jefferson Elementary school with other children in the neighborhood. Kids nowadays all have to be driven everywhere. We really never missed Helena because she was always there for us. She would go to sleep as soon as we left for school and when we got home she would get us changed into our play clothes. While we went out to play, she would fix dinner then call us in to eat and do our homework. At around 7 PM, she would be getting us ready for bed and have just a few hours to herself before gearing up to go back to her job at the factory on the graveyard shift. My father, Harmon, worked at Lyons Veterans Administration Hospital in Lyons, New Jersey as a janitor from 6:30 AM until 3:30 PM. With their work schedules, we had the benefit of both parents being there for us at all times. No sitter was needed and we were not latchkey kids.

Harmon Jr. was the oldest of the four children. He was a complicated child. When he was 3 years old, he was sent to live with our grandmother, Alice, in Baltimore for about a year. Our mother suffered a stroke that left her paralyzed on her left side. Both Darlene and I were just toddlers and my father couldn't handle all three of us while also caring for our mother. So, Harmon was sent to our grandmother. When my mother recovered from the stroke, he came back to New Jersey to live with us. I believe his time in Baltimore had a negative effect on him, but it was not discovered until we went to school. Harmon's elementary school teacher told my mother that his learning was falling behind and that he should go to a special school for the developmentally challenged.

I was the second born. I came along when Harmon Jr. was about 14 months old. I was the first daughter and a daddy's girl. I would run to My Daddy whenever he came in the door and he would pick me up. That was our thing. I loved having all the attention on me and I soaked it up. I guess that was the beginning of the drama queen in me. I always had a flair for the dramatic.

L. Renae Spann

My next younger sister, Darlene, and I were the best of friends because we were so close in age. We were born only 16 months apart. Even though she had a serious personality and I was very playful, together we thought of creative games and things to play with. It was a lot of fun. We went to the same schools together, but I was one grade ahead of Darlene. We had a close childhood and a great relationship that I thought could never be broken.

I was often told a story of when Darlene and I were really young. Darlene was old enough to walk and my father was coming through the door. Darlene ran to My Daddy so he could pick her up the way he usually did me. I, being older, ran past Darlene and pushed her down so that he could pick me up first. Well, My Daddy spanked my little legs and told me that I was wrong to push my little sister, another indication that I would have to learn to share the spotlight. I was the drama queen and Darlene was the smart one.

Darlene was an excellent student. She was always very bright and learned quickly. She still has that ability to this day, just the brightest in the family when it comes to education. I guess that is why my mom didn't think she'd have to be concerned about Darlene. I, on the other hand, was very mischievous, so all the attention was diverted to me. That may be the cause of some form of resentment that eventually developed between us. I didn't know our close relationship would be tested when we became teenagers.

Impossible Things

Marlene was the baby sister that came into our family when I was 9 years old. She was born November 22, 1968. She was an unexpected pregnancy for my mom because my mother was going into menopause. My mother smoked and drank coffee heavily with all her pregnancies before it was confirmed that this could be harmful to a fetus. Marlene was born premature and had many complications. One major issue was seizures. Marlene had seizures for years.

There was a time my mother went to the supermarket and we older kids were watching Marlene when she went into a seizure on the couch. Darlene stepped up to handle her situation while I called the ambulance. I was so scared. I went outside to wave the ambulance down and could not go back into the house again. I couldn't stand to see Marlene in that fragile state. Minutes after the ambulance left with Marlene, my mother pulled up. She told us to take all the bags out of the trunk of the car. Seconds after we got the last bag out and slammed the trunk, she took off to the hospital like a bat out of hell These types of occurrences with Marlene were frequent and nerve racking for me as I was always scared to be left alone with her.

All of us kids agreed that our father was the nurturer and our mother the disciplinarian. My father was a mild-mannered, soft-spoken man of few words, but when he spoke, there was wisdom. Sometimes people mistook his kindness for weakness, but he was anything but weak. He was just patient and not easily angered. When pushed to the edge, our father came out fighting to everyone's surprise. I think I inherited this trait from him. I would fool people into believing that I was a follower when I knew I was a leader. I just kept the peace and did not like confrontation. My Daddy taught us to pray each night before going to bed and Helena, who read the Bible constantly, sent us off to Sunday school every Sunday. Together, they made sure we knew Jesus. This made for a good and balanced childhood growing up.

Buying the house on West 3rd Street was a huge accomplishment for Helena. That made a major shift in our status as not too many black folks we knew owned a house. It was all my mother talked about, buying and maintaining her own house. She said that we should always think about our housing situation and pay the mortgage to keep our house no matter what. Unfortunately, less than a year after the house was purchased, Helena slipped and fell on the job and she had to go on disability. A year after that, My Daddy went on disability as well. This changed things with all the plans Helena had for the house. The focus became to keep the mortgage paid and with just the bare essentials.

There were times when we had to go without lights or gas for a while, but the mortgage was paid. Even when the hot water tank broke and they could not afford another one right away, we boiled water for a bath until I just got tired of bringing a bucket of water upstairs. At that time, I was 18 or 19 years old. I had completed basic training in the US Army and had a job. So, I purchased a new water heater from Rickel Home Centers where I worked as a security guard. Another time the toilet was not working, so we had to pour water in it to make it flush because we didn't have money for a plumber.

Impossible Things

As I recall, we were the last people on our street to get a color television. My mother surprised us one day when she told us to go to the car and get the color television out of the trunk. We were so excited, we nearly lost our minds. Yes, we were truly loved and cared for. Both parents took pride in all of us as we grew up. Eventually, Harmon Jr. and I enlisted in the US Army and Darlene went off to college. The baby girl, Marlene, graduated from high school and also went to college. All of us were raised to be able to provide for ourselves and become good Christians and productive citizens. Our happiness was everything to Helena and Harmon.

My Daddy died of a heart attack when we were young adults, and we lost Helena around Thanksgiving only six years after his death. Our parents died young; both before the age of 60. Their deaths were a devastating loss for us. Even so, we thank God we were able to have their love and wisdom throughout our childhood to help shape our lives for the better.

L. Renae Spann

Chapter 2
My Childhood

In July 1967, I was 9 years old. Our neighborhood was not impoverished, but you wouldn't see families with large modern houses either. It was a working-class community of modest homes where kids typically walked to school in the morning and spent afternoons playing in the street. West 3rd Street would have an annual Memorial Day parade with marching bands, fire trucks and fanfare. There were girl's step teams that danced in white majorette boots and short cheerleading skirts. Young men performed in drill teams wearing military style uniforms, carrying wooden rifles that they skillfully twirled in many directions. These teams were from Plainfield and other black communities throughout New Jersey. It was spectacular as they marched proudly and showcasing their skills in a display of African American culture Many towns had these parades back then. All the neighborhood families and those from out of town would line the street in anticipation. There was clapping, cheering, and laughing as everyone enjoyed the parade. There were balloons and candy for the kids. It was a highlight of the year.

However, less than two months after this wholesome community event in 1967, our neighborhood and the city of Plainfield, New Jersey was overtaken by rioting. The Plainfield riot was only one of more than 150 urban uprisings in the United States during the racially turbulent 1960s. There were many racially based social problems at that time and the country was experiencing unrest. Black communities were becoming resentful due to unfair treatment. In Plainfield, New Jersey, the Black community became frustrated with unfair banking practices like discriminatory lending and Black families being segregated to the West End of the city. There were also issues like high unemployment and harsh treatment by local law enforcement. All these issues came to a head in the middle of July that summer.

My siblings, friends and I were just elementary school kids. We were too young to comprehend the magnitude of the social unrest. We just felt the excitement and wanted to be a part of it all. I am a little embarrassed to share that my siblings and I, along with other neighborhood friends, participated in looting that day.

The rioting started downtown and spread out to other areas of the city. Around the corner on West 4th Street, there was a small grocery store. We saw that older teens had broken the window. We didn't know why everyone was so upset, but we knew it had to do with white people and our chance to be powerful and free. We saw older kids going into the store and getting whatever they wanted without paying for it, so we went too. To us kids, it felt like a free-for-all and we believed we deserved it because we didn't have a lot. We got sodas, candy, chips, cigarettes, and Argo corn starch (the kind you can eat). We went home, left our loot, and went back for more. When we came back home and Helena realized what was happening, she would not let us leave the house again. Had she not stopped us, we would have gone back to the store a third time.

We didn't have a clue how dangerous it was to be on the streets that afternoon. Older kids were letting off steam through looting and vandalism. Police were everywhere. I never saw the neighborhood parents so angry and scared. They were mostly worried about their rebellious teens who, against their wishes, had gone downtown to the epicenter of the unrest. Parents were afraid their children would be hurt or shot by police. Soon, the National Guard arrived in our neighborhood. Army tanks came down Pond Place across from our house with loudspeakers saying, "Everyone off the street now!" I remember it was such a bizarre thing to see.

The newspapers reported that there was one death, 167 arrests, and approximately $700,000 in property damage to businesses due to the riot of July 16 through July 17, 1967. Another result of this rioting was that many White residents moved out of Plainfield, NJ. To put this incident into perspective with this tumultuous time in our national history, Martin Luther King, Jr would be assassinated nine months later (April 1968) and Robert F. Kennedy only two months after that (June 1968). As a little girl, I can say that I had very little understanding of the events of that time. I just knew that some things seemed unfair and that I envisioned a different life for my future. I deserved it.

Impossible Things

When I was eleven or twelve, a white classmate from Hubbard Jr High School invited me to her birthday party. She came to me in school and whispered in my ear, "Here's the invitation. I'd like you to come to my birthday party." She whispered because she didn't want everybody in the class to know that she was not inviting them. It was going to be a bowling party. I had never been bowling or to anything like a bowling party. I was excited.

I told Helena that I had been invited. So, she bought me a new dress. On the day of the party, I put on my new dress. I was all dressed up and My Daddy dropped me off at their house in a beautiful part of town. It was a nice house, and I was the first one there. I went in and met the girl's older brother and sister who were twins. Then we went into the basement. As I looked at their house I was thinking, "Oh my God!"

You see, I always had this thing with the Brady Bunch house. I still love it even today. It was a mid-century style home with a large staircase, open dining room, and a sunken living room. I would always think, "Why can't we have a house like that?" I wanted a house like that. As a little kid from the west side of Plainfield, I was craving it and now here I was in a house that was very similar to the Brady Bunch house only it was on the east end of Plainfield where mostly wealthy whites lived in the 60's and 70's. It was so luxurious.

The girl's mother was getting things ready for the birthday party. She explained that we were all about to get into the van and go to the bowling alley. Again, I had never been bowling before. We arrived at the bowling alley and joined the rest of the kids. There I realized that I was the only one in a dress and the only Black child. The girl's mother initially didn't seem upset about it though. She told her daughter to invite whomever she wanted and I just happened to be one of the kids she invited. But I could tell that the mother wasn't excited about me being there. I could feel it and I would feel it more so when we got back to the house later.

All the children were bowling. I'll never forget, that even though I had on a dress, I was killing it! I was knocking those pins DOWN! It turned out that I was a natural. I still enjoy bowling to this day. I love it. After bowling, we all went back to the house where the party picked up. They had a Build-Your-Own-Sundae ice cream bar all set up. This is when I knew the mother wasn't thrilled about me being there. I could feel that she was only tolerating me. I didn't really know why but now I can understand what was happening.

The mother had all the ice cream and toppings laid out on the kitchen island. We could get our ice cream and toppings, scoop this, and sprinkle that -- whatever we wanted. I had never seen anything like that before. Everybody stood in line. I was about the 4th kid in the line. When it was my turn, I was so excited that my ice cream was going everywhere. Sprinkles were going on the floor. I was piling it up, just piling it up, because we didn't have ice cream like this at my house. My mother never set up anything like that at our house. You see, what I'm saying, right? How would I know about these things if I had never been exposed to them? The girl's mother knew that I didn't fit in. She had known from the minute she saw me.

I had been killing it at the bowling alley and they were just amazed. I was the athletic Black girl, you know? The older twins had taken to me readily. We were talking a lot and laughing together. I was a very excitable child, pretty much the same as I am as an adult. I haven't changed much, always smiling and laughing. Soon after we finished our ice cream, the mother was telling her husband, "Well, maybe it's time to take Renae home now." Yeah, it was time to take me back to my side of town. My Daddy dropped me off and they said they would bring me back. So, her husband took me home.

As we drove back to my part of town, I noticed as we turned a certain corner my mood was starting to change. Even though my family had a house, it was not like theirs. It wasn't the Brady Bunch house. A lot of black families didn't even own a house back then. We owned a house, but it was nowhere near the magnitude of my white friend's house. As we drove back to my neighborhood, I could see people hanging on the corners.

I'm telling you this to say that this childhood experience made me want better even at that young age. Because the only family trips we would take were to Baltimore, Maryland, where my mother's family lived. That was the experience of a lot of Black kids back then going south to visit family. This experience was the first time I had a close look at how the more affluent families lived. It helped to shape my aspirations for a better life in my future and a new spacious dream home. This is when my love of houses began.

Like a lot of Black kids back then, we would go south to visit family during school breaks. That's where we kids would live during the summers. So, I could say I also had a life in Baltimore. When we went to Baltimore every summer, I experienced another style of living that was different from our life in Plainfield. I always wanted to see my cousins and have fun but their homes were not as neat and clean as my mother kept our house. I was always happy to see my cousins but not so happy to be in Baltimore.

Our parents drove us to Baltimore and dropped us off there. We had a choice to live with Helena's sister, Nettie Hodge, or her mother, Alice Fulton. They lived in different areas. Our grandmother, Alice, lived in downtown inner-city Baltimore at 2029 West Lanvale Street. It was a rough, majority-black community. I don't have a lot of specific memories of my grandmother though. She was like a shadow and very mellow.

Our Grandma Alice worked as a nurse's aide. She was a Seventh-Day Adventist and active in her church. I remember her being a medium fair-skinned lady, about 5'5" with a small frame, wearing white utility/nurse-like dresses and frequently attending church. She always had a blue rinse in her hair. That was a thing back then. When women had gray hair, they would go to the salon and get a blue rinse. My grandmother would always carry a bag of money in her apron. It was the weirdest thing. She'd always keep the money in a small brown paper bag.

Impossible Things

When we begged for money when the ice cream man came around, she'd say, "I don't have any money." But we knew she had all that money in a paper bag in her apron. I remember that distinctly, although I was much too young to know what that was all about.

I also remember that there was a padlocked chain wrapped around the freezer at Grandma Alice's house, which I thought was peculiar. We never had anything like that at home in Plainfield. But now, looking back on it and talking with my sister, I believe it was because her adult daughter, Aunt Juanita, lived there. Her son, Harrison, was a heroin dealer who also lived there after Granddaddy died. So, to keep people from stealing things from the freezer, I guess she got in the habit of always locking it up like that.

When my mother was young, she worked two jobs and gave one of the paychecks to my grandmother. I'm sure there must have been a reason for this, but I don't know what it was. With Grandma Alice, I don't know what exactly went on or what kind of family dynamics were present. It just wasn't clear to me as a child.

My grandfather, Pat Garret Fulton, was a handsome man who was extremely light-skinned. His black hair was slightly straight but wavy, almost resembling that of an Italian man. He was very tall, close to seven feet, and with a broad build. We called him Granddaddy. I remember him having to duck as he walked through doorways to keep from bumping his head on the door frame. His height and size made him an intimidating presence, not violent or mean, just daunting in appearance. He was an alcoholic and had been a bootlegger during prohibition. Granddaddy never talked much and if he did, I don't really remember what the topic of discussion was, but I knew he ruled with an iron hand because when he talked, everyone shut up. He carried a flat metal flask of liquor in his back pocket. He wore dark suits with suspenders, I always thought he looked important. I believe there were family secrets that were kept from us children and we can only speculate what type of family dysfunction was under Granddaddy's rule. All I know is that when my mother was able to leave the family house and make a life for herself, she jumped at the chance.

My Uncle Harrison was my mother's brother and a heroin dealer. Once we went to visit Baltimore around Christmas time. This was not our usual summer visit. It was winter and our mother didn't have much money that year. I remember she was in the backroom talking to my Uncle Harrison. I was young, around ten, and eavesdropping on their conversation. Uncle Harrison was as high as a kite, his face was red as he too was very light-skinned like Granddaddy. I could tell because he was mumbling when he talked. He said to Helena, "Well, what is Christmas looking like?" She told him that Christmas was not looking good because of bills and other circumstances, and we kids were not going to have Christmas that year. She just didn't have the money. I'll never forget this. Uncle Harrison reached into his sock and pulled out a wad of money. It was a big roll of bills. He started counting off several 100-dollar bills, maybe $500 or so. Then he gave that money to my mother for Christmas and

Impossible Things

I backed away from the door. I knew we were going to have Christmas that year.

I'm not here to judge and I hope you aren't either. Everybody had to do what they had to do and will answer to God at the appropriate time. But I think that's the way the family accumulated their wealth, my grandfather through bootlegging back in the day and Uncle Harrison selling heroin.

The family lived at 2029 West Lanvale Street in Baltimore. They had a row house with two floors and a basement. Directly across the street from where Grandma Alice and Granddaddy lived was the house where my two aunts lived. Minerva and Juanita were my mother's sisters. Their house, like Grandma's house, was not very clean, in fact messier and more unorganized. It had no proper bedding or furniture that looked nice.

Aunt Minerva was a large overweight, dark-skinned, pretty, and quiet woman who wore glasses. She had a sweet, gentle, spirit and she mostly took care of us by doing our hair and talking to us when we were at that house. I can't remember much more about her but knew she was the youngest of my mother's family. Minerva was never married and had five children. Of the five children, three had the same father and two had different fathers. One of the children was raised by the father. I think this man may have been married and wanted his child to live in better conditions. The Health and Human Services Department pressured Minerva not to have any more children or they would take away her welfare benefits. She did get pregnant after the warnings and attempted a back-alley abortion in Baltimore. After the procedure, she went to work as an aid in the hospital. When she went to the bathroom to handle her excessive bleeding she passed out on the floor and became unconscious. She never did wake up and died from hemorrhaging to death. We are now politically regressing to those days by doing away with legal abortions. However, legislation will not stop desperate women from seeking abortions as a remedy to an unwanted pregnancy. I say let the government stay out of these matters and let the Lord have the final judgment.

I believe Aunt Minerva may have been influenced by her older sister, Aunt Juanita, who I think was a nymphomaniac. Juanita was overweight but light-skinned like my mother and Granddaddy. She was also bossy and mean-spirited. When she talked in her loud raspy voice and heavy Baltimore accent it always sounded authoritative, boisterous, and argumentative to me as a child. As I look back with adult eyes, I believe Juanita ran a little whore house there, right across the street from Grandma and Granddaddy. The reason I suspect that is because when we were kids, we would sleep at their house with our cousins and it was dysfunctional, not an appropriate environment for children. Grandma Alice would have us run over there from her house at night when it was time to go to bed. Some of the things that went on there were not normal for kids to be exposed to. It just wasn't good.

One night our Aunt Juanita had a woman who was very thin and drunk using the room right next to the kid's bedroom.

Impossible Things

The wall had an opening where you could see through from our room into the next room. There was a curtain hung in the opening to obstruct seeing into the other room. The drunk woman had a man come up to have sex with her in the next room. We, the children, were in bed in our room, but the woman kept yelling that we were peeking through the curtains and watching them. The curtain, in fact, was blowing back and forth due to a fan that was on in the room. My cousin, Violet, who was the same age as me, was afraid that we would get into trouble. So, she screamed downstairs to Aunt Jaunita to explain that the fan was causing the curtain to move. We did not want to get into trouble. Back then, you knew if you did something bad, you might get a whooping and nobody wanted that. We were quiet. The drunk woman and her guest continued their encounter. We heard moans, groans, and unfamiliar sounds from that room. Being so young, we did not know what was happening with this strange woman and unknown man. They had no respect for us children in the next room with nothing but a small curtain to separate them from us. Since my sister, brother, and I were only there in the summer, we were not exposed to this as much as our cousins who lived there year-round.

    In the morning, my aunts would wake us up and instead of cooking and feeding us, they would tell us to go back to Grandma's. We would run across the street with just our underwear and T-shirts on. I guess that's what kids did back then. It was no big deal when we were little. We'd go across the street and Grandma would fix us something to eat at her house. That was where we would eat, maybe take a bath, and put on clean clothes. We weren't very well-kept children, but they did take care of us. Looking back on the situation as an adult, I see that they could have done better for us kids. I believe it was a whore house they were operating across the street. Grandma Alice never said anything, it's just the way things were. These were my mother's people in Baltimore and these are my memories.

This was what it was like in the ghetto in Baltimore in the summers. We were not aware that it was the ghetto. It's just how we grew up. People sold snow cones out of their basements through a small window, and we bought them. Black people would come around with horse-drawn wagons selling things like fruit, vegetables, and crabs. I believe they called them Arabs. They would announce what they were selling as they came down the street. They would sing out, "Watermelons!" or "Crabs!" or whatever. We played in the street or on the railroad tracks. It was rough playing there because it was just a rough place.

Darlene and Harmon loved living in Baltimore during the summer. But Darlene would always come back at the end of the summer with injuries. She was accident-prone. So, she would get hurt every year -- stitches, a broken arm, whatever. But that was where she and Harmon Jr. wanted to be for the summer. Less rules, more freedom, free-range range-kids, and more excitement.

They were just rough and that was why I didn't want to stay in Baltimore at Grandma's house. I was a scared kid and

Impossible Things

didn't like to fight. We had a choice. So, I would choose to stay with my other aunt, Nettie Hodge. We called her Aunt Net. Since Aunt Net, her kids, and Uncle Raleigh all looked white, they raised their children like that. In fact, Uncle Raleigh looked a lot like my Granddaddy, Pat Garrett Fulton, extremely light-skinned, tall, and husky. I can say, I liked living with this family. I came out skating every summer, unscathed because I went and stayed where it was safe every day. I went to the white church for Sunday School. It was really like a whole white existence like they were a white family. My mother always told Aunt Net not to raise her children as though they were white. But she did and I think some of them had issues later in life because of it.

Aunt Net lived near Edmondson Village. Today, Edmondson Village really has a terrible reputation. You know neighborhoods go through transitions over time. I believe it's drug-infested now. But back then, it was a good area. Their family lived in a nice neighborhood, had many white neighbors, and went to a white church. It was calmer and settling at Aunt Net's house and that was what I liked. So, my mother would leave me with her. I spent my summers with Aunt Net, Uncle Raleigh, and their kids.

They had 6 kids at the time. Robert Frances was Net's son. She had him out of wedlock and then my grandfather made the man marry my aunt. Back then, that was what they did, but that marriage never worked out. He was abusive and my mother pretty much stepped in and took care of Robert, bought him everything and all that. My mom treated Robert like he was her son. Aunt Net had five children with Uncle Raleigh. Those are the ones I grew up with every summer.

Aunt Net's husband, Uncle Raleigh, didn't drive because he was an alcoholic. A co-worker would pick him up every day and take him to work. Then on the weekends, Uncle Raleigh would take all of us kids in a taxicab to the supermarket in Emerson Village. We'd all walk with him in the aisles and put everything in the cart that was on a list. After he had paid for everything and put the groceries in the back of the cab, he would send us all back home in the cab. Then he would go to the bar. This was a weekly thing that they did. So, looking back at it now, Aunt Net and her children lived a kind of sheltered life. Uncle Raleigh was a provider. He did the responsible thing first. He made sure that he provided for his family.

That's what I said when I gave his eulogy years later, I said he was a provider. I said that he appreciated the institution of marriage. He did what a man was supposed to do traditionally in a marriage. I had to give it to him, a guy who stayed and took care of five kids and a stepson. As I said, my cousin Robert was from a previous marriage and not his biological child. This child was coco brown and everybody else was light-skinned. Uncle Raleigh took on that child as his own. Robert also came to stay with us for a while in Plainfield, New Jersey.

I'm looking back now and thinking about how spending those summers with Aunt Net's family helped shape my outlook on life. It was a whole lot better than Inner City Baltimore. Even though it was a little boring, I felt safer and calmer because there was no drama and roughness like in the city. Aunt Net's family was like a blue-collar white family. As a child, I noticed that the way they lived was better than our family in Plainfield, New Jersey. Although up north we had a much larger house with a big backyard, good schools, and a clean, organized home, the area was experiencing more poverty and "white flight" after the riots. The area where Aunt Net lived was better than ours. Their town was better, I noticed that as a kid. Early on, I noticed that white people had more and I didn't understand why. I thought if they could have all of this, then I could have it too. These observations at a young age left a deep impression on me and guided my understanding of real estate markets and property purchase decisions much later in life.

My mother, Helena, worked hard to take care of us. She worked in a factory, cleaned offices, took care of elderly people, and was a seamstress. She worked to keep the mortgage and bills paid. She wanted to fix up the house and make a better life for us. Her dreams were never realized due to all her ailments and the limitations of working full-time. Then at age 31, Helena suffered a stroke which left permanent damage. She noticed that her good math ability was gone along with her extremely high energy level. My mother eventually had to go on disability but kept a part-time office cleaning job on the side. No matter how much pain she was in, she kept working with an agency cleaning offices at AT&T in Piscataway, New Jersey.

Helena strived to elevate us to at least the lower middle class by becoming a homeowner. She tried desperately to have our house remodeled with nice furniture and décor but never was able to realize that dream. She and my father focused on making the mortgage payments and keeping food in the fridge and pantry. I never remember a time when we were hungry. We kids did not realize the sacrifices that were being made for us. Like most children, we took things for granted.

My brother, Harmon Jr., had a special set of challenges as a kid. We now understand that any child who learns differently because of dyslexia, autism, or educational difficulties is identified as such and given special education services. Back then, I believe Harmon Jr. was just misunderstood and not accurately tested to identify his educational needs. Because of this, he struggled academically and socially.

Harmon Jr. did not care if he had a lot of friends or not. He was not concerned with what people thought and never tried to please others or to fit in. He was a peculiar kid, but he was harmless. He would follow the older kids sometimes and get into trouble. Then they would always blame him if something went wrong. He was an easy scapegoat for them.

One day when Harmon Jr. was 11 years old, he was blamed for something that happened in the neighborhood. My mother believed what they had accused him of, so she gave him a whooping and told him to stay the remainder of the day in his room. Harmon was so upset that he was lied to and punished, that he ran away. When he had not returned by evening, my mother called the police to look for him. He never came home that night. I remember my mother saying that she would never punish Harmon Jr. again for what others said. She was so worried that she waited on the porch all night for news of his whereabouts.

Around 8:30, the next morning, Harmon Jr. came running up to the house breathing heavily. His clothes were ripped and he had scars on his arms and legs. We all wondered what had happened to him. When Helena asked him where he had been, we were all shocked at the answer.

Apparently, Harmon Jr. had walked over 15 miles to a Bradlees department store in South Plainfield, NJ. Once there, he read comic books and played with toys until he became sleepy. At that point, he went to sleep under a rack of clothes in the store. When Harmon woke up several hours later, he found himself alone locked in the dark store and it was closed. He saw a counter with fountain drinks, so he helped himself to a drink and some snacks. After a while, he became afraid of the manikins everywhere in the dim lighting. He knew that he had to get out of there before daylight or he would be in trouble. So, he exited through the back door which immediately triggered an alarm. Terrified, Harmon Jr. climbed over a barbed wire fence and kept running until he got home.

I'm sure there are more details to this story but this is what I remember. I have so many questions like how did he find his way back home? Who runs away to a department store and stays the night? This type of thinking was typical for my brother. He was a strange child, and this was the kind of situation my mother had to deal with. Eventually, the school was able to persuade my mother to place Harmon Jr. in a special school for developmentally challenged students when he was in Junior High school.

My mother was constantly in pain from her many ailments which made her a bit frustrated and irritable although she was still attentive to us kids. She tried to give us everything our hearts desired when she could and cooked the best meals that I still miss today. Helena was not the kind of mother who would hug or kiss us. Her way of showing affection was cooking a good meal, making sure we had the best clothes she could sew for us, and making the house loving, clean, and orderly. All I can say is that I'll always love my momma. No matter how tough the challenges were, she did the absolute best she could for our family.

Chapter 3
Growing Up Too Fast

I feel bad now when I think of my teenage years and how I gave my mother so many problems. I got into much mischief by following my two older cousins, Mirt and Carol. My mother, being sickly, had her hands full with a husband, three teenagers, and a special needs child. She trusted my older cousins to watch out for me when I was out with them. They gave Helena false assurance when they were actually doing the opposite. Mirt and Carol were two high school dropouts who were jealous of my sister and me. I looked up to them like big sisters, but they did not have my best interest at heart. Hanging out with them and their friends, I learned all the wrong things and they had fun teaching me. They taught me things like how to smoke and how to stuff tissue in my bra to look older. They got me hooked on cigarettes and beer by the age of twelve. I had such a bad habit that I sneaked cigarettes from Helena.

I had a way of taking cigarettes from Helena without her knowing. I would take a new pack from her carton of cigarettes and carefully open the pack from the bottom. Then I was able to remove a few cigarettes, glue the pack back together, and place it back in the carton. My plan was ingenious and it was several months before my mother found out. I got greedy and took too many cigarettes from a pack which she noticed. It is amazing what some children can devise to get what they want and circumvent their parents' supervision.

In the fall of 1975, I was fourteen and beginning high school. I was a mischievous girl. I was anxious, not well-disciplined, and already having fun doing things that older girls did. My high school years started pleasant, however. Back then, some high schools had sororities and fraternities. I wanted to be a part of something. So, I decided to join the sorority at my high school. It was called the Iota Psi Omicron Sorority. These high school sororities mimicked the college sororities with pledging and hazing being a big part of the initiation process. So, we were required to do whatever dumb, crazy things they told us to do.

I remember having to come to school in dressy evening gowns one day. We had to do silly, embarrassing things in the hallway. Another time we were at somebody's house for initiation. We didn't have to drink alcohol or anything like that but, we were blindfolded and made to eat a disgusting concoction of food. They spoon-fed it into our mouths and I guess they were expecting us to throw up or something. We were holding this horrible-tasting goulash in our mouths but, it wasn't all that horrible to me. I didn't throw up, it was no big thing. Then they hit our butts with a paddle. I don't remember all the silly things we had to do to join the sisterhood. The sorority thing was a flop for me though. I don't even remember if I completed the initiation process or not. I guess it never really appealed to me to even go further with it, but it was an attempt to be a part of something at Plainfield High School.

Impossible Things

Plainfield, New Jersey was known for having the best-looking girls and the boys would come from Newark, New Jersey to get one of those beautiful Plainfield girls. Well, needless to say, I was one of those girls. I had become boy crazy under Mirt and Carole's tutelage and it was all to my detriment. There were so many handsome guys to choose from and they were gorgeous!

I had my very first boyfriend, Jasper Miller, at age 14. That year, I was going to be 15, and a big birthday party was being planned. Most girls have a Sweet Sixteen, but I had a "Sweet Fifteen" party. I was ahead of myself age-wise and spent my time around the older girls. So, they had a surprise birthday party for me at my house. We all got dressed for the party, and that day was when Jasper and I became close. It wasn't that night, but the following night we became intimate.

As a result of all my boy chasing, I got myself into an early teen pregnancy when I was 15. This caused a lot of grief for my mom, Helena, and trouble for me at school. I was pregnant and I still had to go to school and deal with all the stresses associated with it.

Jasper Miller was my neighbor who lived across the street. He wasn't the best-looking boy on the block, but he had a swagger about him; a certain charisma, and a humorous personality that made him attractive. He was sixteen or seventeen and sexually experienced. He was about 5'8" with a flat nose, cocoa brown skin, and a short, flat-top afro. I thought he was the love of my life. Regardless of how I felt, Jasper never really loved me sincerely. He spent time with many other girls. His mom was a single mother who worked for the United States Post Office on the overnight shift. So, Jasper and his sister, Gail who was only 14, were left alone in the house at night without supervision. So, a lot happened at their house while their mother was at work. Jasper and Gail were both very promiscuous. They would have people over to hang out and to have sex. Gail was already a teen mother.

The day after my Sweet Fifteen birthday party, it was my turn. Jasper and I went to his house late afternoon after his mother left for work at the Post Office. I was a scared virgin, but Jasper had all the moves. He played the record Sweet Sticky Thing (Ohio Players 1975) while having sex with me in his bedroom that night. It was painful but I refused to cry. I wanted to be a woman like the older girls who were not virgins. This was my opportunity to become a woman and I thought I could handle it. Time proved that I couldn't handle it. Jasper and I did not use protection and I didn't realize I would soon be pregnant. After that first time, I fell more and more under Jasper's influence. He was so sweet and cavalier, I believed it was love. So, we carried on the relationship. He was my boyfriend while also dating other girls. He was even occasional sex buddies with my cousin Carol. I didn't know about any of it and at that time, I thought Jasper was the love of my life and exclusively mine.

Seven or eight weeks later, I was at the supermarket with my mother, Helena. I told her that something wasn't right with me. I picked up some cheese and just looking at it made me nauseous. My mother took one look at me and said, "You better

Impossible Things

not be... I know you're not... You better not be pregnant!" She could hardly get the words out, but she knew right away. I was confused. I had suspected that something wasn't right. But, not knowing the symptoms of pregnancy, I didn't know what was wrong. I had missed my period and never shared that with my mother. She said, "If you got yourself in that way, I'm going to tell you right now. You're gonna have that baby. I ain't gonna have no part in any abortion. Because every child I had, I gave birth to and that's it." She said an abortion "would be like a drop of blood from Christ's hand." That was her take on the situation and I would have to go through with the pregnancy. That was Helena's final decision.

When I told Jasper I was pregnant, he talked about getting a part-time job pumping gas or something so he could help with the baby's expenses. But there just wasn't a good way to make it all work. Getting married and having a family wasn't an option for us. We were much too young. While I was pregnant, Jasper continued dating other girls including my cousin and my younger sister, Darlene.

I wanted to be with Jasper, but we didn't have much in common. Jasper was into basketball and other sports. I was not a sports fan. I did not enjoy going to baseball games with him and things like that. I just didn't have any interest in any of it, as it turns out, my younger sister, Darlene did. When he would come over, he and Darlene would talk about those things. She was 14 years old and very interested in sports. She started to hang out with Jasper too. One day there was a basketball game at Plainfield High School and I didn't want to go. So, Darlene and Jasper went together. They would go to school games together. I think that's where they connected but I couldn't see that coming. Through that connection, they grew closer and soon Darlene was also in love with Jasper. I was pregnant with his child and he was dating my 14-year-old sister. This was even more devastating to me than the pregnancy.

Darlene and I were struggling with this. I was walking down Palm Place one day and Darlene came up behind me. Our older cousins, Mert and Carol, were trying to provoke a fight between us and Darlene fell for it. She was going to fight me. I was pregnant and she was going to fight me for Jasper. Encouraged by the older girls, Darlene said things to me like, "You can't hold onto your man! That's why you don't need him!" I couldn't believe it. I was never much of a fighter, to tell the truth. I was scared. I just kept walking until I got home while my sister tried to get me to fight her. Everyone was gathering around to see a fight. Nobody wanted to stop it. They didn't even care that I was pregnant. They all encouraged it. It's sad to even think about what could have happened.

About a week before going into early labor, Helena had taken me to church on Mother's Day. At 15, my stomach was way out there. I looked deformed because, unbeknownst to me, I was carrying two babies. I had on this yellow polka dot maternity dress that Helena got from a secondhand store. I can't remember what the sermon was about, but it was a Mother's Day theme. You know how the Baptist church is. They really go in for whatever holiday it is. I'm sure the sermon must have been something about mothers.

Impossible Things

    There I was, a young teenager sitting there in church with a big belly in this yellow polka dot dress. Although I'm sure everyone had their views about my situation, I found being at church somewhat comforting. I never let people make me feel guilty about being pregnant. I have to give credit to Helena. She did not make a big deal about my pregnancy. She handled the situation with grace. Once in response to my aunt asking why she had not considered an abortion for me, she repeated what she had initially told me, "An abortion is a drop of blood from Christ's hand and I will not be a part of that." I was too young to understand what she meant, but I will never forget what she said. Helena had been raised in the Seventh Day Adventist Church and would have no part in an abortion. Now that I look back on it, I wonder how she was feeling. Was she ashamed of me? I don't know because I was focused on myself. I was scared about how to get the baby out of me.

    I was in my seventh month of pregnancy as I recall. Helena and I came back home from church and had dinner. Everything was fine. Later that evening, we noticed that Darlene wasn't home. My mother was worried about where she was. Helena sat out on the porch practically all night, waiting for Darlene to come back. I came downstairs early in the morning and saw her still sitting there worrying. My mother had a sixth sense or something. Then at 5 – 5:30 AM, Darlene appeared walking across the street from Jasper's house. As she approached the front porch Helena asked, "Where have you been?" Darlene said she just got tired and fell asleep at Jasper's (or some excuse) and I believed that she and Jasper probably consummated their relationship. It was more than friendship between them but, I didn't want to believe it. It was very disturbing.

I experienced constant fear and anxiety during my pregnancy. I was worried about my health. What was going to happen to me? To my body? How painful would it be? I was scared. The physical trauma of the pregnancy took a toll on my body. As the babies grew, I had unbelievable stretch marks covering my entire abdomen. I lost elasticity in my skin and the skin of my whole abdomen turned black. My father was even concerned and asked what the doctor had to say about it. It was years before normal color returned to my skin. To this day, I have deeply embedded marks on my stomach.

Whenever I was upset, I would eat grapefruit and popsicles like crazy. I would eat grapefruits like folk ate oranges but I consumed at least 2 or three grapefruits in one sitting. Popsicles were also a craving of mine; they gave me comfort. Eating allowed me not to concentrate on how unhappy I was due to the pregnancy, Jasper, and Darlene. Everything in my life was devastating.

I went home and cried every night because I was so hurt. Then one morning, I got up and told my mother I wasn't feeling right. I was close to my 8th month by then and I didn't know what was going on. My mother told me that I was probably in labor and took me to Muhlenberg Hospital (also known as "Killingberg") and sure enough, I was in labor. It was too soon but they said, "Looks like she's going to have this kid right now." This was it.

Impossible Things

Being a pregnant teen in the 70s, I did not receive proper prenatal care from the local clinic, no prenatal vitamins, or even education on the birthing process. Back then, Muhlenberg Hospital didn't provide a good standard of care for pregnant, teenage, Black girls. When I went to the hospital in labor, I had no idea what to expect and I was terrified.

They put me in a prep room and shaved my private area with a straight razor. That was how it was done back then. They were shaving me and I was in a lot of discomfort, so it was hard to be still. I was moving around and the nurse said, "You better hold still. You should've thought about all that before you got yourself in this situation!" She was mean and abrupt. She showed me not one ounce of compassion. I can still remember her harsh behavior toward me while they held me down and shaved my privates. Looking back on it now, it was pretty bad. My mother was there just for a minute, but she was not exposed to all the abuse. Once she left the room, they became even more violent.

I told them I was thirsty. They wet a washcloth, stuck it in my mouth, and told me to suck on it. The labor was progressing, with the most intense pain I had ever felt in my life. I could not comprehend being in that level of pain. Soon, they were taking me to another room. I continued to cry and plead for help. I was begging for them to put me to sleep or give me something for the pain. But they said the baby was crowning and there was no time. They numbed the area, gave me an episiotomy, and delivered the baby without pain management. As I was just beginning to feel the slightest sense of relief, I heard someone say, "It appears that another baby is coming." I was giving birth to a second baby. No one even knew I was having twins. They delivered the second baby, and I don't remember much after that. For a 15-year-old girl to give birth to two babies without anesthesia is barbaric and very traumatic.

I woke up later in a recovery room. I remember someone asked me if I would like to see my babies. They told me that both babies were having issues with their lungs because they were premature and they would possibly not survive. They brought two incubators into my room and allowed me to see my baby girls. They were tiny. One was 2.5 pounds and the other 3 pounds. The two of them together weighed 5.5 lbs. They had tubes in their throats because their lungs were not fully developed. It was a horrible thing to see. They were fighting for their lives.

My babies were alive and I had to give them names. They were a part of me, so I decided to give them my names, one was Lucretia and the other was Renae. They both had my last name, Spann. They were Lucretia Spann and Renae Spann. All the while, I was looking at my babies fighting for their lives.

I was later told by my friend Minnie Boggs that Darlene and Jasper, the father of my twins, came up in the elevator of the hospital holding hands as girlfriend and boyfriend. They walked into my room together to see the babies. When my sister saw that I had twins, she remarked, "Oh you have two of them. One for me and one for you!" She was joking, but I couldn't understand why. We were both just children with no idea how to respond appropriately to the situation. I was so young and naïve; I just didn't know what was happening to me. My relationship with my sister had crumbled and my boyfriend was still trying to play the field between the two of us. It was a horrible situation. I believe God in His mercy kept blinders on me, so I could not see how ugly everything was.

    The worst was yet to come when one of my daughters died that same night and the second died 2 days later. My daughters, Lucretia and Renae, were both gone. I remember a nurse coming in and saying to me, "It's for the best. It's for the best. You are young. You can have more children. This is for the best." For the best? As if I should be happy that this was the outcome and I didn't have to take on this responsibility. It felt like a subtle brainwashing technique. It was confusing but it brought me some relief. I thought maybe it was for the best like they said. But I still couldn't understand how they would see a dying child as something for the best. Two lives were taken away.

    Today, I can't help but think that more could have been done to save my babies. The top NICU at that time was in Newark, New Jersey. That was less than 20 miles from Plainfield. Hospitals could airlift babies to Newark in minutes. But I was 15, poor, and Black. Nobody had time or concern for my black babies. I don't even know what happened to their bodies. I did not funeralize and bury them. My mother was distraught with this situation. She was sickly and would not have been able to care for two babies. I was a minor. So, did the hospital get my mother to sign off on something? Were their bodies used for science? Where were my babies? Where are they today? These remain unanswered questions. Current research suggests that Muhlenberg Regional Medical Center really was a horrible hospital and it was eventually shut down on August 13, 2008.

This entire experience was so cruel, and it shaped my life going forward. This trauma scarred my young psyche regarding pregnancy and childbirth. It set the stage for things that would happen later in my life. In my mind, getting pregnant was not a good thing. I feared ever having children again. I knew if I did have a baby again, it would not be good.

I remember my mother coming to get me from the hospital when I was discharged. She hurriedly packed me up and took me home. I thought I would feel better to get back home after all of that. However, I didn't feel comforted or at ease when I got home. It didn't feel like the home that I knew. At that time, our cousin, Marcella, and her three children were living with our family. The house was crowded and not sparkling clean the way my mother preferred it to be. Truth be told, there would have been no room for my twin baby girls. No preparations were made for their arrival. I was still sharing a bedroom with my two sisters. For some reason, everything in the house seemed so dirty to me. We had only one bathroom and I didn't want to sit on the toilet. It seemed so dirty. I remember Helena putting me in my bed, and telling me not to worry about anything. She told me to just lie down and rest, but I was uncomfortable because the sheets were not clean. She reassured me that everything would be alright and tried to comfort me. She knew what it was like to face trauma because she had faced trauma in her life too.

Impossible Things

Somehow my mother knew I would make it past that horrible experience. So, she did everything she could to help me recover and move forward.

My sister, Darlene, at 14 was just a child herself and was persuaded by Jasper to continue the relationship with him. But shortly after seeing what happened to me and how he played the field with other girls, she could no longer tolerate Jasper and decided to end it. She was beginning to mature and become wise. She was realizing what happened but was not yet able to apologize for her part in any of it. Our sisterly relationship was deeply damaged by the whole ordeal, and we continue to bear some of those emotional scars today.

After leaving the hospital, I separated myself from Jasper and the devastation of what my sister did by dating my boyfriend. I just wanted to chill for a while. Helena ensured I went back to high school and resumed my education. I guess she wanted to make me feel like any normal 15-year-old girl who had not been through a terrible experience. I tried to get back to my teenage life still hanging around with older girls. As much as I tried to get back to life and put everything behind me, I had been deeply scarred physically, mentally, and emotionally from the birth and death of my daughters.

I never went to therapy or counseling to help me heal and learn how to move forward. All I knew was that I did not want to ever go through that again. The trauma of that experience set the stage for any future pregnancies. It made me afraid of ever going down the path of childbirth again. But, like most teenage girls, I was still longing to have a boyfriend. I had the romantic idea of a boy who would sincerely love me and that was what I was searching for. I was still that little boy-crazy girl.

Whenever I saw a handsome boy, I was flirtatious. I craved the hugging, kissing, and cuddling of a boyfriend. I was not looking for sex though. I still didn't even understand the whole process of sex. I knew it was a part of being in love with someone. Each time I found a new boyfriend, I believed we were in love. I would picture us getting married. I thought he would be my Prince Charming and we would live happily ever after. Despite my romantic dreams, however, every relationship would eventually lead to sex and a pregnancy. I could not find my happily ever after.

There were several boys, I can't even remember some of their names. Every relationship was ended by a pregnancy. Each time, I would tell the boyfriend that I was pregnant, the relationship would immediately change. He didn't want the baby and there was no fairytale ending. Each relationship would end with an early-term abortion. I knew I couldn't go through the trauma and pain of pregnancy and birth all alone again. So, to protect myself from another horrible experience, I would choose to terminate the pregnancy without letting my mother know.

I found myself in a destructive cycle as a teenager. Chasing boys, looking for love, and finally meeting a handsome Prince. Experiencing what I thought was love, then sex, pregnancy, and a breakup. This was all followed by an early termination to avoid

Impossible Things

the horror of childbirth. In hindsight, I can see that I would have been trapped in Plainfield, a young, single mother with several children. My life could have turned out differently than it had. Now I understand that, but at the time, I was doing what I knew to solve a problem. This cycle would play out into my young adulthood and continue until I was married.

My mother knew I needed help to get me back on the right path, so she took me to a man called Dr. Dallas Moore who was a prophet in Donalsonville, Georgia. A local church in Plainfield sponsored bus rides to see this great man. Seeing him was a form of therapy for me. It was my mother at her wit's end reaching out for help. She needed me to get my priorities in order, finish high school, and become the woman with dreams, and knew I could be. Dr. Dallas Moore was someone I feared as he had a strange way of talking to me. He was spiritual and intense. When he spoke, he was direct and focused, like he knew things about me. In our meeting, he let me know, in no uncertain terms, that he would come to New Jersey and deal with me if I gave my mother any additional problems. He told me I needed to listen to my mother, go to school, and not stress her any further or he would come to New Jersey to see me. This was a direct order and since that day, I feared that if I got too far out of line, Dr. Dallas Moore would follow through on what he had said.

Seeing Dr. Dallas Moore was a turning point for me. His determination made me afraid, and I thought he would come to deal with me on a spiritual level. I was not equipped to fight that type of warfare. Today, I am so grateful to my mother for taking me to him at the age of 16, before my life could take a turn for the worse. Thank God for Dr. Dallas Moore. The following is from his published obituary:

Feb 4, 1915 - Dec 22, 1990 - Dr. Dallas Moore was an amazing, humble, and true man of God. He moved in the power and authority of his Lord and Savior, Jesus Christ. He healed the sick, set the captive free, gave Godly counsel in words of wisdom and words of knowledge, and preached the Gospel with complete dedication. Lovingly known as 'Doc', he devoted every day of his life to doing the work of the LORD from the early 1950s until he passed to his eternal reward in 1990. He affected the lives of many, many thousands of people, always giving all glory to God. Thank you, LORD, for the wonderful life of your servant, Dallas Moore, Jr.

Despite all my teenage turmoil, I pushed myself to finish high school. I didn't do well in school because I had not developed strong study skills. Everything was a struggle. When the guidance counselor advised me what I should plan to do after graduation, he looked at my grades and told me that college would not be a part of my future. I was not college material. He suggested that I choose a secretarial career or learn a trade after high school. So that was what I did. I decided to take secretarial and clerical classes that they offered in high school. I found that I was pretty good at typing, 80 words per minute, and it was kind of fun. I enjoyed it and was focused on those courses.

Still, I was not a great student. I was a mischievous girl and going through a lot of what we now know as PTSD. No one had a clue about such disorders in children and teens in the 70s, at least not in my community. There was no help for me. My mother said it was by some miracle that I was never expelled for smoking in the girl's bathroom, cutting class, or whatever. Sometimes when I was supposed to be in class, I would skip school and take the train over to Newark to hang out. I did it all.

I struggled through all my other courses, English, History, etc., and barely qualified for graduation at the end of my senior year. All along, I was hoping and praying that my name would be on the list of graduating seniors. I made it by the skin of my teeth. I was happy and relieved to be a member of the Plainfield High School class of 1977.

My older brother, Harmon Jr, survived less than a year in the special school. Actually, we started and finished high school together at Plainfield High School. He should have been one grade ahead of me. But he was retained in kindergarten, causing us to be in the same grade throughout school and in the same graduating class. Harmon Jr. and I received our caps and gowns together and were excited about the big celebration. My mother bought me a beautiful off-white dress.

I'll never forget our graduation day on the football field. They called my name, Lucerchia Renae Spann. I walked across the stage and proudly received the leather folder with "Plainfield High School" printed across the cover. I was so tickled because I couldn't believe I was actually graduating. At that moment, I was thinking, "I don't know who made the mistake and put my name on the list, but I'm here!" I looked at that leather folder in my hand and thought, "I have my high school diploma and that's all I need in life."

I proudly walked back to my seat and sat down. I opened the folder excited to see my diploma. Inside there was no beautiful diploma with my name on it. In its place was a letter stating, "You will receive your diploma once you pay a $210 fine for overdue library books that were never returned." I was devastated. I knew there had to be a catch to this whole diploma thing. I was so upset that I cried to my mother. I carried on so badly that she came up with the $210 to pay the fine.

Back then, $210 was quite a bit of money. I don't know how she got that money. It was probably the money for groceries, or bills or something. She sacrificed the money so I could have my high school diploma in hand. And to her, I guess it was worth it. I was able to take the money to the school, pay the fine, and receive my diploma. I don't even know if such a thing was legal, holding my diploma for a book fine. Nevertheless, that was how I got my high school diploma. It was time to become an adult.

Chapter 4
We're in The Army Now

I graduated high school at the age of 17 in June of 1977. It was rough, but I did it. After graduation, Helena took me to sign up for a secretarial/administrative trade school which was in the Empire State Building in New York City, and paid the deposit for the enrollment fee. But I didn't want to go to school anymore. I had narrowly qualified for my high school graduation and couldn't imagine having to take more classes. My guidance counselor confirmed that I was not "college material" due to my grades and just barely qualifying for my high school diploma. Telling certain students, they were not "college material" was a practice some white counselors at Plainfield High would do to discourage young black teens from pursuing higher education. It worked for me, and I was not interested in going to college. However, Helena made it clear, "You've got to go somewhere. If you're not going to college, you're going somewhere." In my teenage arrogance and ignorance, I thought, "Yes, I'm leaving here. I'm going to the Military because I'm tired of being bossed around." I decided to go into the military to get away from Plainfield and Helena's strict discipline. I didn't want to stay in that environment where everybody knew what happened with my pregnancy and my deceased twins. I just wanted to escape all that horror and have a fresh start.

L. Renae Spann

In choosing which branch of service I would join, I looked at the uniforms. I wanted to wear the cutest uniform the United States Armed Forces had to offer. Since they had the best uniform in my opinion, I took the exam to enlist in the US Air Force. I knew that blue uniform would look great on me. Unfortunately, I failed the exam. I was admittedly not a good test taker. I knew that I was smart, but I just didn't seem to perform well on tests. My turbulent high school years left me emotionally scarred. I must credit my mother with the fact that I even graduated. Her encouragement and determination got me through.

After failing the Air Force exam, I went for my second choice of uniform, which was the United States Army. I tested and missed the qualifying score for that exam too. I was zero for two and running out of options. The Army recruiter suggested that I try the Army National Guard. He explained that the exam requirements were not as stringent, and I should be able to qualify there. For the Air Force and Army, I was required to complete the exams at a testing site with other potential candidates. I found the testing environment intimidating and the whole situation made me nervous. But for the Army National Guard, the process was different.

I went to the National Guard Armory in South Plainfield to inquire about enlistment. There, the recruiter told me that I would be able to take the test at the armory instead of a testing site. I was relieved because I was able to test individually and without time constraints. I knew I could perform better under those conditions. Today, people understand the need for specific testing conditions. But in 1978, testing accommodations, even in school, did not exist. The recruiter assured me that I would be just fine. So, I sat alone in a room to complete the exam.

Without the usual time limits, I was able to take my time and do my best work on each question. After failing the two previous exams, I was giving this one all I had. I felt like it was my last chance to get into the armed services. What would I do if I failed this one? I was sure that I was probably taking longer on the test than the average young person. I was trying so hard to get the answers correct. Periodically, the recruiter would come into the room to check on me and see how I was doing. The recruiter was a middle-aged Staff Sergeant in camouflage uniform with combat boots because he was on his weekend drill duty. He was a white man of average height with hair graying at the temples and smelled like sweat. He appeared friendly and smiled a little too much. He encouraged me. Each time he checked on me, he reassured me that I would do just fine and told me not to worry.

After some time and several check-ins, the recruiter came into the room and stood close to me. He asked how it was going and I told him I was almost finished but having difficulty with the last few questions. Then he pointed to my test paper and asked me which questions. As he lifted his hand from the paper, he slowly and deliberately ran his fingers across my breasts and smiled at me. I didn't know how to react. I froze and didn't say a word. Then he proceeded to feed me answers for the final few questions that I had not completed.

L. Renae Spann

When I completed the test, he took my test paper, scored it immediately, and told me I passed. I was excited and relieved to hear it. I was happy that I would be able to enlist in the Army National Guard. My excitement overshadowed the fact that he touched me like that during the test. I just pushed the incident into the back of my mind and never told anyone. I was headed for scheduling and preparation to leave. Soon after that, I entered basic training at Fort Jackson, South Carolina.

I remember the actual day when I was leaving to go on my first airplane flight. The Military scheduled me to fly out of Newark International Airport in January of 1978. On the morning of my scheduled flight, there was a heavy snowstorm. My mother woke me up early to ensure that I made it to the airport in time to catch my flight to South Carolina. I told her that no plane could fly in that weather (as if I had ever flown anywhere in my life). It was my teenage arrogance speaking as I turned over to go back to sleep. But Helena would have none of it. She insisted that I get up and get ready for my flight. She woke my father up so that he could drive me to the airport which was at least fifty minutes away under normal conditions and sure to take longer in the snowstorm. My mother got dressed and went out with a snow shovel and cleared the snow from around the car with resolve. She was determined that I would not be listed absent without official leave (AWOL) for my first day in the Military.

Finally, my dad and I were off to the airport and I was truly excited to fly on a plane "like the rich folks do." I was beside myself when I went to check in and board the plane. One of my

Impossible Things

former high school classmates, a girl named Angela, was also boarding the same plane. When we saw each other, we hoped to sit together on the flight but were unable to. The flight took off into the snowy sky. Then, less than an hour into the flight the pilot made an announcement. We would be landing at the nearest airport due to the weather. I can't remember which city we landed in. What I do remember was the excellent treatment we received once we all got off the plane and entered the terminal.

The airline informed us that we would all be driven to a nearby hotel where we would be given rooms for the night. We would also be provided with meal tickets to cover our dinner and breakfast. The next morning, we would be returned to the airport to catch the first flight out to South Carolina. Both Angela and I were inexperienced with air travel and airline protocol under severe weather conditions. We thought the United States Military was arranging all of this for us and that made us feel important. We felt like we were being treated like royalty with drivers, hotel rooms, and restaurant meals. Looking back now, I realize I had not even been concerned about the possible danger we encountered during that flight. It was my first time flying. It was exciting and I was invincible.

Today, I fly often but I am nervous for every flight. I would probably avoid air travel altogether if I could. My anxiety with flying started at age 55 when I experienced bad turbulence. People were terrified and screaming during the flight. Since that frightening ordeal, I now have to pray earnestly and ask others to pray for me every time I fly. This ritual gives me traveling mercy and stress-free flights. An inflight glass of wine also helps. I'm not letting fear keep me from living and traveling more. I travel more than ever now.

When I arrived at basic training at Fort Jackson, South Carolina, I had a rude awakening. Boot camp would be the catalyst needed to shape me up and develop self-discipline. I thought I was leaving the watchful eye of my mother to be independent. The United States Army immediately let me know that I was not going to have things my way. I would have to follow rules and, if I didn't, there would be harsh consequences. That military environment in 1978, forced me to take stock of myself and realize what I could do and what I couldn't do. The United States Army pushed me to my limits. I needed basic training to help me learn self-discipline even though the drill sergeant was a harsh teacher. I needed to grow up! Waking up early, getting into formation, learning how to utilize an M16-A1 automatic weapon and hand grenades, and feeling the effects of chemical tear gas; I did all of that.

Basic training broke me down physically and mentally. There were times when I thought I could not do it. I remember calling home and telling my mother I was sick. I probably had a cold or something, but what I wanted was for her to rescue me from the hell I had gotten myself into. I told her I thought I had pneumonia again. I had pneumonia once as a preteen. I told her I had pains in my chest and I needed to go to a hospital. I begged her to come and get me. Her complete response was, "You'll be alright," and she hung up the phone. Just like that, I knew there would be no rescue. I would have to finish what I had started.

Impossible Things

It was 1978 and I was among the first group of women who were no longer identified as Women Artillery Core (WAC). We were equal to men. Our training was as extensive as the men's training, and we were the first women to do this. We were the Guinea Pigs. A lot of women got hurt because, physically, we couldn't do what men could do. Still, we fought for that equity. I earned it and benefited from it. I became a disabled veteran because of my training. I dislocated my shoulder in the military and the injury proved to be a problem later in years. But I made it through training and was an ideal soldier.

In basic training, we experienced the effects of tear gas exposure. We were told we would march into a building with our gas masks on and when we were instructed to take a deep breath and then remove the mask so we could feel the effects of the tear gas. They would then tell us to turn right and walk out of the building. It was supposed to be a simple drill. Of course, it was going to be a little painful. Because the effects of tear gas exposure are painful.

I was growing more nervous as the time came for my group to go through the tear gas exercise. Once we were inside, I started to remove my mask when they instructed us to but as I lifted the mask, I also inhaled the gas. I experienced the full effects of the tear gas! It was so painful that I jumped up and just ran out the door coughing and gasping for air. Everybody laughed at me. They thought it was funny, but for me, it was horrible. The drill sergeant said, "Spann, you come back! You go through with the next group. You have not successfully completed the task." That was a pretty bad experience which I repeated and completed successfully. Throughout basic training, it was the running joke to stay away from that gas!

Another requirement we had to complete in basic training was throwing two live hand grenades. There was a large brick wall and the drill sergeant was positioned at the wall. We wore protective gear and were given two hand grenades in a casing. We had to hold the grenades against our chest, walk toward the sergeant at the wall, and then be given instructions on what to do next. After the tear gas incident, I knew I couldn't mess this one up. This was not something I could easily recover from if I made errors or dropped a grenade.

When it was my turn, I held the two live grenades to my chest and walked toward the sergeant. He instructed me to put one grenade down, then take the other grenade out of its casing, and hold it securely. Next, he told me to remove the pin but hold the clamp tightly. He said I should throw the grenade over the wall as far as I could and we would both take cover on the ground when it exploded. I listened intently and did everything he said.

I threw the grenade over the wall. I had no idea how far I threw the grenade, but it wasn't as far as I should have thrown it. When I heard the explosion, I realized that this was dangerous. When I threw the second grenade, I threw it far and the explosion wasn't as loud as the first one. The sergeant said the second one was better. That was my experience with live hand grenades. The only way you graduate from basic training is to qualify for everything.

Impossible Things

When we received our weapon, it was an M-16A1. We had to qualify in one of three categories: marksman, sharpshooter, or expert. Marksman meant that you were good enough to qualify; you got enough targets down, you made it and you earned the marksman pin. That was all I was trying to do. If I didn't qualify the first time, I knew I had up to two more times to get enough targets down to qualify. I was given three attempts to qualify and if I did not qualify during my time at basic training, I would have to go through the whole basic training again. That was my motivation to get those targets down.

I was motivated, but also scared because I had to get into a foxhole. I had to go down into a foxhole with my M-16. Once in the foxhole, I had to put my nose against the charging handle, aim, and fire. Pressing my nose too tightly would cause a kickback from the weapon and a nosebleed. I had to be able to hold the M-16 in a specific way to avoid the kickback. It was a scary experience for me. I tried to master that weapon as quickly as possible. I was amazed at how many targets I was able to hit and I qualified for my marksman badge the first time.

There were a lot of basic marches. We had miles of marches with a backpack, gear, and the "steel pot" on top of our heads. Our helmet was like a steel pot. It was very heavy. We marched out in the field daily. That was when I realized why people with flat feet are not allowed to enlist in the military. With low arches, the long marches caused extensive pain in my legs and feet. I went to Sick Call to complain about the pain and they put an insert in my boots to provide relief. They said it was the best they could do. So, the marches were always painful for me and when

I had to run, it pushed me beyond my limits. I was amazed at how much I could do under those difficult conditions.

At the beginning of basic training, everybody had to be assessed and assigned a partner. This all occurred during the first week. I don't remember my partner's first name, but her last name was Stubblefield. She was a short white woman with black-rimmed glasses. To me, a Black girl from Plainfield, NJ, she was a corny, meek, brainy type. I don't know where she was from, maybe the Midwest. She was not an exciting person; very bland. I wondered why we were put together but once we went through certain maneuvers out in the field, I realized why we had been partnered. I had the drive to run, get through the physical maneuvers, and push through whatever I had to do. She, on the other hand, was very meticulous and detail-oriented. She could pass inspections. We both had something the other partner needed.

We were "The Odd Couple" like that old sitcom. We were Oscar and Felix. We went through conflicts and disagreements but, where the rubber met the road, we were supportive of each other. By the end of basic training, Stubblefield and Spann learned to respect and appreciate each other. It was not a white-black thing or a tall-short thing (I was tall, she was short). It was just a deep regard because we helped each other. Our partnership got us through basic training successfully and by the end, we were respectful and appreciative of one another.

Of course, there were also a lot of men at basic training, gorgeous men and we girls could have our pick of the litter!

Impossible Things

There were many more men than women, but at first, the men did not want to date us because we were competition; doing the same things they were doing. We were drawing weapons. We were marksmen. We were their equals, so they didn't show much interest in us at first. But, once we went through and completed basic training with them, they gained respect for us. Then we became their preference. They wanted to date the girls who had been through the basic training they had.

Another issue that affected dating in the military back then was homophobia. There was a common stereotype that military women were gay. If a female was not a nurse or in some traditionally female role, people would think she was gay. I think many of the men initially thought it was true. I was also concerned about it at first. Leaving home for the first time to go to the military, I wasn't sure what I was getting myself into. Once I was in basic training though, I never experienced anything like that. I never had anybody approach me in that way. If any of my fellow female recruits were gay, I was not aware of it. I realized I had no reason to be concerned about it. We were all just strong, ambitious women in the United States Army.

By graduating from basic training and being physically and mentally challenged during those weeks, I learned I could go much further than I thought I could. It was just about having a winning mindset. Having that tenacious attitude to meet and conquer every challenge made me successful. In the end, I was a model soldier and I was amazed. Being able to pass the written test on my own was hardly relevant anymore. I achieved a major accomplishment and I was proud of myself. I was the ideal of a soldier (test or no test) and I finally got a chance to wear that uniform.

When I completed basic training, my family was not able to make the trip to South Carolina to attend the graduation ceremony. I was proud of myself and deeply disappointed because none of them were there to see me in that uniform. I marched with great pride as one of the first women who graduated equal to the men. There was no longer a Women's Artillery Corp (WAC). Not every woman in that first group made it through to graduation as many could not endure the rigorous physical training. Some failed and were retrained back through basic training. Some were discharged due to injury. It was by the grace of God that I made it through on my first try and did not have to repeat the training. This was all shortly before the beginning of Operation Desert Storm. So, I did not have to apply that extensive training in actual combat because I was not deployed to the conflicts in the Middle East.

After graduation from basic training, I was sent farther south to Fort Gordon, Georgia for Advanced Individual Training (AIT), which is the training you complete to prepare for your Military Occupation (MO); your specification training for your specialty. Fort Gordon was where I first experienced racism as a Black soldier in the United States Army.

One rainy day, a small group of us Black girls and guys were standing outside the mess hall. We were leaving after a meal and decided to wait for the rain to let up. A higher-ranking officer saw us and said in a classic Southern drawl, "Well, what are y'all standing around for? You need to get back to your barracks. What are you afraid of? That shit color won't wash off!" We were all taken aback by his words. We didn't know how to react. We all looked at each other without saying a word because he had a higher rank which demanded our respect as soldiers. It was at that moment when I knew that racism really did exist. To be demeaned like that was humiliating. Even though racism had been ever-present during my childhood, I had never experienced it so blatantly. This was the Deep South. It was staggering to be spoken to in that manner, but my focus was to complete my training there. It was 1978, Georgia and the United States Army wasn't a nice place sometimes. Military training with a side of Southern racism could be degrading for Black soldiers. Dealing with it was a course in self-control and it helped me to develop a thick skin that served me well as I continued through life. I learned not to internalize negativity, but to remain positively focused and keep moving forward.

 Graduating from basic training and AIT changed me. My Military Occupational Specialty (MOS) was an O5C Radio Teletype Operator. By the time I completed basic and AIT, I was physically fit, my mind was clear, and I knew I wanted a better life. Being broken down, challenged, and built up again gave me a new perspective. Being given no way out except to persevere, caused me to grow up quickly and I didn't quit. I was finally successful at something. I had a marketable skill. I was prouder of my military graduation than I had been of my high school graduation. I knew I had to go back to Plainfield but I didn't want to stay in Plainfield. I realized that I did not want to live in poverty. I wanted to do something better.

I wore that uniform home from my training with honor as I knew I had made a major accomplishment and, truth be told, there was nothing in the civilian sector that could supersede what I achieved in my military training. This was the catalyst that spearheaded my persistence, discipline, and endurance, leading to my overall success in the workforce for years to come. As a headstrong 17-year-old, it was all about the nice uniform I would wear, but now I see that God had another idea for my future. From November 1978, I served 4 years in the Army National Guard and 4 years in the Army Reserve as a member of the 250th Signal Battalion in South Plainfield, NJ. I was honorably discharged in October 1986.

After graduation from Fort Gordon, Georgia, I flew into Newark, NJ alone. My parents were going to pick me up at the airport but, when I landed, they were not there to meet me. I had to wait for them alone in the airport at night. Picture me at that moment returning from training. I was slim, trim, mean, lean, and feeling good about myself. I was finally wearing the uniform I always wanted; the uniform made me join the military. I was just waiting there in the airport when I caught the eye of a celebrity.

He was an older gentleman, handsome and well-dressed. He came over, introduced himself, and said, "Do you know who I am?" I really didn't know who he was. He told me he was a singer. I can't remember if he was one of the Temptations or another famous male R&B group. He told me I looked tall and statuesque. So, he just came over and talked to me. Then he invited me to have a drink with him. I had no interest in him, but I said, "Yes," and walked with him to a bar in the airport to have a drink.

In the meantime, my parents arrived at the airport and were looking for me. They searched all over the airport and could not find me. Then Helena thought, "I know where she is!" They came to the bar and found me having a drink. I was so happy to see them, I dropped everything. I told that gentleman goodbye and joined my family, so happy to be home!

Returning home to Plainfield, I reconnected with the older girls that I used to hang around with. They were still in the same position as when I left for the military. They had never even graduated high school. They were still sitting on the porch, drinking beer, hanging out, and talking about what they were going to have and do someday. But, I knew I had to do more than that. I didn't want to spend the rest of my life on the west side of Plainfield.

I got a job as a security guard at Rickel Home Centers company headquarters in South Plainfield. In case you are too young to know, Rickel Home Centers were large home improvement stores. Before there was Lowe's and Home Depot, there was Rickel. My job as a security guard was checking the trucks going in and out. I had to make sure that they had their identification and proper paperwork and then sign them in. It was my first civilian job. I showed up with my military work ethic and took pride in my work.

At Rickel, I worked with a guy from Egypt. His skin tone was darker than mine. We both worked in the evening and had long conversations during our shifts. One day his wife came in and brought him lunch. She brought their two kids along with her. His wife was white and of course, their children were bi-racial. I thought their children were beautiful and it was nice to meet his family. I called the children over to say hello. Both husband and wife immediately said, "No, no…" like they didn't want the children to talk to me. I was wondering what the problem was. I said, "She's white and you're black…" Then he immediately says, "I'm not black. My wife is white, I'm white, and my children are white." So, I said, "Okay," and I left it alone. He obviously was trained early on that. He didn't come to the United States to be associated with the Black Americans. It was that, "Life is alright in America if you're a white in America" mentality. He did not want to acknowledge that he was black. So, at that point, I really didn't trust him anymore because I knew what he thought of me.

While I was there, I looked on the bulletin board and found a job posting for Sign Coordinators. That was the position's title. I didn't know being a Sign Coordinator would require skills in graphic arts. So, I applied and interviewed for the position and they liked me. The manager said they would train me and that I could go to school at night at Middlesex County College to learn the graphic arts aspect of the job. In the meantime, I started the new position assisting with all the signage for Rickel Home

Centers. I worked during the day and went to school at night. Rickel paid for me to take classes in graphic arts.

Being back in Plainfield was shaping up nicely. I was working, doing well, and having a great time. I moved up at Rickel Home Centers and I thought that would be my career goal; to do graphic arts, typesetting, and that line of work. I was taking college classes and felt like I was on my way. So, I started looking for an apartment. I wanted to leave my mom's house and have my place. I wanted to get away from West 3rd Street. I wanted something better.

I would look for apartments in nicer areas that were predominately white. When I was working as a security guard, I would go to see apartments wearing my security guard uniform. I wanted to show potential landlords that I was trustworthy and dependable. But, it didn't matter. I couldn't get approved for any place in a nice area of town. They did not want to rent to me, a young, black woman. I felt like I was stuck and I needed to think of a way to get away from West 3rd Street and out of Plainfield altogether.

I guess that was my state of mind the weekend I decided to go to a Valentine's dance at the Elks Lodge down the street from my house on West 3rd St. So, I went to the dance alone and that was where I met Dr. Thomas Mensah.

L. Renae Spann

Chapter 5
The Doctor

I was living at home in Plainfield after returning from the Army National Guard basic training and A.I.T. at Fort Gordon, Georgia, and Fort Jackson, South Carolina. I was doing well working for Rickel Home Centers corporate office and taking college classes at night. Everything was going great for me, but I was ready to get out of Plainfield. I knew I wanted more for myself and I couldn't find what I wanted if I stayed in Plainfield. Around Valentine's Day, I decided to attend a dance at the Mohawk Lodge which was down the street from my house on West 3rd Street in Plainfield. I asked my two much older cousins, Mirt and Carol, to go with me but neither of them came. They said they had nothing to wear but the truth was they did not have money to get a ticket. So, I went by myself. No need for an entourage.

I was sure my new bright yellow 1979 Toyota Corolla SR-5 with the logo on the side and racing stripes looked impressive, pulling into the Mohawk Elks Lodge parking lot. I boldly walked into the building alone. I had never been shy at all, even when I did things alone. I just had that air of confidence about myself. I don't know where I got that from. I was physically fit, slim, trim, mean, and lean. I was wearing an off-white dress with a fitted bodice flaring at the bottom. It moved when I moved. It

Impossible Things

was the dress I wore to my high school graduation just a year or so before, only it looked even better on my new fit body. I WAS LOOKING GOOD. I walked in and looked around. They were serving drinks. So, I went over to the bar, got a drink, and scanned the room for a place to sit down.

A certain gentleman happened to be at the dance with a date that night and he immediately noticed me. Before I could decide about where to sit, he got up and walked toward me. He was a thin, dark-skinned man, much shorter than me, about 5'7" and I thought he was cute. He came over, introduced himself, and offered me a seat at the table where he and a group of people were sitting. I went over and sat down. He introduced himself as Dr. Thomas Mensah and told me he was a professor at Essex County College in Newark N.J. He told me he was originally from Ghana, Africa, and had been educated in Europe, England, and at The Massachusetts Institute of Technology (MIT) in the United States. He rattled off all his credentials and accomplishments. I was impressed that a Black man had this level of education and that he was so extremely intelligent. He wanted to get my number and to dance with me. So, we talked more and danced a little bit.

As the party was ending, I walked out and he followed me outside. He asked if I could drive him home. He initially came there with friends and I noticed he was no longer with the other young lady who I thought was his date. When I asked about her, he told me she was just a friend. This should have been an indication that he was not honest or a gentleman for leaving her like that.

We walked to my car. My brand new 1979 Toyota Corolla SR-5 was everything. It was bright yellow with black racing stripes, a black interior, and bucket seats. It had a 5-speed stick shift with racing tires and the Toyota logo. I drove a stick shift because I learned to drive Jeeps in the military. My car had been a dealer demo and I bought it off the showroom floor. The dash panel looked like a cockpit. I loved that car. It was my first real sign of success. Dr. Mensah was even more impressed with me when he saw the car. We talked and I drove him back to his apartment which was also in Plainfield, but it was a ratty little apartment. It was terrible. We went upstairs and there was a mattress on the floor with books stacked up all around it. It was worse than the typical bachelor pad.

We talked for a little while and had a good time laughing and joking. He said he would like to take me out or cook me dinner. He said he was a good cook and I thought that was great. The next day, I came back to his apartment and he cooked steak. It was a little tough, but I was really impressed that a man was cooking for me. I thought that was awesome. We scheduled another time to meet up and we were soon dating. I had no idea that those dates were the last time I would ever see that man cook for me, ever.

Thomas Mensah was originally from Ghana, Africa, and described himself as a child prodigy. He told me the story of when he was 3 or 4 years old, his parents found him reading from the newspaper in English to their astonishment, since English was not his native tongue. They knew, at that point, that he should be tested. From that point on, he was considered a child prodigy. His childhood was focused on education, boarding schools, and interest in America.

It was 1980 and we had been dating for two and a half or three months when Dr. Mensah started to talk about marriage. He wanted to marry me! It was surprising to me that everything was going so fast, but I was happy. I was 19 and it was finally time for my life to move forward like I had dreamed. Dr. Mensah felt the appropriate action was to go to my family, introduce himself, and let them know his intentions. He came to our house and met my parents. He told them that he was taken by me and would like to marry me. I didn't know anything about Ghanaian culture, but I believe it may be their custom to pay a dowry for the bride.

He and my father talked and my father mentioned an outstanding bill with the gas and electric company for which a shut-off notice was issued. The bill may have been $800 which would have been an astronomical amount in 1980. My parents were working with the company on payment plans, but they were unable to catch up. The bill just kept growing. My father couldn't believe the company was planning to shut off the service when they had been trying to pay. Upon hearing this, Dr. Thomas Mensah immediately pulled out his checkbook. He wrote my father a check for $800 to pay that bill. To this day, I feel like that was the dowry; the amount he felt I was worth. My father was impressed by the gesture and decided then and there that Dr. Thomas Mensah was a "pretty good young man" because he stepped up in a crisis. My father liked him. My mother, however, had a spiritual eye; a sixth sense. She was uneasy about him, disturbed in her spirit as they say. Helena was concerned that Dr. Mensah would not be genuine in his feelings for me.

Helena brought Dr. Mensah a cup of tea and talked with him some more. After he left, she said, "I don't know but, it's your choice. You say he has the education, and he will be a good provider." She sensed that something just wasn't right, but she couldn't put her finger on it. I was young and arrogant. I told her she just didn't want me to be with a man of status. I said, "What do you know about being up here (gesturing with my hand up high) when you're down here (moving my hand down lower)?" Every time I think about that now, it is a painful memory for me. Not only did I disrespect my mother, but it showed my level of arrogance and cocky attitude. As I matured and gained wisdom in later years, I realized that my mother's knowledge superseded that of Dr. Thomas Mensah because she had great wisdom. She had insight and spiritual discernment. I was just so young, arrogant, and didn't know a thing. I didn't have a clue.

We decided to get married.

But first, Dr. Mensah had an upcoming interview at Air Products and Chemicals in Allentown, PA. He told them he was married and had a son because that was what a lot of companies were looking for, married men with families. He wanted me to go with him to Pennsylvania and pretend to be his wife to help with his job interview. I went along with his plan and accompanied him to Allentown, PA posing as his wife.

Dr. Mensah attended his interview and afterward, we had dinner with his future boss. I had to keep up the charade all that evening. I didn't really mind since our end goal was to get married anyway. He just needed to say he was married beforehand to present an image of the stable family man. When we got back to NJ and he was offered the job in Allentown, PA, he immediately started to play games with me. He told me that maybe we should not get married like he was having second thoughts. I was blindsided by this sudden change of heart. I did not hesitate to let him know how strongly I felt about it. I told him that he just wanted to use me to ensure he landed the job. I was hysterical. After I made such a fuss, he told me we should get married and apologized for suggesting otherwise.

Once he landed the job at Air Products and Chemical, Allentown, PA, we got an apartment in Whitehall, PA. I was not yet able to see the signs of his manipulation and control over me. He would say things like, "Well, you know we don't have to get married. It's okay. Maybe we should do something else. Maybe we should just date." He would make excuses as to why we should rethink our marriage plans. This would make me upset and I would begin to cry uncontrollably. Then he would say, "No, I was just kidding. We will get married." He seemed to enjoy playing with my emotions like that. I had no clue he had another use for me, like gaining U.S. citizenship. It was only two and a half months later that we got married.

In preparing for the wedding, I was afraid to get the New Jersey-required blood test for our marriage license because I feared needles. After everything I had been through with the earlier pregnancy, I was anxious about anything medical. I remember having a physical exam at that time. I imagine it was also required for the license. I saw a Black male doctor for the physical and remember him asking me whether my fiancé knew about the prior pregnancy and birth of my twins. I was surprised by the question. He was insinuating that I was damaged goods because of what I had been through. He was questioning why someone of my fiancé's status wanted someone like me. Regardless of what that doctor or anybody thought, I was about to marry Dr. Thomas O. Mensah, who was a chemical engineer. I was looking forward to my happily ever after. We eventually got married in Plainfield, NJ on May 25, 1979, the birthday of my twin daughters who were born in 1975. Lucretia and Renae would have been 4 years old on that day had they lived.

    Tom and I had a small family wedding at Calvary Baptist Church where I used to go to Sunday School. It was around the corner from our house in Plainfield and my father was still a member of the church. There were only about 6 people at the wedding: my father, mother, Darlene, Marlene, and a couple of friends. I wore the same off-white dress I wore to my high school graduation and to the Valentine's dance where I met my husband-to-be. We did not have premarital counseling but, during the ceremony, the pastor remarked about how beautiful I looked and admonished me to always keep myself beautiful for my husband. That was the extent of his advice. I guess it was meant to help bring longevity to our marriage. That was it, we were married, Dr. and Mrs. Thomas O. Mensah.

Impossible Things

    Because of my veteran status, I was able to rent the VFW hall in South Plainfield NJ for a small fee. So, I could afford an inexpensive wedding reception there. The menu consisted of a large assorted cold-cut platter with fixings and a small wedding cake. We had lots of liquor and beer and one of my friends served as the bartender. We danced while a neighbor who was a DJ played the latest tunes. I believe there were about 30 people at the reception. But they seemed to enjoy themselves in the celebration. Two white women from my job came. We worked together in the print shop at Rickel Home Centers. I don't think my co-workers were very impressed with the makeshift wedding celebration but they faked it and stayed until it was over 4 hours later.

    I was grateful that my sister, Darlene, Helena, and my friend Minnie Boggs picked up the food and helped with the decorations. It was a nice day overall. After giving thanks to our friends and family, Tom and I said goodbye. That night we stayed at the Howard Johnson Hotel on Highway 22 in Watchung, New Jersey. The next day, we drove to our apartment in Whitehall, Pennsylvania. We didn't have a honeymoon.

    When we started our marriage, I couldn't cook. Even though my mother was an excellent cook, I didn't know how. I guess Tom just assumed that I could cook. I used processed foods with a high salt content because that's all I knew how to make. His cholesterol was extremely high because all I ever cooked was steak and Rice-a-Roni. We didn't even have furniture in our apartment right away. Like in Tom's old apartment, we sat on the floor and ate our dinner on the coffee table. We had humble beginnings, but I thought things were just fine. I was married to Dr. Thomas Mensah, a great Chemical Engineer from Ghana. We eventually started buying furniture. It was low-end furniture, but we were moving forward. It was fabulous and I was happy. This was going to be a wonderful life!

I took a job with Merrill Lynch as a wire operator in downtown Allentown. In this job, orders would come through a tube. The wire operator would have to take the paper from the tube and promptly type the order into the system. It had to be done with speed and accuracy as the stock market was ever-changing. That was my job. Since I was a radio teletype operator in the military, the company assumed that job would be a good fit for me to learn quickly and it was. I originally started in the mailroom, but less than three weeks later, I was promoted to a wire operator. In this job, they could better utilize my skills because I worked so rapidly.

By the time I settled into my new job, about 3 months after the wedding, we discovered we were expecting a baby. I was pregnant with my daughter Helena Michelle. This new pregnancy awakened all my fears about pregnancy and childbirth. It brought back all the trauma of my first pregnancy at 15. I was now 20 and scared out of my mind. But this time, I had a husband who was a professional. I thought I would be okay and that he would take care of me. I could depend on my husband, so I was excited.

Three or four months into my pregnancy our relationship shifted somehow. Tom's behavior toward me started to change.

Impossible Things

He became more controlling and we were arguing a lot. He started coming home late. He would say things like, "I am the most important person in this house. You should be grateful." I was pregnant and depending on him to get me through it. But he was treating me so badly and I didn't understand what went wrong. I remember just wanting to get away from him whenever he would get into his arrogant, angry rants.

I was so young. I thought that must be how marriage was supposed to be. After all, Tom was a doctor. He was a highly educated professional. What did I know? I had barely made it out of high school. I felt like he must be right. I tried to shut up and be grateful. But the situation did not make sense. He had nice clothes to wear but I had nothing. I did not have my hair or nails done like the wife of a doctor. He had the money, and he was living the lifestyle to which he felt entitled. He had earned all the university degrees and professional credentials on his own. I had no part in that so I should have been happy to be tagging along and living on his accomplishments. I was confused because he was supposed to be my Prince Charming and treat me like a princess. It just didn't make sense to me.

I soon realized that we were more like oil and water. We were from different cultures. He was extremely overbearing and controlling. He constantly told me that I lacked intelligence and that he was the most important person. At that time, I didn't know much about domestic violence, nor did I realize his behavior was abusive toward me. So as a pregnant wife, I did not feel pampered or cherished.

L. Renae Spann

The situation became so bad between us that I was afraid of him. I once jumped down a flight of stairs to get away from him because he was coming after me. My stomach felt tight and started to hurt. At that point, I settled down as best I could and tried to take better care of myself. It was only by the grace of God that I didn't have an early labor and premature birth with all the stress I was experiencing. It was then I started to think that our marriage was not going to work.

During this time, we moved to a house in Catasauqua, Pennsylvania. I knew nothing of the house before we moved there. I don't remember being involved or consulted about anything concerning the house as far as picking out furniture or anything. I later realized that Tom purchased the house without my knowledge and the property was put in his name only. It was a small row-home type of house, but it was nice. When we moved in, it had the smell of a dog that we could never get out of the carpet. That was where we were living when Michelle was born.

I should have sought counseling during my pregnancy as I was truly afraid of childbirth. I was emotionally scarred by the labor and delivery I had experienced as a 15-year-old girl. It resulted in death: no babies to take home from the hospital. I wondered how it would all go this time. I suffered from anxiety surrounding this issue and I now understand that I would have benefitted from professional support at that time.

Overall, I was blessed to have a healthy, full-term pregnancy this time. Although I was stressed, I was young and fit. My uterus had carried twins before. So, it was easily prepared to carry one baby. I could feel my baby kicking all the time and my stomach was noticeably large as though I might be carrying twins again. It grew even more enormous as my ninth month approached. My weight went up to about 210 pounds. Then it was finally time to get the show on the road and deliver my big baby. The doctors decided to induce labor because of the size of the baby and I was past my due date. It had been such an uncomfortable pregnancy in more ways than one. I was more than agreeable to get the baby out for both our comfort and safety.

I'll never forget that day. I went into labor at home. Tom came home from work and took me to Sacred Heart Hospital, which was a Catholic hospital in Allentown, PA. He dropped me off at the emergency room, said he had to go back to work and left me there. The anesthesiologist, noticing Tom's behavior and considering that I was alone, assumed the role that my husband should've taken. He held my hand and helped me through the labor until they knocked me out. I had to be put under general anesthesia because it was a tough delivery. The labor was hard and painful for 10 hours. I was hollering and screaming from the pain.

Then a priest came into the room, but I didn't know why. So, seeing him there made me even more worried. He did the sign of the cross from his forehead to the chest then right and left, and that scared me. I started asking him, "Why did you do that?" and "What did they tell you?" I was afraid he knew something bad was happening. I did not understand that his visit was routine in a Catholic hospital. The priests would normally come around and bless patients and I needed a blessing. I was there alone, in labor like before. Delirious with pain and afraid of what might happen to me and my baby. They eventually put me to sleep for the delivery.

Tom did not return that night to the hospital and I didn't hear from him. He came back the next day. He went to the nursery to see Michelle and found that other people were looking at her too. She was an amazing baby. She was so long, that she practically exceeded the length of the bassinet. She was like Baby Huey. She did not look at all like a newborn. She couldn't fit into the newborn clothing, they were too tight. They brought her in to me and I'll never forget how she looked up at me when they put her in my arms. I was drinking a cup of ice-cold water and I dropped it. Some of the water splattered onto Michelle's leg and got her gown wet. She didn't even blink an eye at the cold water on her leg and just kept staring at me. I didn't know why she didn't respond to the cold water, but I called the nurse and they took her away to change her clothing.

Tom came into my room and once they took the baby away, he started talking. He started by saying, "Oh what a big, beautiful baby." Then he started to say he didn't know if she was his baby because her skin was light. His skin was much darker. This immediately upset me and I started explaining how my mother had very light skin. That would be why Michelle's skin was lighter than mine. Then he went on to say that he had been told about my behavior during the labor. He said they told him that I was screaming and crying on something terrible and he was embarrassed by the report of my behavior. He only stayed for a few minutes. After he finished scolding me, he went back to work.

He was not there to support me through the delivery of his child and I was scared. So, that was how it went. I was very green and naïve to his manipulation and did not recognize his behavior as a sign of emotional abuse. I thought it was how marriage was supposed to be. He was the head of the household and he handled everything. I thought I should just be grateful and follow along. When I was discharged, Tom came back, and we took our new baby home.

When we got home, I noticed cigarette butts in the ashtray with lipstick on them. I knew that while I was in the hospital, he was entertaining his female friend in our house. He was cheating on me while I was delivering our daughter. I can see now that Tom had many major character flaws that made it clear that he had no intentions of being the family man I thought he would be. But I was only 19 and he was 10 years older. He had all the degrees and I felt inferior. I thought I was supposed to be grateful to be with him but we were like oil and water. I had to take it one day at a time.

Once Michelle was born, there was another shift in our marriage. Because he was from Ghana, Tom had certain cultural expectations of which I was not aware. In my experience, my mother had not breastfed her children. We were all bottle-fed babies. So, I had not planned to breastfeed my baby, but Tom had different plans. He demanded that our baby be breastfed.

There were to be no questions about it. In his culture, mothers breastfeed their babies and his child would be breastfed. I had no choice in the matter whatsoever.

Not only would he decide how the baby would be fed but also when she would be fed. He gave commands like, "Feed that baby now! Breastfeed her now!" and I was expected to quickly obey. Michelle, being a large baby, had a voracious appetite and had to be fed frequently, breastfeeding was a challenge for me. These factors made breastfeeding a horrible, painful experience for me, and without any guidance, I suffered through it for three weeks until I got an infection and had to take medication. When the baby nursed, it felt like her teeth were coming through her gums. I tried using nipple cream for the pain, but it did not help. I would have to grab onto something and squeeze really hard to bear the pain without crying out. It was excruciating and this was how I had to feed my child because Dr. Mensah would have it no other way.

The trauma of these experiences took me right back to the deaths of my twin daughters when the nurse told me it was for the best. I thought maybe they were right to tell me that. This baby thing was not all it's cracked up to be. I had to be a full-time wife and mother. I stayed at home all the time. Tom would not take care of our daughter ever. He would not even change a diaper. It was all my job. I had to cook, clean, and do childcare with no help. Tom would not even pay for a babysitter so I could take a breather. I thought the Army had been tough, yet here was another challenge and I had to stick with it.

Impossible Things

I had to consistently get up during the night to care for Michelle. I was sleep-deprived, exhausted, and stressed out. At night, I was so tired that I did not hear her when she woke. When she cried, Tom would physically shake me awake and say, "Go get the baby!" I would have to get up, delirious from lack of sleep, get the baby, and feed her. He would never jump in and help me out. According to his culture, it was all my job as a woman. I was so exhausted from jumping up and down like that, I felt like I was going crazy. But I thought if I wanted to be in a happy marriage, I had to do all of that. So, I did my best.

Once during the night, I was just beyond exhausted. Michelle started to cry and Tom said, "Get up, the baby's crying. You have to get the baby." His arm was right next to me in bed. I reached out and took Tom's arm thinking it was the baby. I began to shake it as if I were soothing the baby. He pulled his arm away and said, "You crazy. You done lost your mind!" Then I was awake enough to realize, "Oh, I have to get up and the baby."

I tried and tried to breastfeed, but it seemed like it was never enough for the baby. I called my mother and told her the trouble I was having. I was breastfeeding but Michelle just wasn't getting enough. She would wake up crying and her diaper would not be wet at all. She was almost 11 pounds. My mother said, "You need to feed that baby and give her some formula. Breastmilk is not enough." She also told me to mix some baby cereal into the formula for Michelle to have a better meal. I started doing that and Michelle started sleeping through the night. It was like I never really had a brand-new tiny infant.

She was my big baby right from the beginning. I took pride and joy in my baby and felt like I had accomplished something. It was just a strenuous and exhausting process.

Around this time, my sister, Darlene, graduated from college and was looking for a job. While visiting in Plainfield, I suggested that she come and live with us and maybe Tom could get her a job at his company. She was very smart and I knew she would do well. I also thought it would be nice to reconnect with my sister and have her around for company. We used to be best friends when we were little girls and I was so lonely living with Tom. But apparently, Helena overheard my conversation with Darlene.

A little while later, Helena talked to me in the kitchen. She said, "You know Renae, two women in a house with a man is not good." I didn't really get what she meant until I got back home later. I thought about it and realized that the last thing I needed to do was to bring Darlene into my home and possibly start all the madness between her and me again. Lord knows Dr. Mensah could not be trusted. If you don't learn the first time, you're doomed to repeat it. I realized that I didn't know who Darlene was anymore. I thought I knew my sister, but we had both grown up and were different by that point. I had to realize it would not be wise and could have caused more issues between us. Darlene and I had never really bonded again like we were back in the day as little girls. Our sisterhood was still somewhat fractured.

Impossible Things

So, it was life with Dr. Mensah. He let me know that it was my place to cook, clean, and care for the child. It was also my job to help him maintain his professional image. He was very much into his image as "Dr. Mensah: the great inventor, chemical engineer." That was paramount to everything else. And as if that wasn't enough, he soon decided that he needed something else, a son.

Without my knowledge, Tom somehow completed the necessary application process and had us approved. He didn't tell me much about it, but he convinced me that it was a good thing. The next thing I knew, we were accepted as foster parents and the agency brought us a little boy. He was a beautiful little boy about 4 or 5 years old. I talked with him and fed him. I immediately realized that this was going to be an added responsibility for me. I had a 3-month-old baby and now another child. It was more than I could handle. I guess Tom wanted to keep me at home basically "barefoot and pregnant" and this was his way of doing that.

We only had the little boy for a total of 7 or 8 days. It wasn't just because I was exhausted and I didn't know how to handle having another child. I would bathe him and he would scream at the top of his lungs. I didn't understand what was going on. I told Tom and he told the case worker. They told us that the boy's mother would try to drown him and he had a fear of water. I realized this child had special needs that I was not equipped to handle. I was responsible for taking care of the home and children. Tom did not help. He just left the care of the boy to me. He didn't even step in to help when we had a problem. He wanted a son, but he was not willing to participate in the care of the child.

This little boy was also mischievous. Once, when the baby was asleep, I went out to the garage to get something. When I came back, I found the boy closed the door and locked me out of the house. I tried to talk to him, "Please open the door." It must have been 15 or 20 minutes of me trying to convince him when he finally opened the door. At that point, I realized I was in over my head. I would never be able to handle all of this. I was almost in tears pleading with Tom, telling him I just could not do it. I couldn't care for the boy along with the baby. That they would have to find the child a new foster home. Tom finally agreed to take him back to be placed in a different home. I felt bad for the child but there was nothing else I could do. Foster care can take a lot out of you. You have to be prepared for something like that. I think Tom thought he could just thrust that on me. But it didn't work out.

Life there at the house in Catasauqua, Pennsylvania became humdrum. I would drive to my mother's house in Plainfield NJ with the baby just to get away. Tom and I had been fighting and arguing so much that I left my daughter with my mother for 2 weeks. During that time, I went back to the house to see if I could salvage our marriage. I saw it slipping away. Tom wouldn't give me money. He afforded only me a small budget to run the house. It just was not a good situation. I was confused by his behavior. I couldn't understand why he was so bitter toward me and I was afraid to be around him.

Impossible Things

He was coming home late every night and I was starting to feel like I was stuck at home with the baby. I wanted to work and gain my independence back. I chose retail because I had worked at Macy's when I was a teenager in Plainfield. So, I applied for a job with Sears at Whitehall Mall. It was our local mall. I hired a babysitter to care for Michelle when I was at work. After paying the sitter, I was not making much money but at least I was getting out of the house. However, my home situation was not improving. It was getting worse.

Then one day, I came home from work. Tom and I got into a physical confrontation. That day, I left. I called the battered women's shelter and they put Michelle and me up. I continued working at Sears and had a different babysitter, so Tom was unable to find us. He was looking for me and he finally found me at Sears. I was working in the luggage department. He came in and said that he was leaving me. "I'm leaving now. I'm buying luggage and I'm leaving so you don't have to worry about leaving." Then he said, "Where's my baby?" I told him the baby was at a babysitter and he could take his suitcase and go. I told him that he could stay at the house because I was never coming back. I just wanted to have peace and wanted him to leave us alone.

He said, "No. You're going to tell me where my baby is." It was the end of my shift, and it was nighttime. I walked out of the store, and we were still arguing. Another employee noticed and asked if I was okay and if I needed help. I told her yes, that my husband wanted me to get in the car and go with him and I didn't want to go home with him. The coworker went back in and called the police unbeknownst to me, and the police came. We were still arguing but when I saw the police, I just said never mind and I started walking away. The officer followed me. The officer asked me what was going on. I told him that I worked there at Sears, and my husband had followed me to work and he wanted me to get in the car with him and go home. I told him I didn't want to go with him. Then the officer says, "Look, get in my car. We'll go back and work it out." He told me, "Don't worry, just get in the back of the car." So, I got in the back of the police car and he drove back to where Tom was in the parking lot.

Then the police officer got out of the car. When I tried to get out, he said, "Don't panic, you won't be able to get out of the backseat of the car. I'll open the door and let you out." Just at that moment, a state of panic came over me that Tom was getting ready to switch things around like he usually did and make it seem like I was the bad person. The officer opened the door, I got out and Tom started explaining, "She's taking my baby and I need to know where the baby is." So, the officer said to me, "Either you go with your husband to get the child, or we will take you in and find out where the baby is." Instantly, I became the bad guy and Tom was the victim. The police were called to help me. Now the whole situation was flipped. I chose to go in the car with Tom to avoid anything further with the police. I did not want to get back in the police car. I got in the car with Tom and drove with him to the babysitter's house.

The babysitters were white people. Tom came into the sitter's home saying, "Where is my baby? Where is my baby?"

Impossible Things

The sitter hurried to give him the baby and said that she would not be babysitting for me anymore. They were afraid of him and didn't want to care for my child anymore. I was thinking, how could I continue to work at Sears? I would have to find a new babysitter. I got back in the car with Tom and we went back home. I was in that house, but I wanted to go back to the shelter. That was the second time I tried to leave Tom.

There was another time we got into such a serious fight and I ran downstairs to get away from him. I don't remember what the argument was about. I went into the downstairs bathroom. It was a small half-bath. I closed the door. I sat down on the closed toilet and leaned forward over the sink. I put my head down and started praying, "Oh God please help me! God, please help us! Help me! Help me!" That was all I could think of to say, "Help me, God." I thought I had locked the door, but Tom snatched it open. He came into the bathroom and started to hit me on my back. Each time he struck me, he said, "You don't know Jesus! You don't know Jesus!" After he hit me about 3 times, I looked at him. Then he stopped hitting me. He just turned around and walked out of the bathroom without a word.

You see, Tom was the one who put up his picture of Jesus once a week. He would pray, meditate, and fast for one day each week. He was a religious person. He would tell me I didn't know Jesus. He was the one who knew Jesus. He was the most intelligent. He was the most important person in the house and I should be grateful to be in his presence. That was Tom's attitude. I was being beaten down physically and mentally by him, and he was telling me I didn't know Jesus. I just could not understand why he was so hostile or what caused him to be so angry. Later, I found out what it was.

Tom was a womanizer. He tried to come on to his boss's daughter, who was a secretary at Air Products and Chemicals. She reported him and even though he had invented something great, there were consequences for his actions. Dr. Thomas Mensah invented something hugely important in the field of chemical engineering. I did not fully understand the invention as it was beyond my comprehension of the subject. But it was so important that Tom received a $10,000 bonus for his contribution. But once he started sexually harassing the secretary, he was let go. This was the cause of his anger. The company put him in another office and gave him 30 days to find another job and leave. Tom never told me he was fired. He kept that from me. All the same, someone of his accomplishments and credentials had no problem finding another job. Before the 30 days were up, he landed a new position in upstate New York at Corning Glass Works where he eventually earned 10 patents for his inventions.

Thomas would later be well known as a Ghanaian American chemical engineer and inventor, who contributed to the development of fiber optics and nanotechnology. He would eventually hold 14 patents and be inducted into the US National Academy of Inventors. He would also serve as Editor-in-Chief of the textbook, Nanotechnology Commercialization (John Wiley & Sons 2017), and served as President and CEO of Georgia Aerospace Systems Manufacturing. He was a genius who was at the outset of an amazing career. We could have had a wonderful life together.

We packed up and moved to Elmira, New York where things between us got even worse. Landing the new position at Corning Glass Works made Tom feel like a big man. He felt like he was somebody. He received a higher pay and more prestige. His ego grew and he felt he could dominate me even more. We rented a beautiful home in Big Flats, New York. Tom would give me only $40 - $50 to buy groceries and manage the home, which was ridiculous. I didn't even have a washer and dryer. I had to beg him for money to go to a laundromat to do the laundry. It was a horrible life. While he was eating steak, I was shopping in the bent cans and day-old bread section of the supermarket. I'll never forget that. He had all this money that he never shared with me. He just kept telling me that I should be grateful to be with him.

Michelle was 1½ or 2 years old and walking well by the time we had another serious fight. The argument was about the church. Tom said I had to go to church with him, but I was tired and did not want to go. He was determined that I would go. Everything was about the image for him. Wives should go to church with their husbands. Because I refused, Tom drew back his hand and hit me in the mouth with such force that it knocked my tooth loose. My lip immediately started to swell and I was such a mess, he decided I did not have to go to church after all. He said I could go next week and he went alone.

The next day, I went to the dentist, and he asked me what happened. I lied and told the dentist that my daughter had hit me with a toy telephone and knocked my tooth loose. The dentist asked me repeatedly because he knew there was more to the story. I stuck to my story and he treated me. He examined my loose tooth and decided that it would have to come out. I was in tears. I pleaded with him not to have my front tooth extracted. "My smile is everything!" I told him. He said it would have to come out and I would have to wear a false tooth to replace it. I was devastated. So, the dentist decided we could give it a week. He prescribed something for the pain and told me to rinse with a certain solution. Then he scheduled me to come back in a week. I originally had a large gap between my front teeth and that was one of the things that attracted my husband to me. He said in Africa, women with a gap in their teeth were considered attractive.

I followed the dentist's instructions for a week and the pain subsided after a few days. I was afraid to eat so I just had soup. After a week, I went to have him check my tooth. I give God the honor and the praise for what I am about to say. When I went back to the dentist to check my tooth, I didn't have that large gap anymore. The tooth tightened up, shifted, and closed the gap. I couldn't believe how God took that bad incident and turned it around for my good. My smile was even better. The doctor was amazed. He didn't have to remove my tooth after all. This experience let me know that my situation could get much worse than losing a tooth.

Impossible Things

We lived in Big Flats, New York, in a well-to-do neighborhood and my situation was escalating. We soon had another fight and I ran out of the house. I took the baby with me and went to a neighbor. The neighbor was having a dinner party. She put me into one of her rooms and called the police for me. When the police came, I came out and went back over to my house. I was wearing a T-shirt and my hair was a mess. Tom stood there looking like I was a mental case; like I had the problem. He told the police officer, "Oh, she gets hysterical. My name is Dr. Thomas Mensah. Sometimes she gets hysterical like this. There's no need for any issue." The officer looked at me and told me if I didn't calm down, they would have to take me in. Tom was able to turn the whole situation on me. That scared me, the kind of power he had with his finesse and his credentials. To look at me, it was believable that I was the one causing the incident. But it was his actions and secrets that led up to this incident also.

One night, we were watching 60 Minutes and Tom received a phone call. He answered, then walked out of the room and started talking. I didn't pay any attention. The next morning, there was a call on the house phone. I answered. A woman's voice said, "Hello, is this the Mensah residence?" I said, "Yes, this is the Mensah residence," and the person hung up. A couple of minutes later, the phone rang again. When I answered, a woman apologized for hanging up on me. Then she asked again if it was the Mensah residence. I said, "Yes." Then she asked who I was. I told her I was Mrs. Mensah, Thomas' wife. She said,

"Oh my God!" Then she started talking and told me the whole story.

She was an attorney in North Carolina. She and my husband had been dating for several months. Tom would fly in to see her. They would go to church together and he gave her the impression that he was going to marry her. She was wondering why he never wanted her to visit him in Big Flats, New York where he lived. Of course, being an attorney, she was able to do research and find out where he lived. Wanting to surprise Tom, she flew into Elmira Corning Regional Airport and called him from there. She was on the phone like, "I'm here! Come and pick me up." But he said he couldn't pick her up and gave her some silly excuse like he was watching 60 Minutes. That was when she knew something wasn't right. So, she did some research and found out he was married. She was so upset. She told me Tom was buying her things, sending cards and love notes. She said, "If I were barred in the State of New York, I would represent you in a divorce."

She later emailed me all the documentation and evidence of their relationship that she had to help with my case. At that point, I confronted Tom about her: the attorney in North Carolina. I told him what she said about being his girlfriend and the things he had been up to. This infuriated Tom. That was when we had the big fight where I went to my neighbor's house and the police were called.

It was then that I knew I had to leave. I just had to bide my time until I could get out of there. I wouldn't talk to Tom at all. I would sleep in the guest room or the baby's room on the floor. It would be just Michelle and I in there. om tried to make it up to me. He came home with a big screen TV and asked me to help him carry it in. I didn't even come out of the room. I think he knew it was over then. I wasn't interested in anything he had to say. I was done. About a week later, I took Michelle and went to a battered women's shelter. This time, I was determined not to go back.

    I knew I had to find an attorney to represent me, but I had no money. I searched and found an attorney who would take my case pro bono. She was a young, relatively new attorney originally from Poland. I was concerned about what my chances were since Tom had hired Erv Rindy, one of the top lawyers in upstate New York. He paid a $5,000 retainer and brought a case against me to get custody of Michelle.

    I had to apply for welfare and my attorney helped me find an apartment so I could get out of the women's shelter. Her secretary knew of an available apartment that was upstairs in the house where she lived, and I was able to rent it. My baby and I moved there. It wasn't anything special. It was a one-bedroom with an enclosed porch that I made into Michelle's bedroom. It had one of those old refrigerators from the 60s. I was happy to have that place. I was trying to make it on my own and we were starting our new life. The way I looked at it, everything was about to start taking off for Michelle and me. I had broken free. I didn't want the money and prestige of being Dr. Mensah's wife anymore. I just wanted my baby. I knew I was in for a fight because Tom wanted custody of my daughter. He knew that would be the one thing that would bring me back home if he won custody of Michelle.

Just thinking about it now and looking back, I wonder how I made it. We had quite a few days going back and forth to the welfare office trying to get assistance. Being a part of that whole welfare system was trying. Coming from the status of being Dr. Mensah's wife to a welfare recipient, I got to know who my friends were. Tom and I had some friends who I thought I would be able to call for help. I called one woman and asked if I could borrow $100. She found out that Tom and I were separated and getting a divorce. I'll never forget what she said to me. She said, "Well, we are getting ready to board a plane to London. I can call you when I get back." What she was trying to say was, "Please don't call me. We don't want to be associated with a welfare recipient." That was how I looked at it. I fell out of grace with everybody in their high social circles. It was a bad feeling because I thought I had people who were my friends. It was only by the grace of God that I made it to the court hearing.

I knew Tom had the best attorney and I had the young, Polish woman. The court appointed a guardian for Michelle during the case. So, neither of us had legal custody. She lived with me and Tom had visitation every other weekend. The court-appointed guardian, Mark Hutchison, was very nice. He was an attractive, young, white man with curly hair. I would describe him as strikingly handsome. He looked like the guy on Starsky and Hutch. Mark told me everything that was to happen. He said that everyone would be treated fairly, but the child's welfare was of utmost importance. Tom and I were both asking for full custody. The guardian had to take control and make sure everything was done fairly. Once I realized Mark had control of whether or not I got my baby, I knew I had to win his favor. He was a handsome guy. So, it wasn't hard for me to try to butter him up. Unbeknownst to me, he was attracted to me as well.

By this time, I enrolled in classes at Corning Community College (CCC). One evening, when it was Tom's visitation weekend with Michelle, I went down to this little club in Corning, NY with some students after class. Mark Hutchison, the court guardian happened to be there. We had a chance to socialize in a more casual setting and we had a nice conversation. I told him that Michelle was on visitation with her father and I had come down there after class. We talked for a while and then he followed me back to my house where we talked and had a few drinks.

Mark was a handsome man and I was genuinely attracted to him. I also knew I had to secure his favor in my custody case. One thing led to another and I don't have to rehash all of the details. I assumed since I'm Black, he was white, our encounter would probably be just a casual fling; a one-night stand, or whatever. It appeared, however, that he might have intended for it to be more than that. He was telling me about a friend's wedding that he was going to attend and indirectly asked me if I would be his date for the wedding. I found that odd. I had never dated a white man. I thought white men usually kept their Black women a secret. Nevertheless, I gained Mark's favor and that was most important to me. I was completely ignorant of the legal process. I didn't know that the court wouldn't take a child away just because of poverty and that they looked at the character and other things when making a custody decision. I thought a judge could take Michelle away from me because Tom had more money and resources. I was relieved to learn how the process worked. It turned out that Mark and I really liked each other. We continued to date a little longer after that first encounter and eventually, it fizzled out. Nothing further developed between us and we just tapered off.

In preparation for the court hearing, I went to a salon to get my hair done. While in the salon, I heard this woman talking about her boyfriend. She was saying, "My boyfriend likes my hair done this way because Dr. Mensah is very particular." I instantly perked up at the mention of Dr. Mensah's name. The woman went on and on telling everybody about who she was dating, just running her mouth at the beauty salon. I was under the hairdryer and didn't say a word. I just listened discreetly and didn't let on that I was Dr. Mensah's wife. I stayed calm and nonchalant, pretending to read a magazine until the woman left the salon. When my hair was done, I went up to the counter to pay.

I casually asked the receptionist for the woman's name, I told her I knew the woman and wanted to invite her to a gathering. I just could not remember her name. The receptionist gave me the woman's name and address. It was an African name that I cannot remember. She was a Black girl from Africa. I passed her information on to my attorney to help my case. This was a second girlfriend. In addition to the attorney in North Carolina, Tom was dating this nursing student. My attorney

Impossible Things

took the woman's information and subpoenaed her to appear in court. I was told that when they served the subpoena at her address, she fainted because she thought she was going to be arrested and deported.

    The day of the hearing finally came, we went to court to fight for the baby. I'll never forget how I explained in court about the difficult delivery I experienced when having Michelle. I explained how she was 10½ pounds and forceps had been used to pull her out. A couple of people chuckled and thought that was funny. But I was completely serious. I was in the moment and told my story with no filter. I told the court that it was traumatic for me and when I saw my baby, I knew I had to hold on to her. I had lost too many children. Tom didn't have a good case for custody. We decided together to have an abortion after we had Michelle. I couldn't believe he tried to use that against me. He tried to say he knew nothing about it. He had no case and tried to find anything he could to make his custody case, but the Lord prevailed. I won the custody case. It was amazing and it was all God. I was able to keep my baby. Both issues for child support and getting custody of our daughter were resolved that day. After a court hearing on June 14, 1988, I was awarded $600 in monthly maintenance (alimony) and another $450 for monthly child support to be garnished from his salary at Corning Glass Works in Corning, NY.

    After the court case in Elmira, NY, I was able to continue working on my associate degree at Corning Community College. I earned my degree and received a scholarship to attend Elmira College to complete my bachelor's degree.

Unfortunately, I did not finish my last year of college at Elmira as I needed to get a job to support us when the maintenance and child support payments stopped. Eventually, we moved back home to my mom's house on West 3rd Street in Plainfield, NJ.

Following the court case, I received payments for 10 months and never received another payment, EVER. At the time of this writing, Dr. Thomas Mensah owes me over $336,000 (not including interest and cost of living increases over the years) in back alimony and child support that were due to me until Michelle reached 18 years old. My daughter and I received no financial support from Tom after she turned 4 years old because Tom dropped completely out of sight.

I could not find him and we never saw him. He was now officially a deadbeat dad. Over the years, I have attempted to enforce my court order in New Jersey when I lived there. I also tried in Maryland when I moved there years later. In Maryland, they found Tom working at AT&T. There, he was arrested for back child support and ordered to pay me $5,000.00 for his release. Would you believe that he called my mother to complain? He told Helena, "Renae had me charged for back child support and I am in a position to buy my daughter a car and pay for her education one day." My mother told him that I needed the money now to help raise Michelle. I used the $5,000 to buy a 1980 Volvo to get us around in Baltimore, MD. I also purchased groceries and bought clothes for us.

After that, Tom disappeared again. Many years would pass before Michelle and I would see Dr. Thomas Mensah again.

Chapter 6
College and Beyond

Amidst the turmoil of being married to Thomas, I never gave up on myself. Instead, I secretly enrolled in college and during the separation, custody battle, and divorce case, I worked as a college student. I was a 24-year-old freshman in September 1983 and one of the oldest full-time students at Corningj Community College (CCC). I was not an honor roll student by any means. I had to first pass several developmental courses to bring me up to college level studies. I had poor study skills and my GPA was quite low which eventually jeopardized my enrollment. At one point, I was placed on academic probation and petitioned to get back in school. I wrote an appeal letter explaining the circumstances interfering with my studies and promised that, if given another chance, I would bring up my GPA. I was going through so much, but I strived to successfully complete my classes with at least a "C" average. It wasn't easy, but I put in the work to accomplish my goal. As a single mother, I knew I would be better prepared to take care of my daughter and myself if I had a degree. In spite of life's complications, my college years were both challenging and exciting.

I remember a difficult science teacher whose class I failed. As I was going over my college years for this book, I decided to call CCC and ask who my science teacher was back then. They gave me his name and I recently found his obituary. He stood out in my mind because he was, in my opinion, a racist teacher. He failed me in my final semester, making me ineligible to graduate. I would have to retake his class again in the summer to complete the science requirement for my associate degree. Admittedly, science was not my favorite subject and did not come easy for me. The reason I feel he was racist was how he treated me in class.

The professor always compared me with the white students and their work. I remember one time when we were discussing the African continent, an obnoxious white student commented, "If those Africans are so poor why do they keep having babies they can't afford?" Professor Wills just laughed and did not respond to the student's inappropriate comment. Since I was the only black student in class, I felt offended by the comment and slighted by the teacher. There were other indirect actions that showed he was not invested in me as a student. I knew I was on my own and that I could not expect the support I needed to get through his class. As a result, I failed, even though I constantly went to him for help. I asked what I could do to get a passing grade. His only suggestion was that I take the summer class which was my only chance to complete my associate degree. I did not march with my graduating class in May 1985. I already ordered my cap and gown but did not receive my degree until I completed his summer class where I barely passed with a C.

This is important because that was the summer that I met an angel at McDonald's in downtown Corning, NY – who helped me. He was a tall and bearded white man with a large build. He wore bib overalls and had "country polite" manners. I cannot remember his name. He came over to me as I was standing in line and struck up a conversation. Even though he looked odd, like a farmer or something, I found him easy to talk to. I felt comfortable with him. I thought maybe he was lonely and wanted someone to talk to. So, I shared my dilemma with this gentle stranger. I told him about my educational pursuit and how I needed extra credit to pass my science class at CCC. I explained that my last chance to redeem myself was to go to the woods or a park, find several different plant species and identify each of them. It was a daunting task for me and I didn't know how I would ever complete it. The stranger told me that he was willing to go out that Saturday morning and search for the required plants and flowers for me. He said it was what he loved doing, being close to nature. We arranged to meet back at the McDonald's on Monday morning at 8:30 before I went up Spencer Hill to CCC. I now believe this odd gentleman was my personal angel. He showed up Monday morning as promised with a big, brown paper bag containing over 40 different plants. Each plant was neatly placed in a sandwich bag and labeled with its proper name. I was amazed and couldn't thank him enough! Each of those plants would earn an extra credit of 2 points. Submitting that assignment gave me more than enough points to earn a grade of C which my science teacher could not dispute. That meant I qualified to graduate. Oh, my God is an awesome God! He sent an angel to help me when I really needed it. I never saw that kind gentleman again.

Even though I had this great accomplishment, that summer came with a downside. Because I went to summer school, I left my three years old baby, Michelle, with Helena in New Jersey. That was a big help. It helped me better focus on my studies and graduate. At some point, during that summer, my mother left Michelle in the care of my uncle Lewis Spann for a short time while she went shopping. Unfortunately, he turned out to be someone who should not have a small child left in his care. He did not conduct himself appropriately with my young daughter. This experience at such a young age left Michelle with emotional issues, following her into her adult life. I will not share any further details on this subject as it is not my story to tell.

Knowing this incident many years later was a painful and rude awakening for me as well. I often wondered how things would have been different had I not gone to summer school that year and never left my child with anyone. These are always difficult decisions for a single mother because you never know who might hurt your child. I prayed for peace with my decision to finish out my education and get that degree that summer. I also prayed for grace to live with the terrible regret of leaving my child in Plainfield, New Jersey at the very place where my trauma began. I thank God that today my daughter and I are better than okay despite it all. We know that all things work together for good to those who love God. Romans 8:28. As for the science teacher and my uncle, Lewis Spann, it was a great emotional pain and frustration for me. Still, I forgave them in Jesus' name as they both await God's ultimate judgment for their actions.

Impossible Things

Even though I was not considered a good student academically, I was amazed when I was nominated for the 2011 Eileen Collins Professional Achievement Award at CCC. The woman who nominated me for the award was Susan Payne, whom I later met when I moved to Sarasota, Florida. Susan lived seasonally in Sarasota and happened to be on the board of Directors at CCC. She met me at my office at Symtech Corporation and thought I would be a good candidate for the award. I had no idea she even considered me for such an honor. I appreciated her kindness and gracious manner toward me.

The award was named in honor of retired U.S. Air Force Colonel Eileen Collins, a graduate of the CCC class of 1976 and one of the school's most distinguished alumni. She was the first female NASA astronaut to command a space shuttle mission. In July 1999, Colonel Collins piloted the Columbia into Earth's orbit to deploy the Chandra X-Ray Observatory. Being one of CCC's most distinguished alumni, the Eileen Collins Professional Achievement Award honors an alum who has excelled in his/her chosen field. Criteria for the award include evidence of continued growth in one's career.

In 2011, I was honored to have Eileen Collins present the award to me personally. She was humble with a sweet spirit and loved the Lord. She took the time to talk with me and my family at great length before the award ceremony. Even though she traveled in Earth's orbit, she was truly a down-to-earth person. In my acceptance speech, I shared how I wanted to follow Colonel Collins' lead in also being a trailblazer.

Also, while attending CCC, I was elected President of the International and Black Student Union. I was 25 years old, enthusiastic, and open to new experiences. As president, I planned a trip for our student group to visit the nearby city of Toronto in Ontario, Canada. I felt it would be a great opportunity for students to experience the culture of another country. Although Toronto wasn't very far away, many of them had never ventured beyond their hometown of Corning/Elmira. I hoped the trip would be an adventure for them, although I did not anticipate just how much of an adventure it would be for me.

On the day of the trip, more students showed up than I expected, and they were not even on my list. These extra students apparently learned of the trip by word of mouth and showed up without signing up ahead of time. Since there was room on the van, I included them and reserved a few extra rooms on the spot. It was an inexpensive hotel set up much like college dorms. It catered to students with 2 to 4 students per room and shared bathrooms. I planned a detailed itinerary of activities for the duration of our visit. I would drive the van myself and personally supervise all the group excursions. I planned visits to two museums, have group dinners at two restaurants, and have free time for students to hang out in the evening. We stayed for two nights.

I had good control of the group initially for the drive-up and arrival. We checked in at the hotel and had dinner together. The first evening went smoothly. I informed the group of our planned itinerary for the next day. We were to all meet the next morning at 8:30 AM in the lobby of the hotel, then walk together

Impossible Things

to the first museum. However, the next morning, only half the students showed up in the lobby. It turned out that the missing students were the ones who had not initially signed up for the trip.

When I went up to knock on the doors of the missing students, they said they were too tired from the night before and would catch up with us later in the day. I realized at that point that it probably was a mistake to include them on the trip. Those students didn't participate in the planning and preparation for the trip, nor were they committed initially by signing up and making their deposits. It turned out that they were just trouble and uncooperative. The rest of the group and I went to the museum and enjoyed the outing. The others who missed that morning's visit to the museum ensured they showed up for lunch at our designated restaurant for that day. They were careful not to miss a meal. After dinner that night, most of the group went to a nightclub and danced until 11:30 PM. We had a great time.

The next morning was somewhat the same as the first, with latecomers sleeping in and then joining us later at the museum. When it was time to go, everyone packed up, loaded their items into the van, and left Toronto. When we arrived at the border to re-enter the United States, the agent at the gate asked me several questions about where we were headed and any items we might be bringing back into the country with us. These were the standard questions they asked at the border. As I was answering the questions, a few of the male students were joking around in the back of the van which caused the agent to ask me even more questions and take longer to release us to cross the border. Eventually, we crossed safely and headed for home.

Arriving back in Corning, I took most of the students back to the CCC campus where they had parked their cars, and I drove others who lived nearby to their homes. Two of the guys whom I drove to their apartment had taken things from the hotel. As they unloaded their belongings from the van, I discovered they had disassembled one of the wooden and canvas cots from the hotel and brought it home. They also took many other items, anything that was not nailed down. I was furious upon learning this. I felt they had put us all in danger of being detained at the border or worse. I could have been arrested. I was afraid I might lose my position as leader of the International and Black Student Union and possibly be forced to pay for the items taken from the hotel. When I asked them why they would do such a thing, they said that they just moved into their apartment, and they didn't have any furniture. This just showed that I had no idea who I had allowed to come on that trip.

All I wanted to do was give students the experience of seeing another country and broaden their horizons a bit. I was still somewhat naïve, I guess. But God covered me. It was His grace that the hotel never contacted the school about the stolen items. I can say that this is where I started to recognize and develop my leadership skills. This trip taught me a lot. I always meant well and wanted to do good for others. But this experience showed me that it was imperative to stay within the guidelines, follow the rules, and make no exceptions. I was starting to reach a higher level of maturity and learning how to take responsibility for myself and others.

    One of my chosen electives toward my Liberal Arts degree was Contemporary British Theater which included a 10-day trip to London, England to see several popular British plays and then write a critique for each of them. It, of course, required the students to have their passports, meet certain academic requirements, and be able to afford such a trip. This left out a great majority of the students at Corning Community College. The cost was just over $1,000.00 which included airfare and hotel accommodations. I was elated to see this class posted in the student activities center. I had never been out of the country except to Canada and I thought this to be the perfect opportunity to travel abroad. I immediately put down my deposit to secure my spot in the class. I met the criteria. Being very excited, I started to prepare for the trip by buying a few new outfits and arranging for the care of my daughter. In my absence, Michelle would again stay with my mother in New Jersey. This would be the easiest grade of A to help boost my GPA as going to Broadway plays in New York was my thing. I loved plays and to go to another country was just icing on the cake.

    With great anticipation for the upcoming trip, I checked with the coordinator regularly about its status and other details. Just a few months out from our travel date, the administrator announced that the class was canceled due to the low enrollment. Not enough students registered for the class. I expected this might be the reason because CCC was a small college where most students were on financial aid and/or had low incomes. What made me a candidate for the trip was that I was receiving court-ordered child support and alimony from Thomas due to our legal separation and custody of Michelle. That with my savings, made the cost of the class manageable for me.

Needless to say, I was crushed to learn that the trip was canceled. Then I suddenly realized that I did not need the group trip to go to London, I could go by myself. The Army gave me the experience of traveling alone without fear and this would be no different. So, I booked a flight to London on Virgin Atlantic Airlines for only $99.00 and didn't even book a hotel. How bold of me to go to a new country without first securing a place to stay. I was invincible and felt things would be just fine. I thought since Great Britain was an English-speaking country, I would be able to work it all out once I arrived there. So, I boarded a flight at JFK Airport in New York bound for Heathrow Airport in London and my adventure began.

On the plane, I sat next to a beautiful young lady from Nigeria, Africa. She was a college student at a school in Nashville, Tennessee. We both shared our reason for our trip and she was shocked to find out that I was going to London with no reservations for a hotel or even a plan of what to see or do once I got there. Nikki was her name and she shared that she was going to visit her boyfriend who happened to be married and was also a well-to-do African businessman. She told me he was much older than her and that he had a flat in London. She was going to meet him there. Nikki gave me a contact for a bed and breakfast in London where I could stay and gave me her contact information so we could keep in touch while I was there.

Nikki and I talked at least 6 of the 10 hours it took to fly from New York to London. We got to know a lot about each other as we each found the other easy to talk to. We discussed our friends at college and found that we both had several white friends who wanted to know more about our culture. We both found our white friends to be genuine with their intentions to become good friends. One story I remember her telling me was about a white friend she met at college in Nashville who invited Nikki to her house for dinner and to meet her family. They were eager to have her visit and to learn about Nigeria and her culture. When they served dinner, everyone had some kind of casserole but Nikki was served a plate of bones. I could not believe what she was telling me. It appeared that Nikki, like a lot of Black people I knew, had a habit of chewing and sucking on the bones after eating the meat in a meal. This is a cultural practice derived from the fact that many nutrients are found in bones and marrow. The white girl's mother asked about what type of food Nikki liked and the girl responded that she always saw Nikki eating bones. So, the girl's mother prepared a plate of bones. How humiliating for Nikki to have to explain all of this to the ignorant family members who never had the need or interest in trying to learn anything about African culture as it related to blacks. Sadly, these ridiculous misconceptions still existed with many American whites back in the 80s. There was still so much cultural ignorance due to a lack of exposure or willingness to learn. My visit to London was my way to experience, up close and personal, the original white culture and my exploration of what they were all about. I wanted to understand why it seemed vital that we conform to their ways instead of keeping our traditions and culture.

When I landed at Heathrow I went to the baggage claim area. I checked two bags on my flight from New York, a small one with my shoes and a medium-sized suitcase with my clothes. However, only the suitcase was there on the conveyor belt. I was told that they would call me when the other bag was found as it might have been placed on another flight. I didn't get upset about it. My level of joy was still high and I was happy to be in London.

When I arrived at the bed and breakfast Nikki suggested, the lady there took an instant liking to me. She said I looked like the singer, Dione Warwick. She gave me the largest room in the house and made my stay ever so pleasant. I noticed, at the time, I took this trip (1984) that all the people in London were nice to me when they discovered I was from the United States. I felt acceptance and did not feel the undercurrent of racism that seemed ever-present in the United States. People were accommodating at restaurants and shops, wanting to talk with me. They asked questions about where I lived, which sites I was visiting, etc. I went to Piccadilly Circus on my first venture into the city as it was a place where locals shopped and prices were reasonable. My second outing was a visit to Harrods department store which was their high-end store comparable to our Bloomingdales or Saks 5th Ave in New York. It was fun, looking but I didn't purchase anything. Harrod's was much too pricey for my budget.

After two days on my own in London, Nikki called to see how I was doing and invited me to visit her at the flat where she was staying. She offered to show me around and took me to see some of the tourist spots in London. We had a lot of fun on one of the days while we were out. That evening, we went back to the flat and her African boyfriend was there, accompanied by a white American gentleman around the same age. The white man had his 10-year-old son with him as well. I can't remember either of their names. They were friendly and I think Nikki's boyfriend had brought the white guy there to meet me. The gentleman and his son were nice, but I was not attracted to him. We talked for a while and I shared the story about how I ended up in London and how my school canceled the class in British theater. I told him about my love of plays and that I would like to see at least one play while I was there. He suggested that we see Les Misérables which was playing at the Palace Theater. He got the tickets for the two of us to see it the next day.

I went shopping for high heels to wear for an evening out since the airport had not retrieved my bag of shoes. I wore a size 11 women's shoe. When I went to the boutique, it was difficult to find a pair in my size. The sales clerk told me that not many women in London had size 11 feet, so there were not many choices. The shoes I purchased were black patent leather pumps with 5" high heels. They went perfectly with my tight-fitted, black dress. I ended up buying size 10 shoes. That's right, there was pain, pain, and more pain with corns and bunions but I had to look good for the theater. Everyone would be dressed to kill and I wanted to fit in.

That evening, the gentleman and I went to the theater. Once we were seated, I took off the shoes. I remember that night so well, not only because of the tight shoes but because the Palace Theater was so beautiful. The play, however, had a completely white cast and I did not enjoy it at all. Even though the play was still running in both London and New York at the time, I wonder why. I thought it was terrible. I did not understand it and wondered what all the fuss was about. I thought Les Misérables was just miserable but, to be classy and blend in, I lied. I said I enjoyed it. But all I wanted to do was to go back to the flat, change my clothes, and get out of those tight shoes. When we arrived back at the flat, my bag of shoes was delivered from the airport and I thought, "Now my vacation can really begin!"

Nikki's boyfriend suggested that I stay at the flat with Nikki so she wouldn't be alone while he was away on a business trip for 5 days. This worked out well with me because it saved me money and made it easier for me to meet up with Nikki every day. We had a ball visiting all the tourist sites around the city. On my last two days in London, I was back at the bed and breakfast. Nikki was busy with her boyfriend and I was on my own again.

I was getting tired of the fish and chips at most of the restaurants and steakhouses in London. So, I went to Kentucky Fried Chicken to get something I was familiar with. While I was there, I met a young African man named Albert Bafu. He was about 25 and worked as a construction worker remodeling homes. He told me he just broke up with a white girl he dated for several months. He said they broke up because she became too possessive. Surprisingly, he was from Ghana, the same country as Dr. Mensah. However, Albert was more contemporary in his views. He didn't think of a woman as socially lower than him, but more like an equal partner. I thought that once I was divorced from Tom Mensah, I would never date another African man. I thought they would all be like him, not family-oriented and just selfish narcissists. But Albert was nothing like Thomas and he was better looking. I enjoyed Albert's company for my last few days in London. We spent most of that time together and even went to a nightclub. We promised to stay in touch and then I was on a flight headed back home. That was not the last time I would see Albert.

When I returned to CCC, the most memorable experience was the scholar visit of award-winning author, Alex Haley. He was the author of the 1976 best seller, Roots: The Saga of an American Family. Mr. Haley came to speak at our school on November 15-16, 1984, on the topic of The Family: Find the Good and Praise it. I found the message he shared to be timely, and it set the stage for me to change my thinking and build my courage. My estranged husband, Thomas, was also in the audience and witnessed a powerful truth being told.

Alex Haley talked about the single-parent home and thought "Nothing wrong with such an arrangement." He didn't think that a man necessarily made the home. Regarding the single mother head-of-family situation, he said, that in many cases, women could do just as well or better without the man. In his view, it was most important for the roles of each individual to be realized to their full potential. After hearing him say this, I said "That's right" and nodded my head. I felt like he was speaking directly to my situation. Mr. Haley smiled and acknowledged my vocal response. He said, "It looks like we have someone that is really agreeable with this message." I felt a personal connection with the author that day. Thomas just turned around and looked at me as he was sitting several rows in front of me.

That day, Mr. Haley also addressed what he considered to be the greatest challenge facing Black people, the problem of negativity which is still prevalent today. The flawed idea that Black people are inferior and that they can't do or achieve certain things was described as a great barrier and one that would take time to be broken down. I was deeply affected, I found his words enlightening, encouraging, and timely to me at that point in my life. I left that talk feeling like I had been seen and validated.

After graduating from CCC, I applied to Elmira College and the Army ROTC program, which was on the campus of Cornell University, in Ithaca, NY. I was accepted to both the program and the college even though at 25, I was older than most students and already served 5 years in the Army National Guard. I received a waiver to get into the ROTC program because of my age and was not eligible to receive a monetary stipend like all the other cadets. Even more surprisingly, I took the test to get into ROTC and made it by one point. It was amazing. Here I was a student who barely got her Associate of Liberal Arts Degree now in with the Ivy League students, future doctors, lawyers, and Indian chiefs. Classes at Elmira College for Army ROTC were on Tuesday and Thursday. I felt I was right in step with the best of them. In fact, since I was already in the Army, I was ahead of the game. Look at how God elevated my life and placed me so perfectly where I belonged. The last shall be the first and the first shall be the last. Matthew 20:16.

I was starting to feel good about how my life was going. I was progressing to secure a future for Michelle and me. However, my estranged husband, Thomas, wasn't happy about my maturation, becoming formally educated, gaining self-confidence, and developing strong leadership skills. Although we were separated, he did everything he could to suppress my growth and keep me down. He was still controlling and abusive. After six years of this, I decided what was best for my future. It just was not worth it for me. I had to get out of the marriage.

I didn't have my own money. Thomas owned everything. This was when he hired the best attorney in Elmira. He was determined to get custody of our daughter and make me come back home. With my young, pro bono lawyer from Legal Aid, I had to fight Thomas for custody of Michelle, and by God's grace, I won. In addition to granting full custody, the court also awarded me child support and maintenance (alimony). Thomas was so upset at the court's ruling, that he left the country to avoid paying me.

It was after the divorce that Michelle and I moved to Elmira, NY. I already transferred to Elmira College to continue my education. I had one more year to complete my degree. That year, I did everything I could to further my education and grow as a person. Being divorced and no longer connected to Thomas, I felt free to be myself and reach for my dreams. When child support and alimony stopped, I went back to work full-time to support us. Jobs were scarce in Elmira so once I completed one year at Elmira College. I moved back to Plainfield, NJ needing only 18 credits to finish my bachelor's degree.

This was the first time I moved back to my childhood home on West 3rd Street. My father passed away the previous year and Helena was living there with Marlene. Darlene was married and living in her own home with her husband. Hermon Jr was discharged from the army and was also married. He lived out of state with his wife and children. Helena was not doing well at this time. She suffered from rheumatoid arthritis, back pain from an injury, and stomach ulcers but, somehow, she still worked and took care of things.

Michelle was 6 or 7 years old by then and I enrolled her in a Plainfield school. We lived with Helena and Marlene. I spoke to Hermon Jr. on the phone and found that his marriage was ending and he needed a place to go. So, he moved back to Plainfield with us. Eventually, Darlene also ran into some difficulties in her marriage and moved back home. For a time, we were all back together living in our childhood home on West 3rd Street, each patching up our wounds from the battles of life on our own. We each needed a place to regroup and relaunch into the world as independent adults. Of course, our mother welcomed us back with open arms. I immediately picked up a temp job and started working.

It was almost 5 months after my trip to London when Albert Bafu called me. We had kept in touch since we met. He wanted me to come back to London and offered to pay for the trip. My mother was a bit worried about my going but told me she would watch Michelle for me while I traveled. So, off I went back to London to meet Albert. I stayed with him in a small flat with his pregnant cousin. The cousin's boyfriend was out of the country and Albert let her stay with him. She did not speak much English which made it hard to communicate, but I helped her cook and clean while I was there. I got to see another side of London on that trip. I saw an area of the city where the majority of the people lived in poverty. It was the side of London that you don't see on T.V. There, flats were small and folk lived in crowded spaces. I went to the laundromat and even it was crowded. I believed I was poor until I saw how poor people lived there. This gave me a different impression of London. Truth be told, it was no different than American inner cities. It was not a glamorous view when I visited the first time.

Albert really did like me, but his ultimate goal was to get to the United States, and asked if I would help him. He knew America would afford him more opportunities. Since I was already married to a Ghanaian man and understood the culture, he thought I would be willing to help him immigrate. Albert and I did have genuine chemistry but my level of trust with African men was still pretty low after being married to Thomas.

I told Albert I would give some thought to him coming to visit me in America. However, when I got home, I was relieved that I did not choose to venture down that road again with another foreign man. I talked with Albert on the phone for months after that, but never extended the invitation for him to visit me. My ex-husband, Thomas, even talked with Albert over the phone briefly once when he came to Helena's house to visit Michelle. I was talking with Albert on the phone when Thomas stopped by on his way to New York. The only differences between Albert and Thomas were that Albert really fell for me, was the same age as me, and was a more youthful thinker.

Then one day, I called Albert and his cousin told me he was deported. It appeared that the white woman he was dating just before we met dropped a dime on him. She reported him to immigration saying that he was working in London without a visa. So, he was deported back to Ghana and I never heard from him again. Nevertheless, both trips to London sparked my interest in international travel and allowed me to grow not just intellectually but meeting Albert also helped me understand how to handle love relationships more maturely. I learned that my purpose was not just to serve a man or be there for him exclusively. I could see that a relationship needed to be a partnership and not a dictatorship. I started to realize I had worth and value. I knew I brought something to the relationship as an equal.

At this time, Michelle and I were living in Plainfield with my family. I was working two jobs and was on a treadmill going nowhere. The jobs were just enough to keep me going but not enough to pull me up out of my situation. It had been 4-5 months, but I was not able to become independent with my apartment and a permanent job. I was suffocating and had to find a way to get out of my mother's house. I needed to get a home for us and gain back my independence, but it was a struggle. I thought maybe I would move to Baltimore. Maybe I would be able to find better work opportunities there and get better established.

    I asked my mother if she could temporarily care for Michelle again while I relocated for a better opportunity. I moved to Baltimore, MD where my mother's family lived, and took a temporary position as a secretary with a law firm there. The job paid a little more than I was making in New Jersey. I really had gifts when it came to administrative work and I didn't even know it. I was a quick learner and skillful at word processing. I was highly motivated because I had to provide for my child. I didn't have the luxury to quit because I desperately needed the paycheck. God really gave me a gift to learn whatever software packages that were required and learn them quickly. I excelled at my temporary job with the law firm and learned a lot while working there. Things were looking up.

    On a beautiful summer day in August, before I moved to Baltimore, I went to a bank in Piscataway, New Jersey after work to cash my paycheck. Standing in line in front of me was a tall, well-dressed, black man in a dark suit and tie. He was quite obviously a businessman working in the area. As he left the teller's window, he turned and looked at me and smiled saying hello. I replied with a warm gesture of a nod and smiled as well.

Then I stepped up to the window and made a transaction with the teller. After I finished, I left the bank and noticed that the handsome man was standing just below the steps of the bank as if waiting for me to come out. He immediately introduced himself and for the life of me, I couldn't remember his name. He told me that he worked at a large company in Piscataway and was glad that he stopped by the bank that day to see such a beautiful young woman. This made me smile even wider and giggle a little. I noticed that he had a Caribbean accent. When I asked where he was from originally, he said Jamaica. This made him even more fascinating to me. After exchanging niceties and flirting, I told him I would be moving to Maryland in a few weeks and he asked for my number to stay in contact.

I made the move to Baltimore as I planned and 7 months after living there, the Jamaican businessman called saying that he was attending a week-long conference in the D.C. area and that his company put him up on a nice campus in Maryland for the week. He asked if he could visit me and said that we could hang out at the campus as it was nice and I could check out the area. After talking with him on the phone for nearly an hour, laughing and still getting to know him better, I agreed for him to come pick me up. I asked my next-door neighbor to watch my daughter, Michelle, for the day and I would return no later than 8 PM.

My new friend from Jamaica got lost trying to find my house and arrived much later than we arranged. Nevertheless, we stayed with the original plan to go to his work campus and hang out for the rest of the afternoon/evening. Just before

Impossible Things

arriving at his worksite, he stopped off at a liquor store and asked what type of liquor I would like. I was not much of a drinker, just an occasional beer but not liquor. I tried Johnny Walker Red while in the Army. So, I told him he could get that.

We arrived at the campus and went into the building to the 5th floor. We walked down a long hallway with rooms on either side that looked like dorm rooms. His room had a full-size bed, a large desk, a television, a mini fridge, and a bathroom. It was nothing special. I asked him if there were any special things he wanted to show me on campus and whether we were going to the cafe that we saw on the way to get something to eat. He told me that we were just going to have a few drinks, then he made a call, and then we walked the campus and got something to eat.

He went to get ice then gave me a glass and poured the liquor. I drank mine while he went to the bathroom. Then he came out and drank his. I had the TV on as I thought it was weird that he would bring me to such an ordinary place with nothing of great interest and that we went to his room first. When he finished his drink, he started to tell me how attractive I was and that he was glad I decided to come visit for a while. He sat on the bed with me and started to kiss the side of my face and hug me tightly. This was when I became aware of his intentions and got nervous. I told him that I didn't know him well enough to have sex.

He told me that I gave him a different impression and that he believed I was experienced and wanted the same thing he wanted. He continued kissing and hugging me and laid me back on the bed. I did not want to appear childish or let him know just how nervous I was, so I just relaxed and allowed him to continue. I didn't know what else to do. Things quickly got out of hand and he went all the way. I was scared and my body was not ready to have sex. This was apparent when he forcefully and painfully entered me. I was dry and I didn't realize that I was bleeding. After he finished and got up, he noticed all the blood on the sheets. I was not due for my period and I realized that I was not only violated but also injured. His first response was, "What the hell! This was not going to look good. This is my work and it will reflect poorly on me!" He seemed really upset. I was afraid of him and unsure of how much danger I was in. I wanted him to calm down. To diffuse his temper, I said calmly, "Oh don't worry, I will wash the stain out and you can let it dry. The cleaning staff won't know." I immediately took the sheets into the bathroom and used soap to get the stains out. While I was doing this, I stayed calm and was humming. I wanted to appear as if everything was fine.

Then his phone rang and he picked it up. When I stepped out of the bathroom, he waved his hand for me to be quiet while he was on the phone. I listened and he said, "I miss you too, I will be home in a couple of days." I knew then that he was married and that I tried to get out of there as soon as possible. Fear started to set in as I realized this situation could get even worse if I said or did anything to get him more upset. After he finished his phone call, he said to me, "Mike Tyson says he likes to make them bleed." Then he laughed. I was careful not to give any indication that what he said was offensive to me. I chuckled a little bit and told him that I was supposed to be back over an hour ago. I explained that my babysitter would not watch my daughter again if I was late and I did not want her to think I was the kind of person that hung out all night.

 The Jamaican man seemed to be calming down. He saw that my behavior was not anxious or scared and that the sheet was clean of any blood stains. He said we could leave but he could not take me all the way home. He would take me to Union Station in D.C. and I could take the train back home. I told him that would be fine but I only had $10.00 cash on me. He said he would give me the money for the train. As we walked out of the building, he noticed a police car nearby. He looked worried as he thought I may have called the police while he was in the bathroom. He grabbed my arm and turned us to walk in the opposite direction of the police car. Mr. Jamaica was relieved when he noticed the police car was parked and not following us. When we arrived at Union Station in D.C., he looked in his glove compartment and gave me $20.00. I got out of his car and was relieved to get away from him.

 Needless to say, I felt foolish for deciding to even get in the car with him as I did not really know him. The fact that I met him at the bank wearing a suit and tie did not make him a gentleman or a respectable person. I believe this was something that he probably practiced regularly. In hindsight, he was likely a serial rapist; a wolf in sheep's clothing, full of tricks and lies.

 I did not want to share this experience with anyone, but I felt I had to tell someone. The only person who came to my mind right away was my cousin Jean Alice Griffin. Jean and I grew up during those Baltimore summers when we were just 7 to 11 years old and my parents would have us stay with my grandmother at 2029 West Lanvale Street. As a child, I thought living in Baltimore was a rough way of life with row homes of lower-middle-class black folk who I found to be a bit country. Everyone sat on their stoops every day to socialize and watch the summer shenanigans of the neighborhood kids. We and our cousins all became close, but there was something special about Jean.

Jean was a little different with her beautiful chocolate brown complexion and jet-black wavy hair. She was always loud and abrasive. I now realized this was her defense mechanism as she was treated badly by our Aunt Juanita. She would call Jean out of her name by saying things like, "Bring your Black ass over here! What did you do now?" She always referred to Jean negatively and verbally abused her. Lots of times Jean would be singled out and harshly punished with being excluded from the rest of us because of something she said or did. I noticed then that Jean was being treated badly and I was sympathetic. As we grew and I started to gain my walk with the Lord, I discovered who Jean was. A true warrior of God in every sense. She was a fighter and a survivor. She was quite peculiar and said things like, "What was that Lord? I hear you." Over time, I grew to understand that Jean was truly touched by God and highly favored. For that reason, I chose to share my devastating experience with her. So, I called Jean and she came over to my house in Towson, MD the next day.

When Jean walked into my house, she felt an uneasiness and made me aware of it. I didn't think much about it until after we talked and prayed. We sat down and I told Jean everything about the rape without leaving out any detail. I told her I felt foolish and humiliated. Jean's initial response was, "How could you have allowed yourself to be put in that situation?" She was angry not at me but at the incident. Then she bowed her head and said, "Let's pray about this and read scriptures from the Bible." I found out that night that Jean was proficient in reading the scriptures. When she told me to read a certain verse from the King James Version, I stumbled over the words and mispronounced them even though I had several years of college and administrative office experience. When Jean read the Bible, she read with authority and conviction, not once stumbling over words or incorrectly pronouncing anything. She clearly operated with real spiritual gifts. Jean didn't graduate high school. She earned her GED through Job Corp. With her modest level of education, Jean read the Shakespearean language of the King James Bible effortlessly and sounded like a scholar. She was absolutely amazing. Then she began to pray.

Jean started with a prayer of healing for my mind and body. As she was finishing the prayer, her voice became fiercer and more authoritative. She continued to loudly pray to "Remove what is not of God in this house immediately." After about 10 minutes of Jean's loud worship and praise, the woman who lived upstairs started pounding on the floor and yelling for her to stop. After the prayer, Jean confirmed that the woman upstairs practiced witchcraft and that was the source of the uneasy feeling when she first walked into my door. The next morning, I received a call from my landlord saying the woman upstairs was complaining about the loud shouting coming from my apartment downstairs and that she wanted me to stop. I told him that we were praying and that it was a one-time thing. We were not being inconsiderate as it was in the afternoon not late night. Would you believe that the woman moved out less than a week after Jean's visit? She was shaken to her core. Darkness has no place with light and my cousin Jean brought the light.

I was fooled by that handsome, Jamaican businessman. Even after everything I had been through in my life, I thought he might be the one. I believed he could be the man that God sent to me as a spouse—to enhance my life and be my partner. But he turned out to be an imposter. He saw my naive behavior; and my friendly personality and he took advantage. It was a horrific lesson learned and one not to be repeated. It was deeply traumatic as I cannot remember his name or even the location where he took me, and I never reported it to the police. I thanked God for using my cousin Jean to help me get beyond it. I was lifted after her visit and the assault became a distant memory that did not haunt me. I can talk about it and write about it with ease, no more pain.

Thank you, Jesus!

Chapter 7
Marriage No. 2

In Maryland, 1989, my daughter Michelle and I lived in a house that had been converted into a two-family home. We lived on the first floor two-bedroom apartment with a basement. It had a living room, kitchen, and a small bath. It was affordable for a single mom making a secretary's salary. But I was overworked and struggling to keep up—so much so that I started to have problems coping. I could not sleep well, had serious hemorrhoids, and constipation. This condition became debilitating. I went to see a doctor who gave me medication to handle the symptoms but suggested that I see a psychiatrist to handle my anxiety and racing thoughts. I was apprehensive about seeing a psychiatrist but I knew I needed help. After the psychiatrist assessed my condition, he told me that I was headed toward a nervous breakdown. He recommended that I stop working for a while. He advised me to rest and slow down or things would get worse. I resisted at first. I told him I was the only source of income for my daughter and me, so I needed to work. Then the psychiatrist told me that I was under his care and if I did not take his instruction to stop work, he would have to act. He said he would have Child Services take my daughter and have me hospitalized if things progressed. With that fear tactic, I gave notice to my job at Black and Decker in Towson, MD.

L. Renae Spann

Michelle and I went to New Jersey with my used red 1979 Chevy. It had a bumper sticker on the right passenger side that said OUCH! and which covered a large dent. It was not much to look at, but it got us around. I visited with my mom in Plainfield for a few weeks in hopes that I could relax a bit and have someone help me deal with my stress and anxiety.

After feeling a little better, I decided to go back to my home in Towson, MD so Michelle and I started for our four-hour drive home. We left Plainfield around 5 pm. I was just off the New Jersey Turnpike and driving into Delaware on Interstate 95 around 8 pm when my car started to have problems. I exited the interstate and barely made it to the nearest service station. There was a mechanic on call who informed me that the car was inoperable and should be junked. My first thought was to call my mom which I did and she told me to go and see if there was a bus or train that could get us home to Towson. She told me to call her back in 30 minutes to let her know if I found a way home. I only had $30.00 on me and knew that it would not be enough for a taxi because we were over an hour from home. I hoped that I could get a ride to the bus or train station from someone who worked at the service station.

When I got off the phone with my mom, there was a woman and her grandson who overheard my conversation about needing a ride back to Towson. She asked me if I wanted a ride as she and her grandson were going my way. They just so happened to live in Towson. What a blessing and perfect timing! I immediately called my mother back and told her I had a ride

Impossible Things

home. She said that she had gone into prayer and had asked God to send help.

The nice woman drove Michelle and me to our house in Towson. When we arrived, she asked me if she could come in and pray with us before she left. I said yes and invited her in. We prayed in my kitchen. She said a sincere prayer, thanked the Lord for getting us home safely, and asked grace for all of us. As she was going out the door, she asked me if I needed food or anything. I immediately said, "No, we are fine. The ride alone was more than enough. We are thankful that you asked." I said this knowing I did not have any food in the fridge or cabinets and I only had $30.00 in cash. I offered the woman $10.00 but she would not take it.

The next day was Tuesday and I was told that the welfare office knew of a place where I could get food. I just had to come down to the office and get a food voucher. Michelle and I walked to the welfare office. When we got there, I was told that food was only distributed on Fridays at 10:00 am. I immediately got depressed because I knew that all I had was $30 to last us until Friday and no paycheck or assistance coming for weeks.

Michelle and I walked back to our house from the welfare office. When we got home, there were 4 bags of groceries on my doorstep with a note from the woman who had driven us home. The note said, "May the Lord be with you. Have a blessed day." I immediately started to cry while Michelle went through the bags. She said, "Look at all the good stuff Mommy!" We were without a car for almost a year. All I can say here is that we entertain angels unaware. From that day, false pride was stripped away from me. I will never again be too proud to ask for or receive help. Thank God, I am now in a position to give help.

Soon enough, in 1988 I was employed full-time and getting back on my feet. In addition to my temp position at the law firm, I seized the opportunity to start my own business in the evenings which I called Rapid Typing Services. I served students at Morgan State University and Towson University. Back then, the average person (especially men) did not type much. Women were typing a little more, but there was a definite niche market for typing student term papers and I had the skills. I decided to provide a service where I would go to campus, pick up the work, type it up, and then deliver the typed term papers back to the students. Once the word went out, the work picked up and my little business kicked off.

I was proud of myself. It felt great that I was able to supply a genuine need and become an entrepreneur. I had my business going and my full-time job. I had a little more income and life was gradually getting better. I met a really nice Latina girl, Iris, at Gregory Memorial Church in Towson, MD and she offered to do my bookkeeping for free. It was so amazing, she just wanted to help me. She didn't know English very well. So, Iris also taught Michelle Spanish and I helped Iris with her English. We bartered and helped each other. I was finally making money and things were going well in Baltimore, Maryland. I was able to take care of my daughter and was genuinely happy.

Impossible Things

In the summer of 1989, I went to Sears to pick up my word processor and I met Kenneth A. Johnson. He worked part-time as a Sales Associate. He was a husky guy, even slightly overweight, but it was not very obvious due to his muscular physique. He was about 5'9", handsome, and well-spoken. I believe he was drawn to my enthusiasm. I was so happy and motivated at that time in my life. I talked with him about my plans to do this or that. I just radiated a joyful energy and Kenneth was immediately drawn to it. He wanted to scoop me up real quick and get some of whatever it was that I had. I believe he wanted to gain that joy and happiness he saw in me.

Kenneth asked me out and we went on a date. I don't remember where. But, after that, he kept coming to visit me in my apartment in Towson, MD. He quickly became obsessed with me and I became very fond of him as well. One night while he was at work, my phone was off the hook and he had tried to call me over and over again. He eventually became worried and thought that something had happened to me. So, he left work just to come over to check on me. This made me think that our welfare, Michelle and mine, was very important to him and that he would make a good partner for me. Kenneth made me feel loved and protected. Our courtship was fast, only 3 months before he popped the proposal of marriage.

Before the pastor at Gregory Memorial Baptist Church could marry us, we had to have several counseling sessions. At our second meeting, I could tell that the pastor felt we were moving too fast and we did not really know each other. The questions that the pastor asked made us both feel uncomfortable as we could not really give good answers. For example, he asked questions like, "Why do you think you want to marry now?" and "Have you built a trusting bond?" or "Are your families in agreement with your union and will they be attending the wedding?"

Truth be told, we informed our parents just a few weeks before the wedding. My immediate family did not show. I don't believe that either side was excited about this fast wedding because they knew what type of people we both were. My family knew I was spontaneous and eager to be loved. Kenneth's family knew he was a manic-depressive gambler. We were both not well-suited for marriage at that time. We attended all of the required premarital sessions with the pastor because we just wanted to get married and start our life together. I would no longer have to concern myself with what others thought about me not being with someone so long after my divorce from Dr. Thomas Mensah. I wanted to feel chosen and desired again. In the beginning, Kenneth really showed me that he could provide that need.

I had fallen for Kenneth as fast as he had fallen for me. I thought he was handsome with full, kissable lips. He was not much taller than me but the perfect size for me. I thought a real manly man was not thin and short like my first husband. The courtship was short in fact I never did meet his family until our wedding day. I did not realize that maybe there had been a reason for that. Maybe Kenneth was afraid they would share information about him that would make me reconsider dating or marrying him. All I knew was that he moved fast. On one hand, I was curious as to what the rush was all about. On the other hand, my insecurity was telling me this might be my last chance at romance as I was in my mid-30s with no other prospects. Kenneth really wanted to get married and so we did.

We were married shortly after we completed our premarital counseling sessions. The wedding took place at the small chapel at Gregory Memorial First Baptist Church with a total of 8 people at attendance. My maid of honor was my friend, Iris, from Honduras who I had met in that same church.

Only weeks after we were married, I started to realize that we were both still broken and in the healing process. Kenneth would become depressed sometimes. He would just lay around and complain. I, on the other hand, would be running around trying to please him. It was my best attempt at trying to make him happy and keep the peace. But no matter what I did, he never encouraged me or affirmed me. He always found fault with both Michelle and me and complained about everything we did. Later, I would find out what he had not shared with me until that point.

What I didn't know was that Kenneth suffered from severe depression and manic episodes. He actually worked full-time at Clifton T Perkins Hospital Center in Jessup, Maryland, a prison for the criminally insane. He worked there as an orderly since leaving high school. It appeared to me that the work was too much for him emotionally and spiritually. I found that his usual demeanor was very anxious, fatigued, and depressed. This was his usual demeanor. It was like the bad spirits from the criminally insane patients at his work would attach to him and he could not separate himself from it. In meeting me, he found the exact opposite of sad, tired, and depressed. I was full of joy, faith, hope, high spirits, and excitement. He thought he found the answer to his problems. If he could be with me, it would bring him out of his depression. I, however, didn't clearly see or understand any of this until after we were married.

In learning all of this, it made me wonder why I had attracted this kind of person. I now understand that if I didn't learn the first time, I was doomed to repeat the same lesson over again. You have to learn the lesson to gain a sense of discernment. Once you have that, you will gain the ability to see the same thing coming and identify it before you make that mistake again. Ultimately, I repeated the mistake. I jumped blindly into another marriage thinking it was what I needed but I was wrong.

During this time, Kenneth could see that I was working hard and that the Rapid Typing Service business was successful. He became jealous of my minor success and started to sabotage me. He became possessive and controlling, telling me that I couldn't take certain phone calls and other things like that. He then moved us to his old row house on Moreland Avenue in Baltimore City. This was the first indication that things would be rough. The row house was nice with its old 1950s structure. It had a certain charm and quaintness to it. However, it was located in the worst of neighborhoods in Baltimore. I registered my daughter, Michelle, who was nine, in the local public school there. After just three days at that school, she ran from a boy who threw a bottle at her. The bottle hit her in the face and left a cut above her eye. One night, a police helicopter's searchlight shone into our bedroom window looking for a criminal who was on the run. Such incidents were typical for that neighborhood, but it got even worse.

Although being married to Kenneth was quickly becoming another dark period in my life, I can recall one amazingly bright experience I had during dark that time. My daughter, Michelle had a friend named Lona who lived around the corner from us in Baltimore. Michelle would go over and play at Lona's house sometimes after school. One afternoon when I went to pick up Michelle, Lona's mother invited me to an evening with Cicely Tyson in Washington, DC. Ms. Tyson was appearing at a gathering to give a talk followed by a question and answer session. I immediately said, "Yes." Cicely Tyson had been one of my idols when I was a teenager. Two of my favorite movies that she starred in were *The Autobiography of Miss Jane Pittman (1974)* where she played the title role and *Roots (1977)* where she played Binta, the mother of Kunta Kinte. I admired her as a truly remarkable actor.

That weekend, Lona's mother and I went to the event together. I wore a black dress with a white and pink floral print. My hair was styled in a short straight bob and with a natural gray streak in the front. I wanted to look polished when I met Cicely Tyson as the event would be in a small intimate setting. We all were in an auditorium as Cicely Tyson shared about her career, life experiences and, of course, her late husband, Miles Davis. She was poised, well-spoken and confident as she shared details of her life. I appreciated her candor in telling the stories of her personal life. She was transparent and authentic. After the talk, Ms. Tyson joined us for a meet-and-greet in the lobby where she signed autographs and chatted with attendees. I eagerly awaited my turn to speak with her, get an autograph, and take a picture with her. When it was finally my turn, I was too starstruck to speak. My friend took a picture of me with Ms. Tyson and when it was time for me to take a picture of my friend and with her, I froze again. Cicely Tyson hugged her as though there were friends and I missed the photo. Needless to say, my friend was upset with me. I missed her once in a lifetime photo op with Cicely Tyson. This event was just one more time that I found myself in the presence of greatness. I was up close and personal with one of my favorite actresses and it was wonderful. Later in 1994, Cicely Tyson starred in a new television series, *Sweet Justice* in which her character wore a short straight bob haircut and with a gray streak in the front. I could not help but to assume that she got the idea for her hairstyle when she met me. I would like to think that the great Cicely Tyson was influenced by me, Renae Spann. Meeting her was a wonderful experience and a perfect distraction from my life in Baltimore with Kenneth. I love how God always took time to show me that there was something better for me out there if I just keep moving forward.

My marriage to Kenneth was not getting any better. We were always fighting about one thing or another. Once we were arguing about something that I cannot even remember. It escalated to him pushing me into our bedroom closet. This situation felt eerily familiar to me. When I landed on the other side of the closet, I got up calmly, picked up the phone on the nightstand, and called the police. I was telling them to send an officer to our address when the phone was suddenly disconnected. Kenneth snatched the phone from the wall socket. By the grace of God, Michelle heard the commotion, ran to the back room in the office, and called the police again. The voice on the phone told her not to worry because the police were on the way. They traced the address from the disconnected call. I was scared and ran downstairs. By the time I got downstairs, the police were knocking at the front door. I let them in and pointed up the stairs where Kenneth was standing. He was hyperventilating and trying to catch his breath. The officer ran to his aid and helped him calm down to regain control of his breathing. I was looking at him thinking he had been such a bully with Michelle and me, but became a complete coward when the police showed up. The police said that one of us had to leave the house and Kenneth immediately said he would go to his mom's home nearby.

After that incident, I went to a battered women's shelter for two weeks while Michelle was in summer camp. During that time, Kenneth came to my job looking for me and asked me to come home. He was so sweet and accommodating. He brought a balloon that said I love you and we went out to eat afterward. Feeling that he was sorry and remorseful, I returned home with him. Today, I recognize that as the honeymoon phase of the cycle of domestic abuse that battered women experience. It is short-lived happiness. Even on the car ride home after dinner, his sweetness was gone. He scolded me for leaving him and made me promise not to do it again. From that point on, Kenneth slept with a large knife hanging on the bedpost on his side of the bed. He said it was for protection, but I now understand that its purpose was to intimidate me.

Then there were times when Kenneth would shut off his affections. He would just go cold and unloving. His sexual habits were another thing that made me uncomfortable. He likely had a porn addiction and often told me I was inhibited when I refused to accommodate him with far-fetched sex acts. It was many years later that I learned his weird sexual practices were probably considered common for some people. The sexual world may be liberal in some ways to keep it exciting. I, however, found oral, anal, and rough sex to be repulsive. Once while searching around in the basement, I came across several boxes of pornographic video tapes. I did not understand why a married person would watch porn with or without their spouse. I felt it only encouraged sexual fantasies that could be or not be fulfilled by the spouse. Which could be the temptation to venture outside the marriage to live out what they see in these types of movies. I have to refer to the Bible verse of Proverbs 23:7 which says, "As a man thinketh in his heart, so is he." Sex is a natural function and a beautiful thing, for a husband and wife to enjoy and procreate. People should not want to have it on their minds constantly. We are human, let's all practice self-control and unselfishness.

My take on pornography is that watching the act of someone else having sex, live or on video, can trigger a sex

Impossible Things

addiction and/or provoke a desire for other sexual partners and behaviors that are ungodly. I realize that the emotional damage that is done to some children due to molestation, rape, or exposure to sex can cause unhealthy sex practices or behaviors as an adult. All I can say is that more self-control and protecting our children from exposure to such acts may make for more healthy sex practices as adults. Extra stimuli or bizarre types of sex paraphernalia are not needed. I know there are lots of people who may disagree with me, but this is my stand on the matter. Having a conscience is one of the things that caused Kenneth and I to divorce. I had my young daughter to think about, and protect her from possibly being exposed to an unwholesome environment. This was a non-negotiable for me.

On a spiritual note, the row house had a generally bad vibe. My daughter Michelle and I were sitting watching TV one night and I don't know what drew my attention to the wood paneling in the living room. The whole house had wood paneling except the kitchen. I noticed that there was an image of a scary, devil-like face in one of the panels. I thought my eyes were playing tricks on me. Maybe the pattern in the paneling gave that type of image when looked at a certain angle. To confirm what I was seeing, I told my daughter, who was 9 years old at the time, to look at the panel and let me know what she saw. She immediately screamed and said it was a scary evil face in the paneling. We both felt uncomfortable about the area where we were sitting so we went upstairs. As we were walking up the stairs, we noticed that that same pattern/image was in every paneling. We both freaked out and ran to the front door. Once out of the house, we went next door to the neighbor. Our neighbor was an older black lady who had been living in her house for over 30 years. We told her what we were experiencing in the house with the walls and I invited her to come over and look at it. She told me that she did not want to see such a thing and that we could sit at her house for a while until Kenneth got home. Needless to say, it was not much longer before I made my final exit out of that house and the Baltimore hood.

Amid my turmoil that year, I lost my mom shortly after Thanksgiving, only 6 years after My Daddy's death on January 31, 1985. They both died young before 60. I took both my parents' deaths hard, but it was even harder with my mom. I knew I had lost my best friend and the only true advocate for everything I endeavored to accomplish in life. No matter what happened in my life, Helena had been my safe place. Her tough love had given me the confidence to get back up every time I fell. Losing her was devastating.

I remember when Helena was dying and not wanting anyone to come to the house to see her in bed. I came there from Baltimore and helped for a week by washing her hair, cleaning the house, and helping out with my sister Marlene. It was around Thanksgiving when she took a turn for the worst. Even then, she attempted to come downstairs to join the family in the dining room for Thanksgiving dinner. She was at the top of the stairs and called for one of us to bring her the TV tray and a chair so she could sit at the top of the stairway. There she sat and ate Thanksgiving dinner. She could not make it any further. It is only right now while I am writing this that I realize she was in great pain but wanted to give us that last memory of her on Thanksgiving Day. Tears are welling up right now as the memory of her strength and strong constitution overwhelms me. I have not seen anything like it since. I always say if I had just a small amount of Helena's tenacity, strength, and endurance, I would be awesome. She was truly my 'shero.'

She was carried out days later by ambulance to the hospital. Kenneth and I drove back to New Jersey from Baltimore. At the hospital, I read the Bible to her and shared the stories she told about me when I was a baby — how my daddy held me up on the front porch and said, "Who's the prettiest girl on the block?" I could tell from Helena's eyes that she was thinking, "There she goes again being vain and being Renae." These were our last moments together before I left the hospital. I went to the house to cook dinner for the family while Darlene stayed at the hospital. Hours later, she died on December 6, 1991. It was the end of a "good thing" as Helena would always say as you never miss it until it's gone.

We notified all of our family in Baltimore and started preparing for the funeral. The family came as my mother had touched all their lives for the better as well. In my lowest point of grieving, my husband was not very empathic. In fact, he was busy flirting with my first cousin, Bonnie, and she was with him. It was the day before the funeral and we were all feeling down. We decided to go to the mall just to walk around. When I went to get in the car to go with the group, both Bonnie and Kenneth decided at the last minute that they were too tired to go. I immediately sensed that something was amiss, so I went back to the house. The group went without the three of us. I know I made the right choice. I did not need to have more grief if they got together sexually in my mother's house. I believe even now that those two did eventually get together. Because when we got back to Baltimore, I confronted Kenneth about flirting with her. He responded that I should be concerned because he had a dream about Bonnie making advances toward him and they got together in the dream. His response showed that Kenneth could not be trusted. He was lusting after Bonnie and may have picked up with her after our divorce which happened months later. I forgive both of them if that was the case.

I believe my sister, Darlene, probably recognized the danger of what Kenneth could be capable of since he was from Baltimore and worked at a jail for the criminally insane. When I finally left him, my old apartment became available and I was able to move back there. Darlene helped me. She gave me several hundred dollars to help me move. But, Kenneth had been stalking me. Once I came out and saw that his car was parked outside my apartment. I was afraid and called Darlene. She sensed my fear and she immediately called Kenneth. She called him up and said, "If you mess with my sister, I'll send somebody over there to do you in. You better leave her alone." She tore into him, which let me know that she still had love and concern for me. I never knew Darlene had some Jersey Gangster in her. She was incensed about Kenneth stalking me and adamant that she would send someone to deal with him. She said what she had to say to help me. I think that was one of our strongest times as sisters. I can say that Darlene went to bat for me and I appreciated it. Deep down that love was still there. It can't die. It is too strong. She came to my aid and I appreciated the money she gave me and the phone call she made to Kenneth. She knew the urgency of me having to leave Baltimore City. It was a horrible place. After that, I did not see him stalking me anymore and I was able to move on and do what I had to do.

My marriage to Kenneth lasted only six months. My first marriage lasted six years and I could now recognize the signs. I knew the abuse would continue to escalate and I decided not to subject my daughter and myself to that again. I quickly got out of that situation. I told myself, "No more!" No more marriage, no more anything. I didn't want romantic relationships. I was done! I decided I was just going to take care of my daughter and be among the other statistically single Black mothers out there.

By 1993, Michelle and I had our old apartment in Towson again, and I was working as an Executive Secretary at PHH Fleet America in Huntsville, MD. I had not worked there for long, maybe 6 months, and was considered a high performer. I enjoyed being around my co-workers there and we all got along well. One young lady in particular was Dena Pettaway, she was 26 years old, a black, beautiful, dark-skinned young lady who dressed impeccably and showed great professionalism. She had worked her way up from the mailroom where she worked one year with her ex-boyfriend, Preston Robert Fuller, who was also 26. Preston was black, stood around 6'4, 220 pounds, and appeared to be a nice, polite young man. Dena had high goals and wanted to move up in the company. She and I had several things in common but one that I remember is that we both loved

Thanksgiving. We both thought that fall was the best time of the year. We would talk when she came past my desk. One day her ex-boyfriend, Preston, came from the mailroom and brought her a balloon for her birthday but she did not entertain his efforts to win her back.

I, however, had met someone new and thoughts of remaining single were fading. I had been dating a man named Kevin Bland from Glassboro, New Jersey that I met on the New Jersey Turnpike on my travels to NJ. Kevin came with his problems as his mother was dying of cancer as my mother had. This was what bonded us. I thought that he was the perfect mate as he was a Jersey boy who liked to have fun. Maybe too much fun. Kevin was a recovering alcoholic who, at the time we met, had been sober for two years. He was divorced from a nurse who had been the provider while he was a house husband who took care of their two children. Kevin and I were becoming serious and talking about marriage. He took the initiative to move from Glassboro to Towson to live with me. He was there for about a month when my landlord found out that he moved in and asked me to leave. There were only 2 people on the lease, Michelle and myself. Since I was losing my apartment, I decided we would all move back to New Jersey to my mother's house in Plainfield, NJ.

Since Helena's death, my childhood home had been left unoccupied and unattended. I knew it was wrong to move there with Kevin as my mother was against any of her children moving in together with someone without being married. What made me feel guilty and ashamed was that it was her house we were moving into. But I knew, living there would save me money and also allow me to take in my disabled sister, Marlene Kevin could also help me fix up the house and maintain it. The decision was made. I informed my supervisor at PHH Fleet America that I was planning to get married and move to New Jersey. I gave the appropriate two-week notice then we packed up and left for Plainfield once again to live.

I was in New Jersey for less than a week when I decided to call one of my former coworkers at PHH Fleet America to just see how things were with them. One of the supervisors in the department informed me that the beautiful, young, Black woman, Dena, whom I had sat just two desks away from, had been shot and killed while at work in the morning. Her ex-boyfriend, Preston found out that she was in a loving relationship with a 25-year-old vending service driver and was planning to get married because she was also pregnant. This was too much for Preston to bear. So, at 8:30 am on September 16, 1993, he came up from the mailroom, walked over to her desk, and shot her in the head. All the other workers in that area witnessed Dena's murder that day. The company provided a therapist to help everyone through the trauma and issues that they experienced from the incident.

All I know is that if I had been there when this occurred, I would not have been the same because it would have affected me deeply to have known this woman as a former co-worker and to see this type of violence happen in front of me. Knowing that the deranged man could have continued to fire his weapon at everyone in that space would have been too much to add to my personal history of trauma and domestic violence. God's grace and mercy spared me from this experience and it made me even more grateful to know that I had been removed from harm's way days before the incident. Even now as I write about this, it moves my spirit and brings grief that someone so young and promising had her life snuffed out by a demonic spirit. May God rest her soul until Jesus returns and I see her again. God's timing has always been impeccable in my life.

As for my relationship with Kevin, it only lasted a total of 3 months. I later found out that he had made his deceased brother's fiancée pregnant and lied to me the whole time. He was not meant to stay in my life. He definitely had to go. But looking back, I realize he was one of the reasons I left PHH Fleet America and moved back to my mother's house in New Jersey. He was able to help me fix the house up and I was able to take in my disabled sister from a group home. Kevin moving into my apartment and getting us evicted was for my good. I also found out later that Kevin smoked weed which was not okay with me and kept his stash in our house behind the dryer. Even though he was a dynamic lover, a great housekeeper, and an all-around fun guy, he was not my Prince Charming. He was just someone God used to move me away from danger and onto my next phase in life.

Chapter 8
Moving on Without My Mom

I was living in my mother's house again in Plainfield, New Jersey. This time, it was without my mom since she recently passed away. I lived there with my younger sister, Marlene, and Michelle for several years. Before leaving New Jersey again for the last time, I was in the process of selling my mother's home and there was a woman who was interested in purchasing the house. The woman attended a local holy and sanctified church on Front St. in Plainfield. The woman happened to be the girlfriend of the Pastor of the church and she invited me to come visit.

I went to the church one Sunday morning and while in the service, an African pastor with the gift of prophecy came to where I was sitting and prophesied to me right in front of the congregation. He told me that God had a man, a husband for me. I immediately told him that I was not interested. I was emotionally drained. In my mind, marriage would only lead to me having to start all over from scratch when things don't work out. He laughed and said, "This time it will be like something you've never experienced before. It will be a good thing." I was still hesitant to receive this word from the prophet. After two bad marriages, continuing the search for my prince seemed futile. I wasn't looking anymore and not expecting him to show up. But, I never forgot what the prophet told me that Sunday.

By this time, I had been building my resume for years. I had military experience, a college degree, computer training, and a good amount of executive administrative experience. I had been working clerical jobs, as an administrative assistant, executive assistant, and secretary for years. I wanted to get into management to work one job instead of two. I wanted one job that would replace the pay of two jobs, so I could have more time with my daughter and be at home more. I also needed to help Marlene by driving her to and from work. It was quite a bit of responsibility and I was pushing for that managerial job with more pay that would lighten my load. For years, I placed my sister, Darlene, on my resume as a professional reference. Our last names were different because she was married. No one would know she was my sister and she would be able to give me a strong professional reference to help me land a better position. I was constantly applying for jobs and going for interviews. Finally, I was offered a supervisory position. I was excited and relieved to get the position.

After I had been working at the new company for two or three weeks, one of the managers came to check in with me. She told me I was doing well. I was supervising two girls and they were also working well together. She commended me and then added that I might want to remove Darlene Lynch from my resume going forward because she had not given me a good reference. She told me that Darlene told them that I had a nice personality but I made a lot of errors. The manager did not know

Impossible Things

Darlene Lynch was my sister. I thought back over all the jobs that I applied for and wondered how many times I gave her as a reference. How many times had she sabotaged my efforts to advance professionally and that made me question everything. I was really devastated.

If that manager had never told me, I wouldn't have known. The day, I confronted Darlene and told her what the manager said, she had a ready explanation. She is quite clever. She said no one is perfect and she didn't mean any harm. She said she was trying to make it sound like a sincere reference. I told her the manager was clearly telling me it was NOT a good reference. It was so bad that she advised me to remove her from my resume. Darlene just stuck to her story that she was not trying to sabotage me. Regardless of her many excuses, this experience showed that I could not trust my sister in certain areas and it was probably better that we separate for a while. She tried to hold me back, but God knew best. I succeeded despite Darlene and despite myself.

But over time, I realized I had to forgive because nothing could stop me from my own destiny. We are much older now. I'm 65 and she's 64 as I am writing this memoir. We are both off on our own and have put all this in the past.

There was also a time when I betrayed my sister. Darlene allowed me to have my name on her Discover card just after I divorced my first husband, Thomas Mensah. I was desperate as a single mom and thought I could use the card for travel and a down payment on a car and then pay Darlene back without her knowing it. But I only got deeper in debt and she found out. This was something that she held against me. Hoping to make amends many years later, I paid her back the $2,000 that I charged on her card. I also paid for our parents' grave stones and invited all my siblings to stay in a hotel near the cemetery in New Jersey, so we could attend a special memorial Christmas service at the cemetery together. I knew it was wrong of me to have used Darlene's card without her permission all those years ago. It was just one more thing to break our trust in each other. But God has released the pain and frustration of our past and I can honestly say that I forgave my sister for everything and I believe she too had forgiven me. Our relationship has grown much closer in recent years.

Through the years, our sisterhood was a complicated one. There was another incident between Darlene and me during my time living in New Jersey and I believe this experience brought us closer together. Darlene was pregnant with her second child, which was a boy. Darlene called me at work during the day and said that her water broke and she was going into early labor. I immediately knew I had to leave work. I did not have time to tell my boss I had to go because my sister was in labor. It was just that connection between Darlene and me. After everything I had been through with childbirth, I realized how critical things like that could be, so I left work for half a day. I was a temp, so that meant I would lose pay or possibly lose the assignment, but I didn't care. I just left and met Darlene at the hospital.

She was lying in bed with her head lowered and her feet elevated. I'll never forget the fear in her voice when she explained that she was in that position to stop the labor. I thought, "Oh my God! She might lose the baby!" I just cried right there with her. I was thinking, what are we going to do? I was in it with her. I just felt that close to her. I want to talk about that because that was a time that I felt close to her. This was well after Jasper and other things that we went through as kids. I still loved my sister and I was as devastated as she was when she lost that baby. He was born prematurely, around 5 months. Darlene went through her pain and she was then able to identify with the loss of my twins. This loss was especially painful because we all wanted that boy. She and I share a common pain in knowing what it is like to lose a child.

 Not long after this, in the Fall of 1995, my favorite cousin, Jean Alice Griffin, was driving in Baltimore, when the Lord instructed her to drive to Plainfield where I lived at the time. Jean had not been to our house for several years and she had never driven herself to New Jersey before. I do not know how she knew the way to our house, but she came straight away. I found that amazing in itself. She arrived at the house unexpectedly in the late afternoon while I was still at work, but Marlene and Michelle were at home. Since I was working at Macy's in Bridgewater, NJ, the three of them got in the car and drove to the mall. When I saw Jean, she was her usually jolly self, laughing and joking and doing some shopping while I was at the register in the dress department. I got off work an hour later and they followed me over to Darlene's house in East Orange, New Jersey. Unbeknownst to Jean, Darlene was recovering from the recent miscarriage of her son just days earlier and was feeling melancholic. We all talked and laughed into the evening and Darlene's spirits were lifted. After several hours of visiting with Darlene, Jean came back to Plainfield with Marlene, Michelle and me.

When we got back to our house, we were all tired but continued to talk and share memories. All the while, I was thinking that Jean might have been hoping to stay with us for a long period and I started to feel anxious. I was already handling the house after my mother died as well as looking after Marlene, who was disabled with seizures, in addition to handling Michelle, a restless preteen. My hands were full and I did not want another person joining our makeshift family. Working two jobs, driving Marlene back and forth to work, and raising Michelle while she was anxiously trying to "find herself" was too much for me to handle. Just as I was going to ask Jean how long she planned to stay, she said, "Oh well, it's time for me to move on, but before I go, let us pray." We all stood up and formed a small circle holding hands while Jean ushered in the Holy Spirit by speaking in tongues. Jean went on praying earnestly and with the boldness of Christ Jesus. About 5 minutes into prayer, Jean let go of my hand, took both of Michelle's hands, and continued to pray, pleading for the blood of Jesus Christ. I do not remember all of what she prayed for, but Michelle suddenly broke free from Jean and ran to the kitchen where she held her head over the garbage can and vomited. I thought maybe she had become nauseated from the smell of cigarette smoke because Jean was a heavy smoker. I went into the kitchen to attend to Michelle while Marlene started to clean up the floor where Michelle had missed the garbage can. I looked at Michelle and she seemed to glow. I said, "Oh my God! It looks like Michelle has come back to herself." She looked relieved. At that moment, I did not identify this occurrence as a spiritual deliverance, but now I understand that Jean was sent to us on a mission from God that day. She came to remove that unclean spirit from my daughter and to alleviate Darlene's depression because of the miscarriage. When Jean got the word from God to move, she did just that. We all said goodbye to Jean and I was relieved because it was apparent that God sent an earthly angel to cover our house and bring back joy and peace. In hindsight, I would say this was a miraculous experience. Only God knew exactly what we needed and He sent Jean to help us. I love Jean for her obedience to the Holy Spirit.

I was admittedly not the most spiritually mature Christian, but I was learning. All my life, Helena taught me to pray and to trust God above all else. Now, as I was trying to succeed on my own in the absence of my mother, praying, trusting in God, and working hard were all I knew. Around this time, I landed an assignment working at Hoechst Marion Roussel Inc. in Bridgewater NJ as a Clinical Trial Database Assistant. Working for this company was my first substantial career move. I had previously done administrative and secretarial work for several other companies, but this company trained me to manage their clinical trial database for all field personnel. I was responsible for acquiring the information that would allow all Clinical Trial Database Assistants in various company locations to input data into the system. Even though all database assistants were able to access necessary information from reports generated from the database, the process was not comprehensive and user-friendly. At the company headquarters in Frankfurt, Germany, users could convert the data using an "ODBC driver for SQL server which is a single dynamic-link library (DLL) continuing run-time support for applications using native-code APIs to connect to SQL server." Initially, all this technical language was Greek to me and slightly over my head, but I had the ingenuity to figure things out on my own. So, I explored the existing database to teach myself how to manipulate the data. Noticing my tenacity, my manager, who was from France, selected me to travel with a group to the company headquarters in Frankfurt, Germany. There, we would complete a one-week training course on how to effectively use their method to convert the data. Needless to say, I did not have advanced technical training at that time. I was just operating with the gift of administration and walking in blind faith. I was trusting God and He allowed the manager to see that I had the potential to do more.

I was nervous about the training and feared I might be in over my head. I wondered if I would be able to learn the process and do what they wanted me to do. I wasn't sure but, I decided I was going to give it my best effort. In the days before we were scheduled to leave for Germany, I stayed late at work to see if I could figure out exactly how the new process was supposed to work. While exploring different drop-down menus in the database interface, I noticed something that said "input and output." I assumed that this input/output menu might be useful in the uploading and merging of data. I just wanted to have some ideas before the class so I would not be lost. Surprisingly, during the training, I found that the menu I saw was indeed relevant to the process. Because of my extra effort beforehand, I was able to keep up in class and complete the training.

Even more, than doing something out of the ordinary and having the opportunity to become more specialized in my career, my business trip to Frankfurt, Germany was an adventure. I felt like a top executive when the limo showed up at my house on West 3rd Street to take me to Newark International Airport. I had traveled internationally before, but not like this and I had never been to Germany. After my limo ride to the airport, I boarded my international flight and, to my delight, was seated in first class. During the flight, I was served a nice lunch with real silverware and Haagen-Dazs ice cream for dessert. There was also a full-service bar in the back of the first-class section. In my seat, I was able to press a button on the middle armrest to activate a small monitor that showed movies. I felt like I had arrived in the corporate world. This company changed my life for the better by elevating my professional skills and introducing me to business travel.

I had worked for Hoechst for only 4 months when I was selected to go to Germany for training. This caused issues with some of my white co-workers who had been with the company for years. They had never been selected to take such a trip. My managers were also white, but they were originally from Europe. They were not at all concerned with the unspoken racial hierarchy in the United States. All they wanted was someone with the tenacity and work ethic to get the job done. A person who then would bring the training back and help to implement it in our location. Accomplishing this would make us consistent with the clinical trials database management in the rest of the company's locations. I was chosen because I was right for the job.

While I was in Frankfurt for training, a German manager offered to give me a tour around Frankfurt and show me the culture. I tried different German foods. Pork seemed to be a popular dish there along with apple wine. Both were delicious. I also noticed that things were expensive there, especially clothes. Seeing the city, I learned that it was not the old-world Germany that I read about in history books. As a black woman, I was received well with no signs of racism and there was no harsh political environment. It was a new and improved Germany with folks trying hard to show the major change from the country's negative past. As far as I was concerned, the trip only confirmed that I was moving up in the world. I was inspired to continue working hard and trusting God with my future. After the week in Germany, I returned from my business trip with more confidence. Then I was back to working 2 jobs and taking care of our little family.

Since Michelle became a freshman in high school, I had been telling her that she could go to any university that she desired. She just had to keep her grades up and keep the faith. When she was in 11th grade at Piscataway High School in New Jersey, she told me she wanted to go to Spelman College in Atlanta, Georgia, a historically Black, all-female college that is considered part of the Black Ivy League with the price tag and elite level of learning to prove it. I wanted to show her that I meant and believed in what I said about going to the school of her heart's desire.

I did some research and scheduled us for a group tour of Spelman College a few weeks later. My temporary job at Merck Pharmaceutical in Springfield, New Jersey had a raffle and I had won a two-night hotel stay at Embassy Suites. So, I booked with Embassy Suites in downtown Atlanta. Then I got 3 Amtrak tickets to Atlanta for Marlene, Michelle, and myself. I was determined to at least give her the experience and opportunity to see for herself if this school would be a good fit. We could worry about how to finance it later. This is where this story gets interesting.

I went into a deep sleep the night before our trip to Atlanta. My dream/visitation was as follows:

I told my daughter Michelle that she needed to see her father, Dr. Thomas O. Mensah, who she had not seen since she was 3 years old. She was now 16. We went into a building that had steep steps to the top and walked about 3 levels up. When at the top of the stairs, I opened the door and Tom was all balled up in a fetal position at the corner of a king-sized bed. He was short, skinny, and frail. My first response was, "Oh My God, what's wrong with him, is he sick?!" A young Mulatto girl came out of another door in the room with a tray of medicine. She informed me that Tom had AIDS and that he would not be with us much longer. When I heard this, I screamed out, "Oh no, please let it not be so!" My ex-husband, Tom, caused me much grief with both physical and emotional abuse in the 6 years that we were married. He had not paid child support or alimony beyond 6 months after our divorce and custody were settled. Still, I did not want this disease of AIDS to be his plight and cause his death.

I screamed so loudly that I woke myself up in a cold sweat. The dream felt real and the feeling lasted for hours after I woke up. I was happy that it was just a dream. Because of that dream, I no longer hated him or wished him bad. I was released from the unforgiveness that I felt for him. I had only a loving heart and felt the bitterness was lifted.

That morning, we were on our way to Atlanta by train. When we arrived in Atlanta that evening, we checked into the Embassy Suites hotel, had dinner, and then went to bed. The following morning, we went to a presentation in the auditorium, scheduled for 10:00 am. Then we took a guided tour of the campus. At noon, we went to the cafeteria to get lunch. While standing in line selecting my meal, I looked across the room and there he was, Dr. Thomas O. Mensah! I could hardly believe my eyes. He was sitting there in the cafeteria. He was there to talk to new students at the orientation.

When Tom saw me, he had a scared look on his face. I am sure he thought I was going to go into a rage and make a scene about him not paying child support for all those years. Instead, I smiled and went over to him. I told him Michelle was sitting at the table nearby and that he should go over and see her to which he agreed. As Tom approached the table where Michelle and

Marlene were seated, Marlene said, "There is your father, Michelle." Michelle was so shocked and confused that she started crying and shaking. She was so overwhelmed that she could barely speak. Tom realized that my mood was calm and friendly, so he too became friendly and wanted to talk. He asked where we were staying and that night, he came to our hotel lobby and talked with Michelle further. He still did not pay any child support and did not leave his contact info or address. Nevertheless, the dream had prepared me for this encounter with Tom. Years after this encounter, Michelle was working for Child Support Services in Atlanta and found that Dr. Thomas O. Mensah was also not paying support for another daughter. He had fathered this second daughter with a fair-skinned Black woman. That was the Mulatto girl I saw in my dream. This whole experience once again confirmed that my steps are ordered by God. There are no coincidences in my life.

    Before I moved back to New Jersey, Marlene had been living in a group home due to her disability. But soon after Michelle and I moved into my mother's house, both caretakers (husband and wife) at the group home died within a few weeks of each other. So, Marlene moved back home and the three of us lived in our family house in Plainfield for nearly six years. Marlene became more independent because I did not coddle her as Helena did. I still had a bit of military discipline from my years in the Army Reserve. This was to Marlene's benefit as she knew that certain things were expected of her now that Helena and my brother Harmon were no longer able to help. I was working full-time at Hoechst Marion Roussel and then part-time at Macy's at night. I had a teenage daughter to care for. There was no time for me to coddle anyone.

Amazingly, Marlene thrived! She worked part-time, did some of the housekeeping, and even cooked sometimes. She became more and more independent as time passed. When both Marlene and I thought she was ready to move on, so that I too could move on, she went to the library and started looking for subsidized housing. She got her name on the list for subsidized housing in New Jersey. However, the wait for New Jersey locations would be several years. So, Marlene expanded her search to other states and found assisted living housing in Opelousas, Louisiana. We moved her to Louisiana and she lived there for 7 years on her own with the help of staff at her housing complex. Eventually, housing would become available and she would move back to New Jersey.

Her move to independence gave her a fresh start and paved the way for Michelle and me to also make a change for the better. It was time for a new direction. West 3rd Street changed a lot over the years. There were too many bad things going on and it was getting worse. Michelle was a young teenager by now and was affected by the negative influences in the neighborhood. I managed to enroll her in a better high school in an adjacent town where she was doing well. She had good grades, was a cadet in the ROTC program, and also played clarinet in the marching band. That school was good for Michelle, but she still had to come home to our neighborhood every day.

Impossible Things

It is said that an apple doesn't fall too far from the tree. Remembering my own experiences on West 3rd Street as a fourteen-year-old, I knew I had to get my daughter away from there and into a healthier, more stable environment. I felt the responsibility to keep her away from drinking, drugs, smoking, teenage sex, and pregnancy. I refused to see my child repeat my mistakes and waste her God-given talents hanging out with the wrong crowd. The environment was everything. So, the family house in Plainfield, NJ went up for sale and off we went to Hampton, Virginia without a concrete plan for the future. I was stepping out on faith once again, I truly believed my steps were being ordered by God. I just had to trust Him and move forward in faith. I decided to voluntarily give up my red Volvo sports sedan to no longer have a car payment. I cashed in my 401K and pooled all my resources. Then I bought an old brown Chevy and put a large carrier on top, causing the car to lean to the front. We looked like The Beverly Hillbillies! We loaded up the car and headed south to Virginia.

Michelle and I landed near Hampton University, which is another historically black college. I applied for a job at the university and was immediately hired as the Administrative Assistant for Dr. JoAnn W. Haysbert who was a professor and coordinator of graduate studies at that time. Looking back, it was my honor to work for such an exemplary Black woman who went on to have a distinguished career in academia. She became the fifteenth and first female president of Langston University and was the first African-American, female president of any college or university in the state of Oklahoma. Dr. Haysbert, in the spring of 2012, returned to Hampton University as First Chancellor, and recently retired as Executive Vice President, and Provost in 2024.

While working for Dr. Haysbert, she told me that she was the sister-in-law of the actor, Dennis Haysbert, who starred in the movie Waiting to Exhale and many Allstate commercials. Never did I think I would cross paths with someone of this professional caliber once I divorced Dr. Thomas Mensah. In addition to her professional accomplishments, I found Dr. Haysbert to be highly inspiring as a black woman. She was a modest woman who sewed her young daughter's clothes herself. She wore no make-up or flashy outfits. She was my example of a wholesome woman of God. I know now that I was destined to meet her. Dr. Haysbert was my evidence of faith. She loved the Lord and shared with me how God had amazing grace on her when she was near death. Her favorite hymn was Amazing Grace. I thank God that I had the opportunity to meet this extraordinary Black woman. It was no coincidence that she was placed in my path at that specific time in my life. After losing Helena and trying to find my way, Dr. Haysbert was a role model for me.

My old Chevy was on its last legs. It was what we New Jerseyans call a "hooptie." A hooptie is an old used car that is drivable, but barely functional with many mechanical problems. My old Chevy fit the description. It had manual windows that rolled up and down by hand and it would sometimes stall while I was driving it. One day, I was driving and approaching a yellow light that was about to turn red. I slowed down to a stop

Impossible Things

and the car stalled. I had to start it back up before the light turned green again. Before I could get it started and accelerate again, a man driving behind me got out of his car. He came to my car and banged on my window causing the driver-side window to drop down into its casing within the car door. The man started shouting at me, "You could have made that light!" I was so nervous as I tried to explain the malfunctions of the car — telling him I had to start slowly or it would shut off again. That was my first encounter with road rage. I was so shaken by it, that I told Dr. Haysbert about the incident and she started allowing me to drive her Cadillac to run errands. She was so sweet and caring.

While looking for a house to rent with my tax refund, I came across a tiny single-family house just four blocks from the University. It had one bedroom, a small living room, a bathroom with tub only, and a small kitchen that could only fit one person at a time. The kitchen was so small, I barely managed to fit a small two-seater table in there. The house had no air conditioner or fan. The rent was $700 a month which was a lot for me since my job at Hampton University only paid $380 take-home pay a week. This was not much higher than the New Jersey wages that I had been used to, but I was thankful to be in a new place and to have a fresh start. That little house that was less than 800 square feet was all we needed at the time and a true blessing.

Looking back now, I can hardly believe that, with all my responsibilities, I dared to volunteer for the battered women's shelter. As a single mom working full-time, I needed to work a part-time job for extra money. However, I felt compelled to volunteer at the shelter, the same type of shelter that helped me to get out of my abusive situation. I needed to show my gratitude by repaying the kindness I received when I was in desperate situations. I was required to complete special classes to learn how to be a volunteer at the shelter in Hampton, VA. Training was necessary to make sure that the women stayed safe from their spouses. I attended evening classes for 6 weeks and I received a certificate once completed. Volunteering in the battered women's shelter was the most fulfilling thing I had done up to that part of my life.

Here in Hampton, Michelle was thriving. She was a member of the highly rated Piscataway High School Marching Band when we lived in New Jersey. In Hampton, she auditioned and was accepted into Phoebus High School's Marching Band and it changed her life for the better. She was a part of something great. Phoebus High School took after Hampton University's band in their style of performance and we hoped Michelle would one day go to Hampton University to play in their band. I thought since I was working for the University, Michelle could get a scholarship and free or reduced tuition. I too could take courses for free. It seemed like the perfect setup. God's plan is always better than we could ever imagine. All we need to do is follow his lead and obey.

Directly across the street from our new home, there was a Baptist church with a mostly white congregation. I saw that there was a notice posted near their front door that said, "Spiritual Gifts Class." It said the class would be starting that coming Monday at 7:00 pm. The class met twice a week for four weeks and at the end, I got a certificate. That class brought me higher in the knowledge of God and of my purpose. I learned I too had spiritual gifts that I needed to exercise to glorify the Lord and that I should just keep allowing Him to order my footsteps. I have kept the certificate I earned from that class to this day.

One evening, while crossing the street to my house after my Bible class, right near my front door walkway, a strange man looked at me and said, "You shall know them by their name." Then, he continued to walk away without engaging in further conversation. Since I was not an avid reader of the Bible at the time, I did not know what the strange man meant by this. I now believe this to be, "You shall know them by their fruit." (Matthew 7:16). Reading further, "Not everyone who says to me Lord, Lord shall enter the kingdom of heaven, but he who does the will of my father in heaven…", (Matthew 7:21) lets me know I was on the right track and positioned at the right time to get that message from a stranger in front of my house. Another verse that can be referenced here could be, "Fear not, for I have redeemed you: I have called you by name, you are mine." (Isaiah 43:1). God knows your name and He has claimed you as his own. I thought it was weird but years later realized that it was another angelic encounter keeping me on the right path and confirming I was where I was supposed to be at that time. I have a childlike faith, a crazy faith. I am peculiar and God loves me anyway.

Less than two years later, I was headed to Atlanta, GA., for the next phase in my walk with God.

Michelle and I had been living in Hampton for approximately 7 months when I realized that even after working two jobs and volunteering for the battered women's shelter, I could not keep up with the $700 rent for the small one-bedroom house. I had cashed out everything in New Jersey, my bank accounts and 401k, but could barely make enough at Hampton University and a part-time job as a clerk at Kodak. With my bills and living expenses, it was just impossible to keep up. I even applied for food stamps and was told that I made $15 too much and was not eligible. Had I known that, I would have adjusted my application to only show enough income on pay stubs to make me qualified. I was desperate to stay in Hampton and make a life for us. I thought that the small house directly across the street from a Baptist church was blessed. Maybe it was, but there was no other option for me except to move on and I decided that Atlanta, Georgia, was my next choice. Atlanta had been the land of milk and honey for Black people since the 1996 Summer Olympics was held there. I felt I could make a go of it.

When I first moved to Atlanta, Michelle and I stayed in a motel for about a week until I met a woman who told me her husband had a Security Guard Business. She told me he used to date Gladys Knight when he was a teenager. I would soon learn that many people in Atlanta seemed to be somehow connected to someone or something famous. The woman seemed very nice and after learning of my situation, she invited us to visit her home in Decatur, Georgia where she rented out rooms. When I saw her home, I was impressed. She had a swimming pool and a large backyard. Several other people were living there who were renting rooms. She offered me a room there while I continued to look for permanent housing. Her husband also offered me a job as a security officer. The security job would pay for the rent and also give me money to save for a permanent place. I took them up on both offers. Michelle and I moved into a room in their house and I started working security for the husband's company. He sent me out on odd assignments like working at a mall or special parties for Ethiopians when a security officer was required. Many times, I would be a security guard at Krystal which was a fast food place like White Castle in NJ. Since I was a former military, I wore a security uniform and carried a gun. I don't think I considered the level of danger that came with such a job. I only knew I had to get established, even if it wasn't a perfect situation.

I woke up one day and realized that they were just using me and I was not making any progress. The security job was not paying me much and I wasn't making enough money to pay them for the room and also save up to move. I also had to leave Michelle with all the other boarders at the house while I worked mostly at night. It just hit me, all at once, that this was not a workable situation for us and I felt an urgency to leave immediately.

It was around midnight when I told Michelle to get in the car. We took our belongings and drove away from that house. That night, we went to another motel in the Decatur area. The next morning, I was at a temp agency looking for office work. The day after that, I was hired by the temp agency to work in their office. While working there, I met a young Black woman from Africa who also worked there. We got along well and I felt I could share my story with her about how I came to Atlanta. The two of us would always have lunch together and talk. When I told her that Michelle and I were living in a motel, she immediately offered for us to stay at her house. She was a single mom with a 9-year-old and had a beautiful 3-bedroom home. Her spouse was in jail and she allowed us to stay with her for a few hundred dollars a month I also helped with groceries. This young lady turned out to be another earth angel on my journey. She operated in strong spiritual gifts and would have spontaneous premonitions. Once she told me about a car that I purchased. I had not told her that I just purchased a used car from someone at the other house in Decatur that same morning. I planned to pick it up the next day and get it registered and tagged. There was no way she would have known about it. She told me that the car I bought was going to break down and cause me problems. Several months later, that car indeed broke down and gave me problems just as she predicted.

All along I had registered Michelle in the local school district in Decatur and she went to high school every day. It was a rough high school with violent kids. Michelle did not like the school and was apprehensive of the girls who wanted to start fights all the time instead of learning. All I could focus on was work and trying to get us a permanent place to live. I knew Michelle didn't like the school, but it was the best I could do at the time. We lived with my young African coworker and her son for 3 weeks. Then I left after meeting another God-fearing woman while shopping at a clothing store.

This woman was Jamaican. She told me she was divorced and had two kids, a boy about 13 and a girl who was 8. She said that she worked nights and would like to have an adult at home with her kids while she worked. She just added an extra room to her home and turned it into a bedroom with a private bathroom and a large walk-in closet. She said I could rent her guest room and that sounded very nice to me. I thought Michelle and I would be more comfortable with a little more space and a private bath. So, we moved in with the woman and her children.

Her home was nice and we were settling in well. I was on the phone one evening talking to the African young lady that we used to live with and I was telling her about boarding with the Jamaican woman and watching her kids in the evening. While I was on the phone with her, she told me that my daughter was crying and very unhappy. I looked around for Michelle and found her in the closet crying. That African young lady's spiritual gift was powerful. She was able to see something that I was not fully aware of. Michelle was distraught and hadn't told me that the school situation had become unbearable. This gave me the urgency to move to a better area as soon as possible. After only two months, we left the Jamaican lady's home and moved into a motel in Chamblee Tucker, Georgia.

I took the opportunity to register Michelle at Lake Side High in Atlanta, Georgia near Norcross, Georgia where mostly wealthy white children were attending. The area and school were just the perfect educational environment that my daughter needed for her advanced level of study. I should say I "created" the opportunity for Michelle to go to Lakeside High School. I knew what she needed to be successful and I created that opportunity for her. As a mother, there was not much that I would not do in my child's best interest. I got her in the school, and I see now that it made all the difference in the world.

We lived in the motel for a few months going back and forth to my temp jobs and Michelle's school, trying to make the best of the situation. Motel living was getting old though as there was no stove to cook. We were surviving on fast food. I would always stop somewhere and get us a burger, pizza, or Chinese food for dinner. This type of eating affected my health. It made me constipated all the time and caused bleeding hemorrhoids. My health started to decline. I may not have realized it, but I was also depressed. Living from paycheck to paycheck was exhausting. I had to find more permanent housing.

There was an apartment complex across the street from our motel. I noticed it had a lot of Hispanic and Black residents. It was well-kept and also had a swimming pool. I went over to check it out and talked with the office manager there. I told her about my frustration of living in the motel for an extended time, having to give all my paycheck to them, and how that made it hard for me to get established in permanent housing. I told her I did have some savings that I could use to pay a security deposit but my credit was not good. After the manager took my application and ran my credit, she said that it would be a risk to give me the available one-bedroom apartment, but she would give me a try if I could come up with the required deposit. I was so happy. I had a long-term assignment at an accounting firm in Atlanta, so paying the rent would not be a problem. Michelle and I moved in the following week. It was truly a blessing. Even though I did not have any furniture, we slept on blankets on the carpeted floor until I could get us mattresses with my income tax refund. My daughter slept in the living room and I in the one bedroom. Life was looking up for us. We finally had our place again.

At the accounting firm where I worked, I had a coworker named Penny. Penny was a young, single, black woman who wore her hair in long braids and had an upbeat personality. She had a 12-year-old daughter whose name was also Penny. She was a temporary employee like me and we hit it off within my first few days there. Penny would have her Bible on her desk and did not care what others thought about it. She was just bold with her Christian faith, always sharing a good word of encouragement with others. She attended New Birth Missionary Baptist Church where the late Bishop Eddie Long was the pastor. Both Penny and her daughter were in the dance ministry and attended Bible study there. Once she invited me to a special event at her church.

It was an extraordinary cathedral-like building in Lithonia, Georgia with religious statues and beautiful art. Bishop Eddie Long gave a moving sermon that day and I remember being brought to tears. He was a powerful pastor who was a truly anointed man of God. His congregation had over 30,000 members and the bishop was wealthy and did not hesitate to spend lavishly on himself and his family. It's too bad that there was controversy over his sexual behavior with teen boys in the church. In 2010, four young men who were members of his church filed civil lawsuits accusing Bishop Long of sexual misconduct. He eventually died within a few years of all the allegations even though it was medically said that he died from cancer. He was an example of what can happen when we move away from the real purpose of what God has for us and become self-satisfying and self-centered.

One day, Penny came over to my desk and said that I needed to work with her for the employees at our job. There were going to be a lot of layoff announcements coming soon and Penny knew that those who had been with the company for a long time would not take it well. She said that we were temps and were used to bouncing back quickly after finding another job. Others would not fare so well. So, we needed to fast and pray for them to handle the upcoming shift in their lives. After she said this to me, my first thought was, "What is fasting and how would we go about it? How many days would we fast and since we did not live near each other, would we pray on the job?" All of this was foreign to me. Penny said that we would fast for 3 days with just drinking water and she would call me every night so that we could pray for our co-workers. Surprisingly, I was barely eating anyway because money was tight. Each day, I would get Michelle a burger or fast food for dinner. For myself, I would just get something cheap or drink coffee to suppress my appetite. I thought this fasting thing could not be so hard for me because I had been training for it for weeks without knowing.

After our third day of fasting and praying, on the morning of the 4th day, we could eat again. Penny failed to tell me to come off the fast slowly with soups, juices, etc. I woke up early that morning eagerly trying to get to IHOP for breakfast. I gorged myself on 4 large pancakes, eggs, sausage, and bacon. s if that weren't enough, I asked for an additional side of bacon. Needless to say, I went to work not feeling well at all. My stomach started bubbling and I felt like I was going to throw up. I have since learned how to properly break a spiritual fast. Later that day, notices were given out to employees who were terminated and there were many. Some employees were crying, it was difficult to make eye contact with people. I was surprised how many people went over to Penny's desk to share the news of their termination. Penny served as the comforter. I wondered why she chose me to fast and pray with her. I believe God told her to follow the scripture in Matthew 18:20, "For where two or three gather in my name, I am with them." All I remember is that within days of Penny and me being obedient to the word of God, I got another temp position with Coca-Cola in Downtown Atlanta. Penny later moved on to another assignment as well. Before I left the accounting firm, Penny prophesied to me. She told me that I would marry a rich man but there would be an impostor before the real man would be revealed to me.

    Michelle and I had been sleeping on the floor in our nice little apartment and we were happy. When I finally received my income tax refund, I searched for a budget furniture store in Atlanta. The store that looked affordable was Maurice Furniture Store. It had odds-and-ends pieces of furniture and some items that were not good quality, but it was inexpensive. At least I could afford to get the essential items that we needed. I told the owner, Maurice, that I needed two mattresses and two bar stools as well as a few dressers. I shared my dilemma with him and told him that my budget was tight. Looking back on it now, I see that he took advantage of my situation. He sold me a mattress that was returned because of the poor quality and a few more items for only $1,000 and personally delivered them to me.

Maurice was not a handsome man, so I did not see him as someone I would consider dating when he started making advances. He was about 5'9 with a mole on the side of his face and about 45 years old. He asked me to go out to eat and I obliged by going with him to a local restaurant near his store. He got my number and started to call often. I have to admit it was nice to have someone to talk to, but I was not attracted to him and could not see myself becoming intimate with him though I knew that was what he was hoping for. After weeks of his persistence, I found myself getting comfortable with him and settling for a relationship with someone who could help me. Eventually, we became sexually involved which I regretted later, but we were officially in a relationship.

My car was having issues and I needed another car. One day, while I was driving home from work, I saw a red 1979 Volvo for sale on someone's lawn. I told Maurice about it and asked him to come look at it with me. He came with me to check it out and found that it was in good condition. He said the $2,500 asking price was more than reasonable. I told him that I only had $300 to put toward the car but if he would pay the rest, I would pay him back in installments of $366.66 for the next 6 months to pay off the balance. I drew up a contract to that effect. By this time in our relationship, Maurice liked me. So, he agreed to my payment plan and without fail, I went to his store and paid him via money order every month. Maurice was a nice person.

We were only together for a few months. He was nice to me but I was not feeling good about being with him sexually and I still was not really into him like that. I knew it was not morally right and I had my daughter to raise and to be a good example. Finally, I called Maurice and asked him to come over and meet me at the pool. When he arrived, I had my Bible with me. As we sat by the pool, I read to him 1 Corinthians 7:9, "For it is better to Marry than burn in lust." I let him know that I was a Christian and had a teenage daughter who was watching me. I wanted to be pleasing in the eyes of God and do the right thing. I told him I could not continue in the relationship as it was any longer. When I presented that ultimatum, Maurice fled and never called or came by again. What is so interesting is that I had told Maurice about Dr. Dallas Moore from Georgia and that he was a preacher and a prophet with powerful spiritual gifts. Maurice said he knew Dr. Dallas Moore because they were both from the same part of Georgia. Maurice knew to not continue on the path of taking advantage of me and just let me be. That was my confirmation that he was the imposter who had been prophesied.

In the fall of 1998, Michelle and I had been living in the one-bedroom apartment in Chamblee Tucker, Georgia for a few months when one night, I was abruptly woken up by my screams. Michelle ran to me and asked what was the matter. I told her I did not know but I was grieving with sadness for some reason. It was overwhelming. I must have screamed out in sorrow.

After talking with Michelle about how I was feeling for several minutes, we both got back into our beds and went to sleep. Around two hours later, there was a loud pounding on the front door. We both got up and ran to the door. As soon as I opened the door, a young black woman nearly fell into my apartment screaming, "Help me, help me, my baby is not breathing!" I immediately followed her to her apartment next door where the front door was open and her boyfriend, the baby's father, was holding and rocking the two-month-old baby boy. He was rubbing the baby's forehead as though the baby were alive. Somehow, I knew that the baby had died. The baby's spirit had left the lifeless, limp body but the father could not accept it. I stepped in and just started praying to God and crying out for mercy. This felt all too familiar as I too had lost small babies. I truly felt this family's pain. By this time, the mother was going door to door banging and screaming for help. Finally, the ambulance arrived with two paramedics who asked the father to hand the baby over, so they could try to resuscitate him. I believe they knew the baby was dead too. They just did not want to upset the father as it was apparent he was in denial and shock. They didn't want him to freak out and become violent. The paramedics took the child to the back bedroom put some sort of respirator over his nose and started working on him. They had to figure out a way to get the baby out of the house without incident. Soon, they said that they had to hurry and get the baby to the hospital immediately for further care, giving the impression that there was still life in that precious baby boy.

The maternal grandmother of the baby was just coming into the apartment as the paramedics were removing the child. I was in the bathroom doorway continuing to pray and crying out to the Lord to help this family. The grandmother noticed what I was doing and told the mother and father of the child to pray. "Let's all pray," she said as she started crying.

After all the commotion was over, everyone went back to their apartments. When Michelle and I sat down and started talking, we realized that my sudden waking up just a few hours before this incident was a sign that the baby had passed. Since I was sensitive to this, having experienced this type of tragedy myself, I picked up on it and was in grief even before anyone knew what had happened. I realize now that this was a spiritual thing and my first instinct was to pray when the neighbor asked for help. Days later, it was confirmed that the baby died of Sudden Infant Death Syndrome (SIDS). The definition of SIDS is mysterious in itself as it is an unexplained death of a baby younger than 1 year old. A diagnosis of SIDS is made if the baby's death remains unexplained even after a death scene investigation, an autopsy, and a review of the clinical history. Even though it is hard to accept, some things are God's will. There are no warning signs or precautions as a baby can be healthy with no signs of struggle and are often found in the same position as when they were placed in the bed. No one can figure this one out.

L. Renae Spann

I truly believe that the baby's soul was released at that very time that I woke up screaming. The feeling of grief came over me and I was obedient with prayer when it was required. The couple never returned to the apartment next door and just weeks later, we too moved out. I found it all very disturbing and I did not want to stay there any longer. I could identify with what that young couple was experiencing and I became depressed. It was not much longer before my mother's house in Plainfield would be sold and I would finally have an opportunity to buy a house. I knew even with my bad credit, it was time for me to try.

I started looking for work again to be closer to my new location and found a temporary position as an Administrative Assistant at Lockheed in Norcross, Georgia. That was where I met Cathy Talbot, another of my earthly angels even to this day. Cathy was a gorgeous white woman, about 5'4". A Christian powerhouse who was gentle in her delivery when giving someone a word from God. She was never judgmental, condescending, or harsh. She led with love and empathy. She not only helped me in my walk with the Lord but convinced me not to be afraid of the Holy Spirit or anything that was of God. Cathy was unlike the Black holy and sanctified churches I had visited in New Jersey, New York, or even in Georgia. I was always scared about spiritual things as I did not fully understand. Watching the movie the Exorcist, at the age of 13, had me afraid of anything supernatural. I believed I was not right with the Lord at that time and I thought if I was around anything spiritual, a demon would jump into me. That movie terrified me and I don't watch movies like that even now.

Impossible Things

God placed Cathy in my life to help me eliminate fear by letting me know that God's power superseded the Devil. She taught me that all I needed to do was to put my trust and love in Him and it would bring me closer to my calling and my destiny, therefore, allowing me to hear from Him and continue my faith walk. Cathy and I became best friends right from the start when we met at Lockheed and I gave her my resume for employment there. She was helpful with prayer, support, and things needed whenever I asked. Her husband, Bill, was also a total blessing to Michelle and me.

There was a time when Cathy took me to a revival at a storefront church in Atlanta. It was a Black church and we went there to see a white preacher who was a prophet, Wesley Van Johnson of Petersburg, Virginia. Cathy was confident that he was of God and that he would have a word for me. The Prophet entered the church accompanied by two deacons, with both men on either side of him as he walked down the aisle. The men ushered him to the pulpit and then he preached. After the Prophet preached, he walked among the congregation and spoke in the ears of certain people. He went to a few people and then made his way down to where I was sitting. He came to me and told me that my steps were ordered by God. He said more than that, but I was so nervous, I barely remember anything else. What made this man so genuine was that he only went to maybe 5 people that night and gave them a word from God. Shortly after that, he left the church the same way he came in, with the two deacons walking him out. That experience still sticks with me today. I know God has been and still is ordering my footsteps in life.

It wasn't long after that experience with the Prophet, that my mother's house was sold and I received $7,500. I used that money to purchase a condo in Chamblee Tucker. It had two bedrooms on the second floor and a small front enclosed patio area. The condo was a dream come true, the first of many houses that I would purchase in my life. As far back as I can remember, I always dreamed of having a house. As a child, I drew pictures of houses. In my adult life, I would have recurring dreams of owning homes with lots of rooms. In my dreams, I would go into the house and see doors I had not noticed before then realize that there were additional rooms in the house. It was such a good feeling to know that I had even more house than I had initially thought. I have had many types of dreams but the ones with a house always seemed real to me. I did not have the gift of interpreting these dreams, but I knew that they meant something. My new condo in Chamblee Tucker was in a prime location, near the Centers for Disease Control and Prevention (CDC) and close to a metro station that took me to my work at Georgia Lottery in downtown Atlanta. I loved my new home and felt I could stay there forever. The mortgage was only $450.00 a month with a small association fee. I even had a housewarming party and invited a few friends. It was just marvelous, a dream come true.

Just when I became totally content at being in the condo and telling myself I could live there for life, that very night I had a dream. I dreamt about a house near a lake. This was my dream:

Impossible Things

I saw a big white house near a large lake and tennis court. A worship group with white robes was going into the back of the house to have a prayer meeting and Bible study. I told them that they could not go into that house as it was vacant and they did not own the house. The leader of the group told me that I should buy the house so they can use it for Bible study. I told them, "That's crazy, I can't afford such a house!"

Then I woke up feeling that the dream was real and that now there was a desire placed in me for a house near a lake. Our condo community had shared laundry facilities. As I was doing laundry that day, I saw a newspaper ad that said, "House Near Lake for Sale in Lithonia, GA." It described this house as being an ideal home for folks who like water sports and recreation. It had tennis courts, a club house, and the lake could be used for boating and fishing. The house was described as a split-level with fireplace, large back porch, 3 bedrooms, master with on suite bath, a full bath near the other bedrooms, and a two-car garage. The asking price was $107,000. Even though this house seemed more than I would need and was completely out of my price range, I still wanted to check it out.

I called the number in the ad and was given directions to the house. I drove to the house and saw its location right on the lake. The next day, when I arrived to see the house, the owner told me that they had accepted an offer and it was no longer available. I was disappointed. The area itself was awesome with many homes nestled around the lake. A small bridge crossed over a running brook spilling over rocks. It looked like something out of a Norman Rockwell painting, a wholesome and picturesque subdivision. I took the opportunity to ride around and see more of the area. Then I came across a white house that looked familiar and had a for sale sign on the lawn. I experienced a feeling of déjà vu and my curiosity was peaked. I really wanted to take a look at the inside of the house. Was this the house in my dream last night? I called the realtor who had helped me purchase my condo, Mary Jane Parker. Mary Jane happened to be showing a house in Snellville which was the next town over. So, she was able to meet me at the house within the hour.

Soon, Mary Jane Parker met me at the house and we went inside. Once, she opened the door, I rushed in ahead of her in my eagerness. Immediately, I went up the stairs. The inside was even better than the outside. The kitchen was equipped with all updated appliances and open space to the living room. Just off the living room was another room that could be used as an office or recreation room. On the other side of the house were the 3 bedrooms, with a master bedroom that looked out over the tennis court. On the lower level was a den with a fireplace and a two-car garage with a washer and dryer. It was just perfect, more than I could have wished for. This, in fact, was quite similar to the house in the dream. Surprisingly, the subdivision was called "The Promised Land." What was the chance that I would find such a place of peace and tranquility?

Mary Jane asked if I wanted to put in an offer for the house. Because of my income, I would have to sell my condo for more than $63,000 to qualify for a loan for the house. I had two jobs but still would have to come up with a substantial down payment to be able to get the house. The seed had been planted and that was all the hope I needed. That evening, I went to my second job at Macy's and couldn't stop thinking about the house. I was talking to a customer at the register, telling her about the house I saw earlier that day. I told her I could buy the house only if I was able to sell my condo in Chamblee Tucker. That sale would give me the necessary down payment. The woman said that she and her husband were looking for an affordable house near the CDC and asked if they could come and see my condo the next day. Needless to say, that couple bought my condo for $85000 allowing me to purchase the house in Lithonia. I put in an offer for $104,000 and the owner took it. I only lived at my Chamblee Tucker condo for a little over a year and God moved me higher, from glory to glory. I thought that the condo in Chamblee Tucker was awesome and I felt I could have been there for the rest of my life. But the Lord showed me favor and grace, giving me double for my trouble. My daughter and I had gone from homelessness, living in motels and with strangers (earthly angels) to a big, executive style home near a beautiful lake in an upscale community. Won't He do it? I was in a house that I had literally dreamed about. It was amazing. Moving in was not difficult at all. I purchased items from the clearance section of furniture stores and also from Rent-A-Center. I bought items that had been repossessed and were in good condition. I was able to furnish my beautiful 3-bedroom house with ease.

Chapter 9
Just Michelle and Me

It was a blessed season for Michelle and me around this time. We were living in my dream house by the lake and Michelle was finishing up a successful senior year in high school. I felt like celebrating. To commemorate Michelle's graduation and to bless our new home, I invited our family and friends to come and celebrate with us. My sister Darlene flew in from New Jersey with her husband and daughters. My sister, Marlene, flew in from Louisiana. My brother, Harmon, and his new wife, Janet, flew in from New York. My family as well as my newfound family, Cathy and Bill Talbert, all joined us for the graduation and a weekend of planned activities at our new house in Lithonia. It was so good to have all the family together for this occasion and to let them see how the Lord had blessed Michelle and me with a house in "The Promised Land," as the subdivision was called.

Even Thomas O. Mensah found out about the graduation and decided to attend. He had his limo pick us up and take my whole family to the graduation. Tom sat in front right next to me as if he participated in Michelle's success. It was shocking. Cathy and Bill met us at the graduation and we all sat together. It was a proud day for me and my genius baby girl. In less than 2 years, we conquered Atlanta and achieved what only God could do for us. We were living evidence of His word that "We can do all things through Christ who strengthens us."

The family stayed with us for a long weekend and we all enjoyed the lake and tennis courts in my new community. I obtained tickets and we all took a tour of The World of Coca-Cola, a popular attraction in Atlanta. It was a great friends and family reunion. Michelle would be heading to the University of West Georgia in Carrollton, Georgia the next day to begin a summer program. I rented a van and drove everyone up to Carrollton to drop her off.

When we dropped Michelle off at the University of West Georgia, she was understandably quite nervous. The weekend had been a whirlwind of activity and things were happening fast. She received a scholarship from Georgia Lottery which covered her tuition and required her to complete a summer program leading into her freshman year. Michelle excelled in high school even though she attended a few different schools. She was brilliant, young, gifted, and Black. We met her college roommate briefly. She was quite different from Michelle and seemed to be less than excited about having a roommate. She was not very welcoming and had several tattoos which made Michelle a little leery. I didn't want to judge this girl on a first impression but, I was a bit concerned and worried if they would get along.

As we prepared to leave Michelle at her dorm, she started tearing up. I knew she was nervous, but I was thinking, "I've had it." Single parenting was starting to wear on me and I was eager to get back home. I told Michelle, "You've got everything you need. I will check up on you next week. You can do this!" We had our friends, Cathy and Bill Talbert, with us. The whole family; Marlene, Darlene, her husband Doug, their two daughters, Rachel and Mia, and my brother Harmon and his wife, Janet, were all there. We all drove up to drop her off at college for the first time at the University of West Georgia. But, it was time for everyone to head back home. Michelle was visibly teary-eyed and nervous. She did not know her roommate and had never been separated from me as a young adult. Nevertheless, I had to go and get some rest. So, we all got into the van and drove home.

My family members left that Sunday afternoon to fly back home and I was left alone in my big house on the lake. I felt relieved that I did not have to worry about my daughter. I could just focus on myself for a change. I was thinking this may be the perfect opportunity to start the book that Cathy prophesied I would write.

Still working 2 jobs, I decided to let my part-time job also be my social time and I took on more evening hours at Macy's. I met all kinds of fascinating people at Macy's and loved handling the beautiful clothes and merchandise. While working at night, I met Annette Pullman who was yet another earthly angel. She was looking for sheets that would fit her large mattress and I recommended deep-cut sheets for larger mattresses. We started talking and immediately clicked. She had such a sweet spirit and was very caring. I was talking to her about my life and about my daughter going off to college. We exchanged phone numbers and continued to talk often.

Annette was an encouraging friend and she truly loved the Lord. This woman had only known me for two months when she loaned me $1,000 to pay my mortgage. I know God used her at that time and she was obedient. A few weeks later, a Discover Card came in the mail for Michelle and she took out an advance and repaid the $1,000 loan to Annette. It was a perfect time for me to meet this new friend as I was entering a new phase in my life. I was an empty nester without Michelle living with me at home. It took a while for me to get used to it but working two jobs kept me busy. Annette is still a good friend to this day, always sending me text messages and emails with encouraging words. I thank God for placing her along my journey.

Michelle was at the University of West Georgia beginning her college life. She was making new friends and finding her way like many young adults her age. Despite all her efforts, however, she was not able to settle in there. The transition from home to living away at college can be particularly problematic for some young people and Michelle was one of them. She was unhappy at the University of West Georgia and, without my knowledge, left there and enrolled at a small two-year college in Valdosta, Georgia. In hindsight, I believe Michelle was taking a page from my playbook. She had seen me make many transitions while she was growing up. When a situation wasn't working out, I was never too afraid to move to a new place or make a necessary pivot to find a better opportunity and improve our lives. I believe this was Michelle's intention when she left for a new school all on her own. She was attempting to walk in her adult independence. But she would soon learn that life can be more challenging than she ever anticipated.

Shortly after enrolling at the 2-year college, Michelle and some other students were expelled from the school due to dorm violations. The school made an example of them. As quickly as she moved there, she was out again, but she still didn't call me. She went to her best friend from high school who was attending Valdosta State University. Her friend lived on campus there and Michelle stayed with her while deciding her next move. While all this was going on, I was completely unaware. I thought everything was fine. Michelle kept all of this from me and never divulged the details of her struggle. I was at home adjusting to my empty nest and considering what my life should look like as I was living all alone in my dream home by the lake. I was working and beginning to feel it might be the ideal time to start writing my book. Since I had more time on my hands, I thought to myself, "I'm going to sit down and write the book." I was planning to do other things too. Then I received an unexpected phone call.

The mother of Michelle's high school best friend called me. She was upset that Michelle showed up at Valdosta State University unannounced and moved in with her daughter. She told me that it wasn't fair to her daughter that Michelle should bring her problems there and disrupt her daughter's college experience. I was flabbergasted and confused. To my knowledge, my daughter was safely settled at the University of West Georgia where I dropped her off several weeks before. The mother explained to me that this was no longer the case. Michelle was living in her daughter's dorm room. I felt bad because this mother thought that I was not looking after my daughter. I apologized to her and immediately contacted Michelle who had been diligently working on getting herself enrolled in Valdosta State University.

Believe it or not, Michelle managed to get herself enrolled, registered for classes, and acquired campus housing in short order. She became a legitimate student at Valdosta State University all on her own. Again, I believe she was trying hard to demonstrate her adult independence. I think she wanted me (and everyone) to know that she was fully capable of managing her own life. She was always strong-willed and capable. So, I couldn't be surprised at what she managed to accomplish without my help. Although I was not happy that all this happened without my knowledge, I was impressed at her ability to emulate things she saw me do while she was growing up.

Michelle seemed to find her place at Valdosta State University and finally settled in. She made new friends and joined the marching band which was something she excelled at. She played the clarinet and was a member of the Phoebus High School marching band when we lived in Hampton, Virginia. That band was truly the best in their league. They danced while playing in the style of the great historically Black university (HBCU) marching band of Hampton University, "The Marching Force". I believed that this would be Michelle's outlet and that she could thrive there in Valdosta. She had the band, new friends, and even a part-time job. She was finishing her second semester at Valdosta State University when Michelle called me one night.

That phone call from Michelle caused great depression. She said, "Mom, come get me. I'm not feeling right. I don't feel like myself." She said she wanted to stop everything and she just didn't feel good at all, mentally or emotionally. She just wanted to leave. I tried to tell her that her semester would be over in a couple of weeks and then she could come home. She said, "No, come and get me now. I need to leave right now." So, I jumped in my car and drove three hours from Lithonia to Valdosta, Georgia. It was a long drive, but I knew Michelle did not sound good on the phone. Her spirit was heavy and saddened for some reason. She told me to come get her and I did.

I arrived to pick her up and she was sitting inside her dorm room, against the door covered in a blanket. I tried to push the door open but she was on the other side. So, she stood up to let me in. I looked into her eyes and it was like she wasn't there. We gathered her things and left. When she got into the car, she laid back in the seat. She wasn't asleep, just lying back. As I started to drive, I asked her what happened and she finally told me that her mind was not right. She was not feeling right. I thought she would feel better once we got home. I didn't understand that this was an episode with mental illness; a chemical imbalance or something related. I didn't understand how it all worked.

That night Michelle slept with me because she was afraid. We got up the next morning and she got dressed. Then she said, "Mom, take me to the hospital. I need to go to the hospital." I

Impossible Things

asked if she was sure and she said, "Yes, take me to the hospital. I need to go to the hospital." She started to tell me what was going on. She told me about her fears, how she was not feeling like herself, and how she was feeling overwhelmed. Her past was starting to overwhelm her and she never shared any of it with me before. As we were driving to the hospital, she started to tell me bits and pieces of what she could remember from her childhood. She shared how her great uncle, Lewis Spann molested her when she was just 3 years old. She was starting to remember things, traumatic experiences that caused her painful memories and added to her emotional distress.

At the hospital, we saw a young, Black, female doctor. As soon as Michelle saw her, she started saying, "No, no, she's got chains around her neck! No, no!" The young doctor was offended by Michelle's reaction and became aggressive with Michelle instead of realizing that she was having a mental breakdown. Then they called in a white, male doctor. Michelle was crying, and repeating, "No, no, no." I just hugged her. The male doctor told me to continue to hold her because she needed comfort at that time. He said, "Just hold her. It's going to be okay." He spoke with Michelle briefly and then told us that the female doctor would be handling her treatment. Then he arranged for the county police to transport her to the mental ward in Gwinnett County.

I was shocked. I couldn't believe that this was happening. I refused to accept any of it. What really disturbed me was when the female doctor came over and explained that Michelle was having severe psychosis. She was talking over my head. I couldn't follow all of the medical terminology, but I could tell it was serious by her delivery and tone. I asked her when Michelle would be able to go back to school and if could she return for the next semester. I clearly remember the doctor's response to this day. That doctor told me that the likelihood of Michelle going back to school and finishing college was slim to none. My immediate reaction was oh no, oh no. I just never let those words sink in and I refused to accept that lie from the pit. The doctor further predicted that Michelle would be in the psych ward for several months. I told her that I needed to go with Michelle when the police came for her. But she said that I would not be able to go with her. So, I tried to explain to Michelle that they were coming to transport her to a different hospital. She said, "Mama don't let them put chains on me! I can't have any chains!" I said, "What are you talking about? What chains? Why would someone put you in chains?" I didn't understand the logic. I asked Michelle why she would think that. She just kept telling me not to let them. So, I tried to comfort her by saying, "Okay, okay, I won't let them."

Sure enough, when the police arrived, a female officer had chains that she was about to use to restrain Michelle. I said, "No, she has made it clear that she can't be in chains. She is going to go ballistic." I begged, "Please, for God's sake, don't do it." Regardless, the female officer attempted to put the chains on Michelle. You can call it a coincidence, but those chains would not lock. They did not work. They jammed. They could not get the chains on her. Eventually, the officer said she would walk Michelle out. She walked her out without those chains and put her in the car. The police told me not to follow them. They gave me the address and told me to wait 30 minutes before coming so they could get her settled in first.

It was very difficult to find the place, but I found it. I got there and at the door, they told me I wouldn't be able to see Michelle until 3:00 PM the next day after the doctor came. No one would be allowed to see or talk to the patient until then. I realized they didn't want to tell me that at the first hospital when they were taking her away. That was when I started to panic because I was no longer in control of her welfare. It was a terrifying situation, one that I knew I had to take to prayer. I called my prayer warriors, my earthly angels, Annette, and Cathy all at different times. I told each of them what was transpiring and they all went before God in the prayer on Michelle's behalf. We all committed to pray earnestly for however long it would be until I could see her. I was severely distraught. I could not believe that this was happening. My brain was not fully comprehending the situation. It was just too much. But I had more faith than a mustard seed that my baby was not going to be in the psych ward indefinitely or even for months. I just could not fathom that. Finally, a day and a half later when she was taken there, I was able to call and talk to Michelle.

Once we were on the phone, Michelle started to plead with me saying, "Mommy, get me out of here! Get me out of here now!" That made me even more anxious when I heard her begging me to get her out. I was calling her from work. I had a temporary position at the time and I had to talk to her on the phone and try to calm her down without drawing attention to myself. I calmly responded to her, "I will come to see you. They say I can come, so don't worry. You'll be okay." She said, "Mom, I've got to get out of here." She told me about an experience she had. When they had a group meeting and everybody left, she remained in the room and sat on the sofa by herself. She told me that my mother, Helena, who died when Michelle was 11 years old, came and sat on the other end of the sofa. Helena said to her, "Well, what's wrong with you? You get yourself together. You know you can do better." Michelle said, "She was talking to me, Mom, she was talking to me." The first thing I was thinking was, "Oh my God! There's been a psychotic break. It's probably worse than when I took her to the hospital." I thought things were getting worse instead of better. It scared me when Michelle said she saw Helena.

Eventually, they let me see her. I went in briefly. It was a room with a couple of other teenagers like her. There was a soda fountain where we could get soft drinks. Michelle and I sat down to talk for a while and she reiterated that she needed to get out of here. She kept asking me to let her out. I reassured her that we were working on it and I was doing everything I could to get her out. It was a stressful time and I am sure I have forgotten some of the details of what all transpired. What I did know was that Annette and Cathy continued to hold me up in prayer through this difficult time. Those two women of God earnestly prayed as I prayed. I had been trying to start writing this book, but I had to put it to the side. Nothing meant more to me than to get Michelle out of there as soon as possible.

Finally, I received a call early in the morning on the third day after Michelle was admitted to the hospital. They told me Michelle was prescribed a certain medication and was responding well to it. She seemed to be relaxing, which meant that the medication was working. They said she would be released the next day and I could come and pick her up. When I heard this, I nearly fell out of my chair. It had only been a three-day hospital stay and Michelle was coming home. Her quick release defied what the Black, female doctor originally predicted about her being hospitalized for several months. I was learning in real time that there is no limit to what God can do and that the power of prayer is real.

I arrived at the hospital early the next morning, well before release time. I took the day off from my temporary job. When you take time off from a temporary job, you don't know if you're going to be able to work there the next day. You could be instantly replaced and lose the assignment. But Michelle was the top priority. I had to wait for her to be released. Finally, I saw her peek out of the door and I said, "It's okay, come on out Michelle, come on out." She was hesitant like a little kitten. She didn't know what was going to happen. So, I took her hand and walked her out to the car. I was happy and relieved to have her back. At that moment, I decided that I would never lose control over my daughter's well-being again. I would never again be in a circumstance where the state would have custody of Michelle and be able to dictate when I could or could not see her. I decided that, with God's help, she would never go back to a place like that. I would do whatever I could to prevent it.

I took Michelle home, gave her a nice hot bath, and fixed a meal. She had been through so much, I could still see that she was depressed and feeling down. We sat down at the table and ate. She said to me, "Mom, the only reason why I'm still here and I'm still okay is because of you. I worry about you. I don't want you to be alone and unhappy." She shared that with me because she already knew that she was my world and that it would crush me if I lost her. I told her, "I don't care what it is that is keeping you here. If that's the reason, then so be it. I need you to be strong, Michelle. I have to go back to work because both of us can't be out of work We have to maintain a steady income. So, in the next four days, I have to go back to work. But I don't want to leave you here by yourself. I had to come up with a way to take care of Michelle and get back to work at the same time. This is the ongoing struggle of a single mother and it doesn't end when your child turns 18. An adult child needs her mother too. One wise older mother once told me, "The older the children, the bigger the problems." I imagine this is why mothers' prayers are so powerful.

The day before I had to go back to work, I went to the bank and took Michelle with me. While I was there, I was talking to the banker, not knowing she was the manager of the bank. was telling her briefly that my daughter had to take a break from school for a while. I explained that Michelle was taking too many credits and became overwhelmed and anxious. Because of that, she would need to take some time off and go back next semester. In the interim, the doctor said it was a good idea for her to stay busy. Upon hearing this, the bank manager told me that they were hiring tellers and the next training session would begin in a couple of days. She offered to hire Michelle to work at the bank. I was shocked. She said, "Yes, she will have to take the test and then she can join the program. Where is she?" I said, 'She's right here in the lobby." The manager went out to talk to her.

As Michelle talked with the bank manager, I could see life coming back into her eyes. She could feel the acceptance. She knew that somebody needed her help and wanted her to work for them. So, she signed up to become a bank teller. Once again, you might call that a coincidence because I had only one more day off from work. Timing is everything but, more importantly, is God's timing. Because of my encounter with the bank manager, the following day I could go back to work and not worry about leaving my daughter at home alone. Michelle would be in the teller training program. God is everything. He knows what to do and when to do it. He sent an earthly angel once again to intervene on my behalf because my faith was strong. His divine intervention worked everything out in perfect timing.

I left my job at Georgia Lottery. It was too far to travel into downtown Atlanta from Lithonia and get back home to support Michelle. Her well-being took priority over everything at that time. I took a part-time job at Rhodes Furniture store nearby in Snellville to keep my mortgage current. I was good at sales. But selling furniture was a different type of sales than I had done at Macy's. It was more difficult in my opinion. Since I needed to make more money on commissions, I went looking at other furniture stores to become more knowledgeable about the business. I went into Haverty's furniture store and there I met a man who reminded me of Jasper, my first boyfriend. I was immediately attracted to him as he felt familiar to me. He was a successful furniture salesman, but his passion was stand-up comedy and talent promotions. At that time, I really needed a distraction from everything. So, we dated and had a lot of fun. I could not manage to get my furniture sales up enough to cover everything and was falling behind on my mortgage. I needed a lot more sales or another job so I went back to temping and that was where I met Gladys Dark.

Gladys was assisting recruiters at the temp agency in Norris Lake, Georgia when I walked in looking for work. They immediately found an assignment for me, but I was really in no shape to focus on my job. I was too worried about Michelle. Gladys would talk to me and encourage me all the time. She too turned out to be an earthly angel who was sent my way to assist in my journey. I was thinking that it might be best for Michelle and me to move closer to my family in Maryland or New Jersey. Selling my house was a hard decision as I felt I would never get such a house like that again. When I asked Gladys if I should sell my home or refinance, she said, "Let's pray about it," and we did. The next morning, it was clear that I had to let go and let God. He was teaching me to continue to trust His plan for my life and He would take me from glory to glory.

I was just starting to meet my neighbors at my Lithonia house and became good friends with Evelyn Harrison who owned the house next to me with her disabled daughter. She had a pottery wheel in her garage where she made vases and other ceramic items. She gave me a cookbook that she and her other two sisters wrote. I still have it and may start to pick up the hobby of cooking and try some of their delicious recipes. She passed on about two years after I moved away but not before she told Dr. Thomas Mensah about himself. Thomas came to visit me at my house one day after he saw me at a Burger King drive-through. He was getting out of his limo at Red Lobster next to Burger King when he spotted me and called my name.

Thomas immediately ran over to my car smiling and asking for Michelle. We had not been in touch since Michelle's high school graduation and he did not know about her recent crisis. He did not keep in touch nor provided any financial support. I told Thomas I was getting a burger for Michelle and then driving back to my house in Lithonia. He asked me to first have dinner with him at Red Lobster and then take him to see Michelle after I got her burger. I had dinner with him. As we talked at dinner, he told me that I was right about how people were just using him and that he had lost a lot of money trusting the wrong people. As he was sharing all of this, I was thinking, "How in the world did this all happen just now?" and I noticed that his communication with me had a different tone now. Thomas was talking to me and not at me. His demeanor was upbeat and pleasant. But, I had no desire for him as a spouse anymore. Too much damage had been done in the past. However, I was not bitter either. In fact, I felt nothing. After dinner, I thought it a good idea to drive him home to see Michelle.

I drove Thomas to my house. When we got there, Michelle came to the door asking for her burger and I told her that her father was coming in to see her. She did not talk much to him. She just ate her burger and listened to whatever he was talking about. Then he walked around my house and said something like, "This is ok but Alpharetta is better." He walked outside on the back porch where there was a beautiful view of the lake and tennis courts. My neighbor Evelyn happened to be at her gate in the back. I introduced Evelyn to my ex-husband and the first thing she said was, "How do you like Renae's new house? Are you jealous?" I couldn't believe she said that. I never shared with her about the things this man did to me. She just had a sixth sense and knew he was not genuine. Thomas was embarrassed and asked if we could go back into the house. Now that I am thinking about it, Evelyn may very well have been an earthy angel too.

Gladys not only worked as a recruiter but also as a licensed realtor. Once we prayed about it and I made the decision to sell, she sold my lake house in less than 4 weeks. Dr. Gladys Dark was a conduit that God used to take me to the next phase in my life. Currently, she is serving people halfway around the world with her African Ministry and Jael Women Group. They are a group of Christian women who are serious prayer warriors. So, began my transition to the next phase of my life.

Michelle worked at her bank job for the rest of that semester. She rebuilt her confidence, took her medication, and got back to her life. She wanted to go to Howard University in Washington, DC. So I decided we would move to Arlington,

VA. Michelle inquired at Howard and realized she couldn't get a scholarship there. Then we found out that she could get a full scholarship back in Georgia at Clayton State University. So she had to go there. We were in Arlington for several months and then Michelle went back to Georgia to enroll at Clayton State University.

Michelle's breakdown had been terrifying for me. I felt helpless as a mother, but God's grace brought her through it. It is remarkable that she made a complete recovery and successfully graduated from Clayton State University. She also met her husband there, Sundiata Bradshaw. Michelle and Sundiata met as students, dated for several months, and married after graduation. Everything doctors had told me about what Michelle was not capable of, she eventually accomplished on her own. She did it.

She got married, bought a house, and went through all the rigamarole that average people go through. Unfortunately, the marriage didn't work out after a couple of years. She had to go through the experience of a divorce, losing her house and car, and starting over from scratch. Situations like these might set a person back, but not Michelle. I find her to be a most remarkable person. Through all of these life changes she still found the strength to work through her challenge with anxiety and the trauma that happened to her in the past that were not fully understood before that point.

As a result of therapy, Michelle eventually uncovered a childhood trauma that had been long suppressed. She remembered that she had been a victim of sexual molestation when she was just 4 years old. It was perpetrated by my uncle, a retired military officer in New Jersey, and we were completely unaware of it. This was the root of Michelle's issues with anxiety. She suppressed the memory for all those years. When she went to therapy, it all came out. That was the root of her nervous breakdown, along with the obvious pressures from college. Finding this left me devastated. I went through debilitating feelings of guilt and regret. My thoughts raced through the issues of who was at fault for this grave breach of my child's safety. Was it my fault for not being there? Was it my mom's fault for leaving my baby in someone else's care? Was it my uncle's fault for being a deceitful and depraved predator? Was it Tom's fault for leaving us out with no financial support and leaving me to figure it all out on my own? I was overwhelmed with a whirlwind of racing thoughts about what my baby had gone through. My heart still aches today at the thought of this violation.

I just felt helpless and hurt that my child had experienced such a thing. But with God, in His grace and mercy, my daughter has now healed and is helping others. She runs a successful business as an independent support coordinator for the State of Florida and helps disabled adults to live better lives. She's walking in her calling and I could not be prouder of her. I am beyond grateful that she has maintained and expanded her business over the past several years on her own. I am so impressed with her success and I could talk about her forever. I am a proud Momma! I love Michelle dearly. She has become the woman that God intended for her to be despite all her challenges. To God, be the Glory!

I no longer beat myself up for being imperfect and a single mom. I went above and beyond to do the best I could. I believe I exceeded more than a lot of other single mothers according to statistics, because Michelle graduated from college and went on to have a full life. She bought a house, got married, divorced, lost everything, and started over. Today, she has a bigger and better house, a newer car, and a wonderful, supportive husband. She's a successful entrepreneur and business owner. God has blessed Michelle's hard work and tenacity. He has given her the strength to get back up when life has knocked her down. Sharing some of her story was difficult for me but necessary because it is my story as well.

I remember a time when I went to pay an overdue electric bill before our service would be shut off, Michelle was 3 years old and big for her age. She looked more like a 4-year-old. I fastened her in her car seat and I parked the car across the street which was a two-way highway. I left her in the car and ran to the billing office across the street for less than 5 minutes. I paid the bill and just as I was getting the payment receipt, I turned around and Michelle was coming through the door saying, "Mommy..." In that short time, she apparently got out of her car seat and ran across the street to where I was. I think about this often and know that God had both of us safely in His hands protecting us from danger.

L. Renae Spann

Another time, Michelle and I were in a major car accident when she was 9 years old. We were driving on the interstate from Maryland to my sister Darlene's house in New Jersey. I attempted the trip earlier that morning but was stopped at a toll booth and I did not have my purse or any money. I pulled over to the side and spoke with a police officer. He noticed that my registration expired and my sticker was out of date. The officer told me that he would have to have the car towed and I could not drive it. I told him I had no way to get back home with my daughter and it was snowing. Then just as he was writing up the ticket, he received a call on his radio about a major accident on the highway and he had to respond immediately. Due to this incident, he instructed me to take the next exit back to Towson, Maryland, and he let me go. I went back home which was nearly 40 miles away and called Darlene to let her know what happened and that Michelle and I could not make it to her family Christmas gathering. She was disappointed as she had her husband's family there and everyone was expecting us. I felt bad and made a terrible choice to make a second attempt to go to New Jersey.

We got about 30 miles north on the interstate from my home. While I was driving the speed limit in the center lane, a drunk driver hit me from behind as he was trying to pass me and misjudged the spacing. He was speeding and hit my left bumper so hard that it put my 1989 Volvo 240 DL into a spin. It caused us to spin and hit the center divider facing the fast-lane traffic. As we were spinning out of control, Michelle looked at me in fear and I could not say anything. I didn't know how this was

Impossible Things

going to turn out. With God's grace, we were in the right car at the right time. My car stayed on the ground and did not jump the divider going into the oncoming traffic. We hit the divider hard but were not hurt. When our car stopped, Michelle said that she could not move so I thought she was injured. A woman who was watching the drunk driver from miles back pulled over to the side to offer her assistance. She came to the car and I got out of the driver's side. When I realized that I was standing in the fast lane, I almost passed out. The ambulance came and took Michelle on a stretcher. I panicked and I got into the ambulance with her. The EMTs told me to calm down or I would go into shock and they would have to treat me as well. Once we were at the hospital, they examined Michelle and she was more relaxed and could move with no problem. We were both released. A friend from our church picked us up and took us home. The car was considered totaled, so they towed it to a nearby lot for an insurance adjuster to examine.

When Michelle and I got home I called Darlene once again and told her what happened. This time she understood. There would be no Christmas for Michelle and me that year. I made us peanut butter and jelly sandwiches and we started to watch TV. Michelle said to me, "Mom, isn't it good that we can bite these sandwiches with our teeth and that we are alright?" That was when I felt like crying. I made so many mistakes, but I was doing my best with what I had. I just thank God that He was looking out for us at every turn. I used to torment myself with all the bad choices and decisions I made as a parent, but I gave it my all. We experienced several near misses over the years, but God was faithful. Both Michelle and I were spared physical harm.

At 65, I am now totally free to tell my story without concern for the judgment of others. My daughter Michelle has been a major part of my life. I hope one day she will feel free to tell her extraordinary story in its entirety and in her own words. All generational curses have been broken for us. There is no more emotional pain and suffering with fear, anxiety, guilt, or embarrassment of the past. I declare in the name of Jesus that we will have good mental and physical health and a long life as stated in Psalm 91 which I have read every morning for the last 2 years before prayer. I have been told that I speak Michelle's name in conversation as if she is my whole world. After giving birth and losing my first children, Michelle has been my blessing. I thank God that I was allowed to keep and raise her. I may have been a little overprotective and for that, I pray she forgives me. I also ask that she forgive me for my mistakes and shortcomings as a single parent. Looking back, I had hoped she would be raised and protected by two dedicated parents. Being married, I expected her father, Thomas Mensah, would be there for us and that I would be a stay-at-home mom for her younger years. Her father was a gifted scientist and successful professional. As her mother, I did my best with the limited choices I had. I take full responsibility and ask forgiveness for any instance where I fell short.

Chapter 10
The Real Prince Charming

"He that finds a wife, finds a good thing and obtains favor from the Lord."

Proverbs 18:22

Because of God's grace and mercy, we were able to move on from Michelle's crisis. She was feeling much better and decided that she wanted to continue her college education at Howard University in Washington, DC. Howard is considered by many to be the top historically Black university (HBCU) in the country. Many great names can be found among its distinguished alumni, including leaders in every field and industry. So, to support Michelle's dreams and to also move closer to my familial support system, I decided the Washington, DC area, also known as the "DMV", would be our new home. I sold my beautiful lake house in Lithonia, packed up everything we had, and we were on the move again.

Michelle and I headed north to the DMV (DC-Maryland-Virginia metropolitan area). Without a concrete plan, we reached Washington, DC, where I checked into a motel and registered with an employment agency. I knew how to get myself quickly established in a new place since I had done it so many times before. The first order was a job and permanent housing. I found a real estate agent and started to look for homes in the city. Washington, DC is a historic city with numerous sites and attractions. In addition, there are beautiful neighborhoods with lovely homes on tree-lined, walkable streets that still have a city vibe. Although I loved the district, I was not able to find a home that fit my criteria and budget. So, my realtor suggested I look in nearby Arlington, VA.

Arlington is a beautiful city in Northern Virginia and is just minutes away from Washington, DC by car or public transit. It, too, has beautiful neighborhoods with parks, open spaces, and lovely town centers that provide shopping, dining, and entertainment. Arlington seemed like a breath of fresh air and a new start for me. After seeing some homes in Arlington, I settled on a small, second-floor condo with two bedrooms and one bath. It was in a lovely garden-style community, and Michelle liked it too. She noticed that a bus stop was just steps from the front door and said, "Mom, you can take the bus to work from here!" The decision was made. The little condo was perfect for us and would be our new home. Soon, I had two jobs, one as an Administrative Supervisor at Cassady & Pinkard, a commercial real estate company in D.C., and the other as a part-time sales associate with Macy's at Pentagon City Mall in Arlington. Michelle also got right to work inquiring at the University, and we were on our way. We were settling into our new environment, and I was thanking God for a fresh start.

In our new home, the downstairs neighbor was a nice lady named Lois Barksdale. Lois was a secretary and was just getting back to work after a recent knee surgery. Her boss was a kind gentleman who helped out by giving her a ride to and from the office while she was still healing. His name was Seymour Metters III. One day, when Mr. Metters was bringing Lois home after work, he noticed me from his car as I got off a bus and walked to my door. He asked Lois, "Who is she? I would like to meet her, she is beautiful." Lois told him that I was her new neighbor who recently moved there from Atlanta. Mr. Metters insisted that she somehow introduce us or at least tell me about his interest in me. The next day, Lois told me that her boss saw me coming from the bus and was interested in meeting me. I immediately told her that I was not interested. I told her with my two jobs and, more importantly, my teenage daughter that I was trying to raise and get into college, I had no time or interest in meeting her boss. Lois laughed and said that he was really nice. She further described him as a complete gentleman and encouraged me to at least meet him. Because she spoke so highly of her boss, I agreed to meet him. I had an extra ticket for my company picnic that coming weekend, and Michelle was not able to attend with me. So, I told Lois that Mr. Metters could come to the picnic in Chesapeake, and I would meet him there. It would be a blind date for me, as he had seen me and was inclined to meet me.

When I arrived at the picnic, I assisted my co-workers with setting up for the day's festivities. We had to prepare for serving food, playing games, and various activities. When I was done helping, I went to rinse my legs and feet in an outdoor shower. Just as I was getting done, Mr. Seymour Metters III approached me from behind. I was sure he got a good look at my legs before I turned around. (Seymour is a leg man.) He was slightly shorter than I and had my same shade of cocoa brown skin. He was a well-groomed man with a small mustache, curly, black, freshly cut hair, and a serious demeanor. He looked crisp in his casual outfit, but his vibe was all business. I could tell that he was a little older, and I always preferred older men. I cannot say that I felt any immediate chemistry, but I did feel a sense of familiarity. He approached me and introduced himself with a smile.

He really was the perfect gentleman as Lois described. We started to walk and talk as if we already knew each other. We settled under the picnic pavilion overlooking the water. He showed me two peaches he had in his hands, and his pick-up line was, "I love Georgia Peaches." Since Lois told him I moved to Arlington from Atlanta, he assumed that I was from Georgia. I told him I was not a Georgia Peach, but a Jersey Girl. We laughed and continued to talk for the duration of the picnic. We never even left our seats. My co-workers seemed disappointed that I had not participated in any of the activities, and I don't even remember eating anything. We just talked and talked all afternoon.

It turned out that Seymour was a successful business executive. He was the CEO and founder of Symtech Corporation and had recently been featured in Black Enterprise Magazine. He was a former U. S. Air Force veteran, which made him even more appealing to me since I was a U. S. Army veteran. I was definitely impressed, more like smitten with Mr. Seymour Metters III. He was easy to talk to and a great listener. I shared a lot with him about the reasons for my move to Virginia. It was perfect timing for me to meet someone like him. I was stressed about things and just getting situated in a new location. He listened and then told me that he would grow on me like moss, and he was right. We continued to see each other every day from that day until he asked me to marry him 3 months later.

Seymour would come by my house every day after work, even if only to talk for a short while. On the evenings that I worked at Macy's, he would come there and hang around while I worked. He would even help me by folding shirts to pass the time. We started to spend a lot of time together, and he would take me out every weekend. Our first date was to see the movie "Shaft" starring Samuel L. Jackson, followed by dinner at Olive Garden. I was thoroughly impressed with all our dates, as he always picked up the bill without hesitation. He took me out so much, I had to buy new outfits to wear on dates. I only had business attire for the office, no dressy cocktail or evening wear. This was where my part-time job at Macy's came in handy. When you live on the edge, you learn to maximize your resources. At Macy's, I was able to get deeply discounted, very nice clothing by paying attention to clearance markdowns and utilizing my employee discount. Thanks to Macy's, I was able to dress the part.

The dinner date that really blew me away was when he took me to Timothy Dean's restaurant in DC. It was an upscale restaurant owned by Timothy Dean, a well-known black chef. It was classy, and I had never been to a place like that before. The food was so good, I found myself commenting after every bite. I kept saying, "Oh my god, this is delicious!" often followed by "Mmm, mmm, mmm!" because my mouth was full. Seymour was tickled by my reaction to the food, and we were having the best time. In my sheer delight, I didn't realize I had been drawing attention. With all the excitement I was creating, Chef Timothy Dean appeared from the kitchen and approached our table. He came to greet Seymour and me and to confirm that I was truly enjoying my dinner. I told him it was absolutely delicious. As my mother used to say, "You can tell a person who never had anything." It was me. I was that person.

Seymour did not officially propose to me right away. But, after several weeks of dating, I brought up the subject because I needed to know his intentions. Although we were having a great time getting to know each other, I reminded him that I had a teenage daughter who was watching my every move, and I had to be an example for her. I told him I didn't have time to get involved if the relationship was not going anywhere. I was straight with him because I had been through enough, and I was not willing to complicate my life any further.

I was holding it down on my own in Arlington, with two jobs and still dealing with Michelle's teenage antics. Although Michelle was doing much better with her mental health, she was behaving like a spoiled, rebellious teenager. Once we moved to Virginia, she insisted that I buy her a car. I thought she would need it for school, so I bought her a car, only to have her start going everywhere she pleased whenever she wanted without my knowledge or permission. Although she was legally an adult, Michelle was still living with me and depending on me for

Impossible Things

everything. She met new friends and would be away from home for days at a time. I never knew where she was or what she was doing. I was always worried about her. This was beyond stressful for me, and my patience was wearing thin in dealing with her unmanageable behavior.

So, when I asked Seymour about his intentions, he told me he hoped our relationship would continue to progress and lead to marriage. He let me know he was clearly hoping for a wife. With that response, I started planning the wedding. The formal proposal came a little while later when Seymour planned a romantic weekend trip to Philadelphia, PA.

We checked into a beautiful luxury Hotel, then ventured out to take in the sights. We visited the Liberty Bell and all the historical sites, including a ghost tour. I am generally a scaredy cat and don't like anything like ghosts. But Seymour had planned such a romantic weekend that I wanted to accommodate him, and I went on the ghost tour. We saw the city and ended the day with a lovely dinner at a fine dining restaurant. The next morning, we went to the diamond district of the city to go ring shopping.

At the first jewelry store we came to, I could not contain my excitement. I immediately opened the door for myself and rushed in. I knew exactly what I wanted, the diamond ring I had dreamed of – the perfect 2-carat marquise diamond ring with a platinum band. That was pretty much all I knew about diamond rings, as I remember the diamond I got from my 2nd husband, who took me to a local jeweler in Baltimore. I didn't know anything about diamonds. All I knew was that I wanted a marquise-cut diamond that was twice the size of what I had before, and the band not to be made of gold. Now, I was in a large jewelry store in the famous diamond district of Philadelphia. I would finally get the perfect ring that I could show off to friends and family, one that would truly display my fiancé's love for me. After seeing what I thought was the perfect ring, I was determined to select it without even going through the appropriate procedures before purchasing it.

Seymour did not seem happy with my choice. He suggested that we look around at other options, as this was the first store that we went to. But I was insistent that it was the ring I wanted as it was very large. He asked the store associate to let him look at it through the jeweler's magnifying glass to inspect the clarity and started to ask other questions that were relevant to examining the diamond. But I became impatient and wanted the ring right away. Seymour saw that I was getting agitated at the delay caused by his questions. He stopped asking questions and then fitted the ring for me. He wanted me to be happy. He purchased the ring, and I wore it out of the store. After walking a few blocks, I started to feel different about the ring and told him. It looked different. I told him it no longer had the shine and sparkle. Outside in the daylight, it just looked like glass to me. I changed my mind and told Seymour I did not want that ring.

He immediately walked me back to the jewelry store and demanded that we look at the ring under the magnifying glass. Once we did, I realized that the diamond had a long black mark running through it, causing it to be dull and lifeless. Seymour

Impossible Things

asked for a refund and told the clerk that we would be back after we had eaten to continue shopping for the right ring. He, in fact, had no intention of going back to that jeweler as he attempted to take advantage of us. We left and went to a store just two doors down. When we approached the door, Seymour opened it before I got to it. Then he let me into the store first as he followed. Without saying a word, he reminded me that he was there to treat me like his queen.

The salespeople in the second store were Asian. They were pleasant and accommodating. They talked with us first to get an idea of what we were looking for and to understand our preferences. Once I searched every marquise-cut diamond in the cases, I selected my flawless marquise diamond. Then the jeweler fitted me for the platinum ring and set the diamond while we waited. When he was done, he gave the ring to Seymour. At that point, Seymour kneeled on one knee in front of me and proposed to me while the jeweler took a picture of us. I said, "Yes!" he put the ring on my finger. It was a perfect weekend.

It was official, I was really getting married to Seymour Metters III. I called Darlene to share this wonderful news. Our relationship progressed rather quickly, and I had not told Darlene about Seymour yet. I was bursting on the phone, trying to tell her everything. I told her he was a CEO, a millionaire, and I was just overjoyed. I couldn't believe everything was happening so quickly. I told her I was going to marry Seymour, and I wanted her to be my Maid of Honor. I wanted the whole family to come to the wedding. But Darlene was not happy for me and told me she didn't want to be my Maid of Honor. She said she didn't feel like being at my wedding and gave no excuse. I told her I wanted her two little daughters, my nieces, to be my flower girls. She said she might be able to do that. So, I invited her and Doug to have dinner with Seymour and me so everyone could meet and discuss the particulars. I really wanted her to meet Seymour.

I already planned to come to New Jersey and meet up with my friend, Debbie, for dinner and introduce her to Seymour, also. Debbie chose a restaurant in South Orange, which was not far from Darlene's house in East Orange. She chose that restaurant because she knew the owner, and it would be convenient for Darlene and Doug, too. I thought that would be a great place for us all to meet. But when I called Darlene to give her the name of the restaurant and settle our dinner plans, she declined, saying she couldn't come because of work. I was disappointed, but told her that we would stop by to see the family since we would be in the area. She responded that she did not want to go to dinner with us, nor did she want us to come to her house to visit. I was shocked and a little bit hurt by her response. I wanted her to be happy for me and to join in the celebration. But Darlene was not at all interested in sharing my joy.

Seymour and I drove up from Virginia on a rainy afternoon. When we got to New Jersey, I was having some trouble finding the restaurant. I knew we were close, but it was pouring rain and I didn't know the area as well as I thought I did. So, I thought we could stop at Darlene's house, and Doug would be able to give us directions to the restaurant. When we arrived at the house, I got out with my umbrella and went up the steps to the door. I knocked and someone opened the door. My little niece, Rachel, Darlene's daughter, was happy to see me and called my name. Aunt Nae Nae! Aunt Nae Nae! Then Darlene appeared at the door, pushed Rachel back, and slammed the door in my face. It was pouring rain, but I was standing on the enclosed porch. At first, I thought it was just a joke. I thought to myself, "Darlene is just joking." By this time, Seymour was also on the porch. He was supposed to stay in the car, but he was too much of a gentleman to do that. I'm sure he also wanted to say hello and meet my family. Now that he had seen the door slammed in my face, I was embarrassed. I looked at him and said, "Oh, she's just playing. Darlene plays jokes like that." Then I knocked on the door again, and no one answered. I knocked for a while. Still no answer. I tried to make a fast excuse because I was humiliated in front of my fiancé. "I guess she is not feeling well," I said. Then we got back in the car.

We eventually found the restaurant, but we were late. My New Jersey friends, Debbie and Deborah, were there waiting for us. I told them what had happened at Darlene's house. They were such good friends, they would not let me be upset. They made me shake it off, and we laughed about it. We were three divorced, single moms, and they were overjoyed about my engagement. They were happy to meet the wonderful man I had told them so much about. In the back of my mind, I knew I couldn't depend on Darlene to bring her kids to be a part of my wedding. So, I tried to focus on planning the wedding to cushion the blow. Debbie offered to have her daughters step in as flower girls. Coincidentally, they were two delightful little girls who were exactly the same age as Darlene's daughters. By the end of dinner, it was all settled. Debbie would be my bridesmaid. My friend, Cathy, would be my Maid of Honor, and Deborah would sing at the wedding. We had a really wonderful dinner and meeting that evening. Jersey girls know how to pull things together.

 I never received a formal apology from Darlene, just an explanation saying that it was really my fault. She said I shouldn't have come to her house and that I brought it on myself by not listening to her. She told me not to come, and I came anyway. Now, looking back at everything as a 63-year-old woman, I feel there is no justification for slamming the door in your sister's face. Especially when she knew the trauma I had been through and that she was a part of that trauma. There was no justification to subject me to additional humiliation in front of Seymour. She should have just come out and said that she was not willing to celebrate when something good happened to me. Being a coward and closing the door in my face should not have been an option. I was offended and hurt by her actions.

 Just days before the wedding, I decided to call Darlene again. I thought maybe we could talk it out in time for her to still attend the wedding. I asked, "What have I ever done to you that would cause you not to attend my wedding?" She didn't answer the question. She only changed the subject to deflect. Darlene never answered me, and she didn't show up for my wedding. Nor did she ever apologize or send her regrets. Although I was deeply disappointed, I did not let it ruin my day. Our wedding was absolutely beautiful, and everyone who was meant to be there was there.

It is only the grace of God that only now in our 60's have we become closer. Both of us went through a lot back then but I appreciate and am very proud of the women that she has become. After raising her two daughters and retired as a Sr. Systems Analyst for a major insurance company, we did not allow the past to destroy our sister relationship indefinitely.

When it was time to make wedding plans, I had a limited amount of funds to put toward the occasion. In usual fashion, I started thinking of ways to save on the various things I would need while still having a beautiful event. Fortunately, I had previously been a member of the Assemblies of God Church in Decatur, GA. So, I decided to contact a local Assemblies of God church in Arlington, VA, and ask if the pastor could marry us there. Since I was a member, Pastor Rick Hudock said he would have no problem performing our ceremony, but we would be required to complete premarital counseling with him before the wedding, and we would have to abstain from sex until we were married.

Seymour and I were both divorced, and Pastor Hudock required that we also not live together before the wedding. I had already listed my condo for rent. It had been leased to a new tenant, and I was in the process of moving in with Seymour. Once we shared this with the pastor, he said that he would not be able to perform the wedding if we continued to live together.

L. Renae Spann

Pastor Hudock then offered a room in his home for me to live in until the wedding. I accepted the offer and stayed with the pastor and his family for 6 weeks until the wedding. This is where I met Earth Angel # 4, the pastor's wife, Ruth Hudock.

Ruth treated me like a family member right away and refused to accept any payment for my stay. She also volunteered to serve as my wedding coordinator and was able to work creatively within my meager budget. She arranged the entire wedding ceremony at the church, including a string quartet, and even managed to have some of the wedding items donated to make it extra beautiful. However, once I found out that Seymour's sisters and niece would be flying in from Oakland, CA, I realized that I needed to elevate the style of the wedding reception dinner from an informal gathering to an elegantly formal event more befitting of the Metters family. Because of this change, I had to "come clean" and let Seymour know that I needed his help with the wedding budget to plan a more elegant event to appropriately receive his family. I wanted them all to feel warmly welcomed on our special day.

Seymour did not hesitate in paying an additional $10,000 to make our wedding reception a Cinderella-style soirée at the Mark Center Hilton in Arlington. This beautiful venue provided an enchanting fall ambiance with elegant fireside dining and a view of a decorative outdoor fountain beyond the windows. It was perfectly apropos for a gathering during the Thanksgiving holiday season. We had about 60 guests, making the day flawlessly intimate as I finally married my Prince Charming.

Impossible Things

I could not thank Ruth Hudock, my wedding coordinator and now a good friend, enough for going the extra mile to make our special day a blessed and memorable occasion for all. Ruth and I still share fond memories of the wedding and all the miraculous things that took place to keep me within my budget. Ruth and her daughters remain in our lives today, and they visit us from time to time.

Now let me tell you about my Prince Charming, Seymour Metters, III. He is the son of a Baptist preacher, Reverend Seymour Metters II, pastor of Saint Rest Baptist Church in Oakland, California. He had the perfect start in life as the Word was deposited into him at birth. Seymour is from a generation of believers who are close-knit. All of his siblings, who consist of two brothers, Samuel and David, and four sisters, Mary, Ester, Betty, and Gladys, have helped to direct Seymour into the ideal husband and father. Their mother, Lillie B. Metters, was a true matriarch who served as the glue to bond the family together, and she kept them moving forward. Pastor Seymour Metters, II had a strong desire to formally educate all his children as he knew that knowledge is power. As a father, he knew it would honor God and the family for his children to all excel to their full potential and do the will of God, which they have accomplished. Seymour and his siblings are all successful, caring, loving, ambitious, and driven Christians. I admire them immensely. In meeting the Metters family, I saw the epitome of excellence in how a family should function as a unit to help ensure that everyone is taken care of and loved. The extended family is all successful as well, and I believe it is a result of the prayers of

Pastor Seymour Metters, II. He produced a son who followed in his footsteps to become a Minister as well, Reverend David Metters. Seymour, too, is a faithful, devoted believer who is dedicated to prayer and worship every morning, which is a habit that I, too, have now adopted.

In marrying Seymour Metters III, I finally fulfilled my desire for a son, in fact I got two sons, Seaton and Marlin Metters. Seaton has two sons Samaji and Isaiah. Marlin has two daughters, Jahida and Eliana. Our grandson Samaji has two sons, Roman and Valor, and a daughter, Anastasia. The addition of two sons, beautiful grandchildren and great-grandchildren gave Michelle and me a more blessed family life with so much love to go around.

Two months after our wedding, Seymour and I purchased a newly built, 3,786 square foot house in Fort Washington, MD. It was a colonial-style home with three levels and two sets of stairs leading to the upper level on each side of the house. It had a grand foyer with 2-story ceilings, 4 bedrooms, 3.5 baths, and luxury walk-in closets. There was a gourmet kitchen, a sunroom, and a 2-car garage. The home was on a nearly an acre lot and brand new. Before this, I would have said the lake house in Lithonia was my dream house. But apparently, God had bigger dreams than what I was able to imagine. This house was truly a dream for this little girl from West 3rd Street. It was palatial and grand, much more so than the Brady Bunch house of my childhood dreams. In March of 2001, we purchased it for $330,000. For me, it was a dream come true.

Impossible Things

    Moving into our new home, we had a budget of just $22,000 to purchase new furniture. We decided to buy a rosewood formal dining room set and a matching rosewood master bedroom set. These were signature furniture and would be heirlooms representing our fresh start in life together. We used all the other furniture pieces from our apartment to fill in until we could get the rest of the house properly furnished. We could not have been happier. A few months later, reality quickly brought us back down to earth.

    It was about 6 months into our marriage when Symtech Corporation, Seymour's government contracting company of 12 years, was experiencing difficulties. Our current office space had failed to pass OSHA standards due to the noise produced by another business on an upper floor of the building. Their running equipment produced a loud noise that could be heard in our office, and the landlord refused to relocate Symtech to a more appropriate location that would pass OSHA standards. Since Symtech was under a lease, Seymour had taken the landlord to court for this issue, but lost the case and was ordered to pay the 2-year lease in full. This was a major expenditure in addition to losing our company office space. At the same time, Symtech was not getting as many new contracts as usual, which made it difficult to meet payroll and other expenses. This put Symtech in a financially vulnerable state. It was like a perfect storm. To cut expenses and remain afloat, we relocated Symtech headquarters from Arlington, VA, to the basement of our house. This move saved us money on office space. Our basement was unfinished, but we were able to finish and organize our office nicely there, and it all worked out. We had a staff of just 5 people in the corporate office at that time.

On top of all this, Seymour and his younger son, Marlin, had been in business together for several years with Members Carlink, an online car lot that worked with credit unions and their members to purchase cars. Seymour wanted to diversify with another company, as government contracts were not coming in soon enough to sustain things. He also wanted to make sure that his adult sons would have generational wealth and thought that Marlin's idea to sell cars on the internet through credit unions would be a good investment. I admired Seymour for continuing to help his sons excel after his divorce from their mother. In him, I saw a caring father who truly loved his children. In contrast, my ex-husband, Dr. Thomas Mensah, had not even thought about our daughter, Michelle, after we divorced. Seymour was a great father and role model for his children.

Unfortunately, we soon discovered that the Members Carlink business was in the red. It was starting to collapse financially. It became a money pit for Seymour, who was the sole financier. Before he could pull out as instructed by his accountant, the company went belly up. This put Seymour's main business, which he had built over 12 years, Symtech, in jeopardy. This all happened just months after Seymour and I got married and bought our home. Now our new home was in jeopardy of being foreclosed on in less than a year after purchasing it. All I can say is that the Devil is a liar.

Impossible Things

Seymour realized that bankruptcy was the only solution to salvage things and to keep our new home and the company. After he shared the bad news with me and explained that bankruptcy was our way out of this dilemma, I told him not to worry because I had filed for bankruptcy twice before. I was not upset or afraid. I knew that together we would get through this with God's help, and everything would be ok. Seymour was surprised by my attitude toward all this. But my joy and commitment came from the fact that I knew I had finally found a true partner after all these years. One who really loved me and wanted to take care of me, my Prince Charming. I knew we could work everything out together. I was no longer by myself out in this world. We would recover financially even faster because we had each other.

Over the next few weeks, Seymour worked with a company lawyer and our accountant to prepare for the bankruptcy. When all the documents were completed and ready to be signed off, Seymour and I headed to the garage. We were leaving to go to the lawyer's office when the phone in the kitchen started to ring. We were running late for our appointment, but I decided to answer the phone anyway. Much to my surprise, it was someone calling from the Small Business Administration (SBA) asking to speak to Seymour, the CEO of Symtech. He was inquiring as to when Mr. Metters would be coming down to sign off on the $350,000 loan he applied for. Seymour spoke with the man on the phone, and the rest was an absolute miracle. To acquire this loan, my Condo in Arlington, which I kept as a rental property, had to be put up as collateral. There were some other stipulations, but we were rolling without incident. I was glad that I had something to bring to the table and to truly be a good helpmate to my husband. From that point, things got better than we ever expected. Not only were we able to keep and fully furnish our beautiful home, but Symtech Corporation was saved, and business got even better.

Our company's Business Developer, David Albis, was growing concerned about the number of contracts available to Symtech. We did not want to find ourselves in the same financial situation again. David explained to Seymour that more government contracts were available as set-asides for service-disabled veteran women-owned businesses. Since I was classified as Black, female, and a service-disabled veteran, having me as CEO would greatly increase the availability of contracts for Symtech. I had shown my faith in Seymour when I used my Arlington condo to secure the SBA loan. Now it was his opportunity to show faith in me. Even though I was nervous about taking on the responsibility of this major leadership role, I knew I could do it with Seymour's guidance and direction. We had only known each other for a little more than one year when Seymour stepped out on faith, sold the company to me for $1.00, and I became the CEO and President of Symtech Corporation. He assured me that under his instruction and guidance, I would become an effective CEO. Thus, began my new station in life as CEO and President of Symtech Corporation for over 15 years, the longest I have ever been at any job. The Lord blessed us tremendously over the years, and we have not looked back.

Impossible Things

This proved to be the right business strategy when, 2 years later, we won our biggest contract shortly after we moved to Sarasota, Florida. Our company went from 60 to 350 employees when we won the Waco/Austin, Texas, contract for the Military accounting department. We were on our way to great success. All the jobs I had worked up until that point prepared me for the challenges of the task ahead of me. I also became the company's FSO (Facility Security Officer). Both Seymour and I had to acquire Top Secret Clearance to make Symtech Corporation a Top Secret Cleared company. I was required to be recertified and updated annually as a service-disabled veteran and be approved by the SBA. My gift of administration proved to be useful, as well as my military experience.

In 2014, I was nominated for SBA Woman-Owned Small Business Person of the Year by Arleen A. Wilson of AW Enterprises Consulting, LLC. I appreciated Seymour having so much faith and trust in me, and I did not want to let him or the company down. All along the way, Seymour and I worked together, and our marriage did not suffer. Seymour was a true partner in every sense of the word. He is extremely intelligent and has a head for business and finance. He loved and respected me and was my source of constant encouragement. He showed me that I could do whatever I put my mind to and that he would be there to support my efforts. Never did he try to discourage me from advancing or try to keep me down, like my past husbands and relationships. He recognized the light and fire in me as the makings of a good leader and wife. Seymour is patient and generous to a fault, always giving to anyone in need. He has a genuinely peaceful and kind spirit. Our relationship is even better now that we are retired.

During our years of running Symtech together, our company supported political candidates on both sides of the aisle. Since Symtech was a government contractor, we thought it was important to be politically active in our community and participate in elections. Once, Seymour and I met Ohio Governor John Kasich while taking a walk near our home in Sarasota, Florida. We saw the governor while we were taking a walk on the bridge. At that time, he was a Republican candidate for the presidential nomination (2016). As we approached the governor, we were met by his security. We told them we were constituents and would like to say hello. Governor Kasich was welcoming, chatted with us briefly, and took a picture with us on the bridge.

During that same campaign season for the election of the 45th president of the United States of America, Senator Hillary Clinton was running for president. I thought, could this be the time of the woman? Would the world finally witness a woman leading America like in England? One who would run this country with grace, honor, and great diplomacy? I felt like it was our time to shine as women and to be completely respected as equals to men. I was so invested in this idea of the first woman president that Symtech donated $10,000 for Seymour and me to attend a fundraiser for Senator Clinton in New York City. There, she would meet with a small group of her constituents and speak about her plans for the presidency should she be elected.

Impossible Things

The event was to be held at the Manhattan home of a young, male, gay couple, and we felt honored to be invited. Their apartment was on an upper level, and before anyone could enter, they had to be identified and searched by the Secret Service. Although it was a group of only about 50 people, security was rigid and vigilant. Once we arrived in New York, I learned that I could not bring a large purse to the event due to security, and the only purse I had with me would be too big. So, I had to go shopping for a smaller purse that would meet the criteria for this special evening. I went to Bloomingdale's and told a sales clerk about my dilemma and how I wanted to make a good impression on Hillary Clinton. I wanted my outfit and accessories to be perfectly coordinated. The sales clerk immediately took me over to the expensive small handbags and showed me a designer purse by Chloé. It was pale yellow leather with a gold chain. She said it would be "just the thing," and that "Beyonce had that very bag but in pale blue." That was all I needed to hear, and I purchased the bag for $400.00. I had never paid that much for a purse before, but this was a once-in-a-lifetime event, and I needed to blend in with the aristocrats.

The evening started with the security checks before we entered a room where there were pre-poured glasses of white and red wines arranged on a large table for guests to take as they passed into the living room of the apartment. I opted not to have any wine because I did not want to be tipsy when meeting Hillary Clinton. As we entered the living room, I found a seat up front on a large leather chair. Senator Clinton entered from the back of the room, walked up to the front of the group, and began to talk. She was very personable, first sharing about her grandchild and then talking about her run for the presidency. As she talked, I noticed that my new Chloé bag had caught her eye. Every so often, as she was talking, she would look down at it lying on my lap. I believe she liked it as much as I did. After her speech, everyone took pictures with Senator Clinton in the library. That was where I was able to speak with her briefly to let her know that I support her efforts and was excited that she was running for president. I believe she was also interested in my husband's thoughts as she would look over at him while she and I were chatting. Mainly, I was caught up in the moment of just being in her presence. I remembered years earlier when a prophet at Women of Hope Ministries in Atlanta, Georgia, told me that I would someday be in the presence of political figures. I thought the prophet must have been referring to this moment. When the prophet told me this back in 1998, it sounded impossible. I had no political ties or affiliations, nor could I relate to what she was saying. What high political figures would I come in contact with? Now I understand that she was foretelling another major growth spurt for me. God was taking me to new places in life. Senator Clinton lost that presidential election, and so went my hope of a woman president. It wasn't meant to be, but I was honored to have met Senator Hillary Clinton all the same.

While things were going well with Symtech, Seymour and I thought it would be a good idea to make additional investments with our expendable cash. I told him about how my struggles in Atlanta had been as a single parent and how challenging it was to acquire and maintain housing. I suggested that we try purchasing homes in Atlanta and maintaining them as affordable rentals. I contacted Andrew Malone, a young realtor there, who found our first Atlanta property in East Point, GA, for only $22,000.00. My daughter, Michelle, had just gone through a divorce and needed to relocate. So, we leased the house to her at a low rent.

    We created Metters-Spann Investments LLC, and Michelle eventually became our property manager for all the other 19 homes we purchased thereafter. As we acquired each new property, we renovated it and started renting to Section 8 tenants. Most of our tenants were single moms who were struggling to maintain housing just like I had. We did not make much money at first. Whatever profit we made went back into the homes to pay for repairs and modifications. Michelle worked with us to secure the best tenants for the properties and kept us out of court with evictions by physically collecting the rents each month. I focused on acquiring properties with the help of our realtor. I selected and collaborated with contractors to renovate the homes. Seymour handled the financial side of things, making sure the accounting was timely and completed with accuracy. He kept us in the black and always on budget. The three of us made a great team.

    We were blessed by the success of this new venture. I had always been interested in real estate and was enjoying the process of discovering, purchasing, and renovating homes. I felt that God was guiding me to make all the right decisions, and I was able to assist some low-income, single mothers in the way I prayed for help when I was in those circumstances. I was feeling great about what we were doing through Metters-Spann Investments. Then in 2005, just before the Easter holiday, I was about to fly from Sarasota to Atlanta to close on our 4th East Point, Georgia rental property. We planned to purchase this particular house to rent to my daughter, Michelle, and her fiancé, Sundiata Bradshaw. They reunited and decided to take another chance at marriage together. I was pleased that they were getting back together and that they were willing to rent from Metters-Spann Investments. The property was a large 1960s house with 4 bedrooms. It had two levels, two bathrooms, a large den with a fireplace, a dining room, and a living room. It also had a spacious backyard. It was located in the same East Point subdivision where we previously purchased our first three rental homes. This one would be the fourth. It needed work, but I had my carpenter, Ben Morlas, who could update it beautifully and increase its value. The house was a great investment as it was selling for only $45,000. Another winner, I thought. Metters-Spann Investments was on a roll.

    I remember arriving at Sarasota Bradenton International Airport around 8:30 AM that rainy morning. As I was approaching the counter to check in for my flight, an announcement came over the PA saying that the 10:00 AM flight to Atlanta had been canceled due to stormy weather conditions in Atlanta. I immediately called my realtor, Andrew Malone, to let him know that I was going to miss the 1:30 PM closing due to my flight being canceled. He responded, "Never mind, don't worry about getting here today." Andrew went on to explain that the house we were closing on had been split in half by a large tree that stood in front of it. The tree was struck by lightning in the storm, which caused it to fall and demolish half of the house. The house next door had an enormously large branch fall and crush one of its upstairs rooms, causing extensive damage to that home too.

I could not believe it. My first thoughts were, "Did anyone get hurt?" and "What do we do at this point?" I had been moving so fast on finalizing that deal while still working at Symtech, and I failed to obtain homeowners insurance for the house to be covered when we closed. I had so many questions. What will become of my down payment? Would the damage be repaired by the seller before closing? I did not know how it would all work out, but it did. The Lord was covering us, and timing was everything. The miracle of it all was that no one was hurt. Since we were making a cash purchase, I had the house inspected just days before the tree fell and had paid the inspector $400.00. So, I had an earnest deposit and the inspection cost on the line.

I still wanted to fly into Atlanta the next day to see the situation for myself. I went to visit the house and took pictures of the humongous tree that had fallen. A local news station covered the incident the day before and stated that an "out-of-state company" planned to purchase the house that the tree fell on. That was how big of an event this had been. I walked around the tree and looked at the once two-story house now flattened on one side. The next-door neighbor was outside, and he told me that the event was scary. He invited me into his house. It had a large blue tarp covering one side of the roof where the tree branch had fallen. I was uneasy about the safety of his house, but my curiosity got the best of me and I followed him in. He described how he had just come halfway down the stairs from his upstairs office to get a drink when the tree fell. The large limb crushed the roof of that upstairs office. The desk where he was sitting minutes before was destroyed as well. While the young man was telling me about this experience, he was trembling and had tears in his eyes. He was still visibly shaken the day after the event. I could feel his emotional state, and I was just thankful that he was not hurt in the event. Eventually, my earnest money on the house was returned to me, and I still count my blessings today for God's perfect timing and protection. That house was intended for my daughter and her fiancé. It was to become their new home only weeks after the purchase and remodel. By God's grace, we were able to avoid something that could have been catastrophic for our family.

After about 8 years and 20 homes purchased in East Point, we discovered that Tyler Perry purchased the old Fort McPherson Military base for $30 million and was planning to build his new production facilities there. It just so happened that all of the Metters-Spann Investments properties were located near Fort McPherson. The building of Tyler Perry Studios would have a positive effect on the local economy and initiate a significant rise in property values there. I had no way of knowing such a thing would happen when I decided to invest in that area. Our strategy of selecting the worst homes and renovating them made improvements to the neighborhood and gave some low-income families a nice, affordable place to live.

Impossible Things

The news of Tyler Perry Studios coming to the area was an unexpected blessing. In my experience, God can always bless you in ways you may never have considered.

It had been 10 years since the start of Metters-Spann Investments when we decided to sell. We were able to sell all the homes for top market value. It was just before the COVID-19 pandemic gripped the world, and the entire country shut down in March of 2020. At the start of this real estate venture, Seymour and I agreed that we would purchase at least 20 homes in cash, ranging from $22,000 to $89,000. The purpose of this investment was to enable us to maintain the lifestyle to which we had grown accustomed and remain debt-free. When we cashed out and sold all of the rental properties, we cleared well over $1 million.

Seymour Metters III and I have enjoyed all the years of our marriage, and now in our retirement years. We are currently enjoying five homes that we have acquired over the years for our personal use. Two are generating income as short-term rentals when we are not there. Seymour suggested we keep them for that purpose. We have a condo in Downtown Sarasota, FL in a beautiful high-rise overlooking the Gulf of Mexico, a quiet retreat on 5.5 acres with a pond out in the country also in Sarasota, FL, a remodeled garden condo near Shirlington Village in Arlington, my original guest condo also in Arlington where we met, and my favorite, the log cabin on Sebago Lake in Naples, Maine.

Seymour's brilliant financial savvy and my childlike faith (allowing God to order my footsteps) have made for our debt-free retirement. As of November 25, 2024, we have been blissfully married and blessed for 24 wonderful years. Thank you, Jesus! In our new phase of life, we are seeing the world. We have cruised all of the Caribbean, visited Alaska, the Panama Canal, Hawaii, and the west coast of the United States. Internationally, we have visited London, Germany, France, Italy, Switzerland, and the Netherlands. In celebration of our 25th wedding anniversary in 2025, we will complete a 15-day land tour from Porto, Portugal, to Barcelona, Spain, followed by a 15-day cruise back to Fort Lauderdale, Florida. This little Black girl has found her happily ever after. The third husband was a charm -- a Prince Charming that is!

Chapter 11
Happily, Ever After

I really believe my dreams have driven my life. That was the channel God used to speak to me since my daytime life was so busy and my mind was always racing. I guess the only time I was able to pay attention was during my sleep, so God would show me dreams. However, I did not learn to interpret my dreams until later in life. Since childhood, I had recurring dreams about houses which sparked my strong desire to have a beautiful home. My Mother, Helena, was also a dreamer and a woman of great insight and vision. She read the Bible constantly and was spiritually intuitive. She could always sense danger. Helena was born on Easter Sunday with a veil over her face. Some beliefs may be considered old wives' tales that say a baby born with a veil has many spiritual gifts and is highly favored by God. My mother was one of those babies. I believe I have a gift of dreams due to my childlike faith.

During my homeless period in Atlanta in 1996, I had unwavering faith in God that He would provide a solution. We first moved to Decatur, Georgia, where Michelle and I lived for several months with Christians I met along the way. I enrolled Michelle in a high school in Decatur and found out that the kids there were violent and mean. My daughter was a good student. She was focused on learning and tried to make friends, but she just did not fit in there. She would cry every night about having to go to that school. This troubled me deeply, and I was frustrated that I had no way to get her into a better school. When we left the Jamaican woman's house where I rented a room, we moved to a motel in Chamblee Tucker, Georgia. While there, I noticed large, beautiful homes in that area.

The high school for that neighborhood was Lakeside High School. It was in the upper-class area and looked like it had mostly white students. I wished my daughter Michelle could be in such a school, but we would have to live in that neighborhood to enroll her at Lakeside. I was desperate to get my daughter out of the school that was tormenting her. I would drive through nearby neighborhoods, looking at the homes, wishing we lived there. When I saw a house for sale in the area, I was not in any position to buy it, but I had an idea. I decided to put in an order with the phone company to have a phone line connected at the vacant house. By completing that order, the phone company connected the phone and provided me with a phone number and a utility bill with that home address. I was able to take that to Lakeside High School and enroll my daughter there. It made a major difference in my daughter's well-being as well as her ability to excel in school. She did so well that she received the Georgia Lottery Hope College Scholarship given to students with a 3.0 GPA and higher.

I am not proud of having done this. I don't even know how I came up with such an idea. I just know that single mothers will sometimes do desperate things when it comes to the well-being of their children. I realize now that doing that might be considered illegal, and I learned much later that parents have been prosecuted for using a different address to enroll their child in a better school. Once again, grace and mercy were extended to me by God. Only four months later, I was able to purchase a condo in Chamblee Tucker, Georgia, which placed us legally in the district of Lakeside High School. All I needed to do was continue to trust God.

My first condo, which I bought for $43,000, was all I needed, or so I thought. I was so content with this small, two-bedroom, two-level condo just blocks away from the Centers for Disease Control (CDC) in Chamblee Tucker, Georgia. A year later, it was a dream that moved me forward to my second house in Lithonia, Georgia. I woke up from that dream, not knowing that God deposited the desire for me to have a larger home by a lake. The rest of this story is the miracle of how God worked it out for me to buy my beautiful house on the lake in "The Promised Land." I believe it was because I was content with the small house and keeping it up that God gave me a bigger house. The night before I dreamt about the lake house, I said to myself, "I can be in this condo for the rest of my life, paying only $450 a month for a mortgage." For God to take me higher, he had to deposit the desire for something bigger in me, and I moved toward it. Yes, I will continue to allow God to order my footsteps. He continues to place beautiful desires in my heart and wonderful angels in my path.

Let me tell you about the day God sent messengers to meet me at the store. While visiting my daughter one day in October 2012, I noticed that she did not have any fall decorations on her porch. Since I rented the house to her and checked on all our properties of Metters-Spann Investments in East Point, Georgia, Michelle's rental stood out because it did not have any fall adornments. Wanting to bring in the cheer of autumn, off I went to Lowe's to purchase pumpkins and mums for her front porch. While I was inspecting and choosing plants, one dropped to the floor. I discreetly picked it up and put it back on the shelf, thinking no one was looking. However, a police officer saw me do this and came over to me. She said, "I saw you drop that plant and leave all the dirt on the floor." I was ready to tell a lie to defend myself when I noticed she was smiling.

We both started to laugh, and an easy conversation ensued. I told her why I was at the store in the first place: to spruce up my daughter's front porch with fall decor. Somehow, we began talking about our mothers, and I shared with her that my mother had died of colon cancer over 20 years ago, and it still felt like yesterday. "You never really get over losing your best friend, advocate, and biggest fan," I said. The officer told me that her mother had cancer, too, but she survived. We both started to get teary-eyed. She shared more about what a miracle it was that God allowed their family to have their mom still. It was truly by grace.

Then I proceeded to tell the officer that it must be a generational curse on my family because all our elders died before age 60 with some form of cancer or heart disease. My hidden fear at the time was that I had the cancer gene. I did not want to suffer that fate as I witnessed the pain and agony my mom went through. For years 35 through 45, I became more and

Impossible Things

more concerned and started to develop stomach problems, hemorrhoids, and constipation. I was relieved after my first colonoscopy at 37 because no polyps or cancer were found, but I was still not completely over my fear. It was starting to affect my way of thinking as I believed my life expectancy would not make it to 60. Depression was slowly creeping in. I thought, why make long-term plans when there may be a good possibility that I might not be around to enjoy the fruits of my labor?

    As I was going on and on with this negative narrative, the police officer just started praying, saying, "Lord, let her know that she will never have to worry about cancer in her lifetime as that generation curse is broken." I thought this was strange as she did not know me or anyone in my family, but she was so sure of what she was praying about, so I touched, agreed, and thanked her for the heartfelt prayer. We shared a few more stories, and then I was on my way to another part of the store to continue looking for fall decor. As I was going down the aisle near the cleaning products, I saw an old man dressed in a black suit with a white shirt pushing a shopping cart. In the seat of the cart was a small, brown, wooden box that was hand-carved in some sort of pattern. Surprisingly, he had a pale pink ribbon on his lapel, so I asked him if that was a cancer support pin. He said, "Yes, I minister to cancer patients." Needless to say, I did a double-take as I had just left the subject of cancer minutes prior. The pastor said to me with great conviction, "Let me give you a special ribbon just for you to wear." He reached into his wooden box and pulled out a bright pink ribbon and pinned it on my sweater. He then proceeded to say, "You will never have to worry about cancer another day of your life as the generational curse has been broken." At that point, I began to go into full-fledged crying and coughing. I realized at that moment I was being delivered from the fear of cancer being my cause of early death. After the encounter with these two angels, never will I allow that fear of cancer to rule my emotions and rob me of my joy. The message came twice in the same day for me to completely receive it, and I thank you, Jesus!

Another area in which I have experienced major changes is my relationship with money. At different stages of my life, money has played different roles. As far back as when I was 15 years old, I started to realize the importance of money when I found myself pregnant and unprepared. I was just a young girl, unmarried, living at home with my parents, and my boyfriend didn't have a job. How were we going to handle all that was needed? My mother and father were living on disability, and there were four of us children still in school with no jobs. How was this all going to play out? The real issue was being a poor, Black, teenage mother. Statistically, I did not matter. Money could have made a real difference. Financial resources would have meant access to proper medical care both prenatally and for my premature newborns. In addition to no medical care, no preparation was made to receive new babies. I had no way to purchase baby clothes or furniture to set up a nursery at home. We didn't even have an extra bedroom in our house. There was no room at the inn. Our family was already crowded with the addition of my older cousin and her three children, whom Helena took in temporarily. We were all living in my family's 3-

bedroom house with one bathroom. It seems that fate saved me from the doom of being a statistic and continuing the cycle of poverty. Unfortunately, fate did not spare me the trauma of being a child, having children, and then experiencing the death of my children. Being poor meant no bereavement care, no counseling, or adolescent therapy to help me process this dreadful experience. So, I internalized it all and, with my mother's support, moved forward as best I could. I buried it somewhere deep inside, and I am still healing to this day.

    The second stage where money made a major impact in my life was when I met and married Dr. Thomas O. Mensah, a famous Chemical Engineer and businessman who later died in 2024. At the time I married Tom, I was 19 and he was 29. I just came back from US Army basic training and Advanced Individual Training (A.I.T.). I was at my best physically, and my savings provided a large down payment on my first brand-new car. I was in control. I thought I was on a great career path, and by marrying a Black man with a PhD, I would have no more problems with money, or so I thought. However, due to his control and manipulation, I became totally dependent on Dr. Mensah, and he was selfish. After giving birth to our baby girl, Michelle, the issue of money started to creep back up. He used money to control me, and he had all the power in the relationship. The marriage ended in divorce after 6 years, and I had no savings. When Dr. Mensah left the country to avoid paying alimony and child support, I was left with nothing. He was originally from Ghana and married me to obtain his US citizenship. When the marriage was over, Michelle and I were no longer of any concern to him. The divorce left me struggling to provide for my daughter by working secretarial jobs in addition to part-time retail jobs simultaneously, but this was not sustainable. Bankruptcy was inevitable and the very thing I tried to escape, I ran right back to. I went home to my parents in New Jersey as a single mom.

The third stage, where money played a critical part in my life, was when I married my second husband, Kenneth Johnson. Our marriage turned out to be unsustainable and lasted only 6 months. I worked for a bank in Baltimore near the Inner Harbor. I knew I had to leave the marriage, but I was not making enough to get an apartment on my own. I had to bide my time and wait for the opportunity to leave. Kenneth was also an abuser, and the lack of money was preventing me from getting my daughter and me out of a dangerous situation. Eventually, I was blessed to go back to my previous apartment in Towson, Maryland, where I lived when I met Kenneth. Getting my old apartment back allowed me to start again, but only after filing a second bankruptcy to clear my debt.

The fourth stage, where money played a significant role in the direction of my life, was when I met my true love, Seymour Metters III, the son of a preacher. His family was from Oakland, California, all well-educated, and all financially established. Seymour had a government contracting business at the time for 15 years. By the time I married him, I had worked for over 10 years in major companies as an Executive Assistant and supervisor, learning all there was to learn about administrative details. Less than one year after our marriage, Seymour asked me to become the CEO of his company because I held value in government contracting as an Army service-disabled veteran and a Black woman. There were government contracts set aside for that group classification. My taking on the role of CEO brought contracts into the company and kept it afloat during a rough time. To my surprise, all my struggles, work experiences, administrative jobs, and, more importantly, military training prepared me well for handling government contracts and personnel. Both Seymour and I received Top Secret clearance for the company, as he was an Air Force Veteran. This helped us to qualify for even more set-aside contracts. Together, we went from 50 to 360 employees in less than one year. We were not only a good match in marriage, Seymour and I turned out to be a great match in business and finance. We lived below our means for years and invested our discretionary cash. We are now blissfully retired, and money is no longer an issue for me. When I met Seymour, he saw my value as a life partner, and we brought the best out of each other. That was our recipe for success. I know I will NEVER be poor another day in my life as my steps are truly ordered by God.

L. Renae Spann

Impossible Things

My favorite movie as a young adult was "Claudine" (1974). It starred the beautiful actress, Dianne Carroll, and actor, James Earl Jones. The movie portrayed a Black, single mother, Claudine, who was raising 5 children on welfare in the ghetto of New York City. It showed all the struggles she went through to provide for her family while still searching for her own happiness. All her past relationships had not panned out, but each one left her with more heartache and another mouth to feed. She cheated the system by secretly working as a maid in the suburbs while receiving welfare benefits from the city. Even with that, her income was not sufficient to provide for her family. Claudine needed a Prince Charming. One who could love her and her children. She knew the addition of a good man would give them a better life and relieve some of her burden as a mother. I still like this movie because it is a constant reminder that without God's grace and mercy, this could have been my life.

Starting out as a pregnant teenager, my life could have gone in the same direction as Claudine. The trauma of giving birth and suffering the death of my twin girls at age 15 left an emptiness that I didn't know how to fill. I went in search of a fairytale kind of love that would be the answer to all my issues. I wanted to find a charming prince who would make everything better, but I could not find him. I would meet a boy, fall in love, and get pregnant. Then I would find out that the boy did not want the problem of a pregnant girlfriend and reality would set in. I was terrified to go through the pain of childbirth and become a single mother. So, I would be off to the abortion clinic. In the 70s and 80s, many young girls used abortion as a form of birth control. I found myself stuck in a destructive cycle. My ignorance and fear resulted in my having several abortions as I repeated the same mistake over again. I later discovered that terminating my pregnancies was sin against God. Each of those embryos was a human life, and I had no right to snuff them out due to my fear and selfishness. I was ashamed and disgusted with myself. If I had received proper sex education and been offered appropriate trauma therapy in my youth, it could have all been prevented. Maybe I would have understood how to break the cycle and conduct myself in a more disciplined manner. There are, however, no excuses for my behavior. I have to take full responsibility for my part in these unwanted pregnancies and terminations. I just thank God daily for His grace, mercy and forgiveness of my greatest sin and shame. "But where sin increased, grace increased all the more" (Romans 5:20). It is because of my love for Jesus and His love for me that my life now is peaceful and happy. The guilt has been lifted. Negative thoughts and feelings have all been resolved. I now walk in the favor and love of God.

In writing this book, I know that God is moving me toward my next chapter as it had been prophesied to me over 25 years ago by my Christian sister and earthly angel, Cathy Talbot from Bethlehem, Georgia. Since then, each time I have attempted to start writing, something has come up. Like my daughter getting sick or my having to work two jobs to pay bills for 10 years, I allowed myself to be distracted by life's ups and downs and I procrastinated. As women, we are so used to feeding into the success of our families that we often put ourselves on the back burner. We say, "I will do this or that for myself later." Then before you know it, later becomes so far down the road that you give up hope of ever pursuing your own dreams. In my case, I felt that I needed a man to be complete, useful, or of any value. I thought my Prince Charming would take care of all my needs and desires. He just had to find me first.

When it came to writing, I was also frozen by fear of being rejected by my friends and family for what I shared in this book. Most of all, I doubted that I could intelligently write and publish a book that would make a difference for other struggling and troubled young women. But I've been set free like the woman at the well. Jesus met me where I was and released me from the shame of my past. By grace, my faith finally superseded my fear, and I was ready to receive direction and guidance from the Holy Spirit. I was able to just go with the flow. Sharing my true deepest darkest secrets has served as a balm. This book has finally come to fruition in God's perfect timing so that it could best be received by those who need to restore and strengthen their faith.

Along my journey, I had the privilege of meeting and talking with a few famous icons like Cicely Tyson, Hillary Clinton, Alex Haley, and Colonel Eileen Collins, the first woman to pilot the Space Shuttle. Meeting each of them had a positive impact on me. Their lives and accomplishments showed me that anything is possible. They had different careers, but all were brilliant in their respective fields.

L. Renae Spann

Meeting Cicely Tyson many years ago was unforgettable. Recently, I listened to her latest book, *Just as I Am: A Memoir,* and it changed my life. Cicely Tyson's life story let me know that she and I had some things in common. She operated in spiritual gifts, and she loved the Lord like I do. She rose to success from a secretary to an award-winning actress and model, beautiful and blessed. Like my mother, Cicely was born with a veil over her face. She had great wisdom and remained true to her convictions throughout her life. Most importantly, Cicely Tyson left a rich legacy on this Earth before she died at 96 years old. It is not by coincidence that she died just 2 days after her book was published on January 28, 2021. I believe it was by divine design that her book was published to share her life journey and her memoirs with the world. I highly recommend *Just as I Am: A Memoir* by Cicely Tyson. It is a great inspirational read written by a truly phenomenal woman. May she rejoice in heaven.

The one role model I would love to have met in person was Muhammad Ali. He had a God-given talent with boxing, but even more so, he displayed an undying faith in his ability to accomplish whatever he set out to do. He was fierce, uncompromising, and unapologetic about his beliefs and had an unbreakable will to win. I bought everything I could that was related to Muhammad Ali. Among the pieces of paraphernalia, I obtained over the years is my prized possession. It is a large 3ft x 2.5 ft cherry wood shadow box picture frame. Encased in the frame are a pair of Ali's autographed burgundy colored boxing gloves and the famous photograph of his first championship fight against Sonny Liston (Feb 25, 1964). Muhammad Ali, only

Impossible Things

22 years old, knocked Liston out in the sixth round as he predicted. At that point, he was unstoppable. Over the next 4 years, Ali defended his title nine times. The caption under the enclosed picture has these inspiring words that I thrive from, "I AM THE GREATEST!" It has become a personal affirmation for me.

Some other notable quotes from Muhammad Ali that I find edifying:

Affirmation: "I figured if I repeated it enough, I would convince the world that I really am the greatest."

Confidence: "It's lack of faith that makes people afraid of meeting challenges, and I believe in myself."

Imagination: "The man who has no imagination has no wings."

Pride: "I am the greatest. Not only do I knock 'em out, I pick the round!"

In reading this book, I hope that women and men will see that they are never alone if they would just trust their instincts and value who they are in Christ Jesus. This is my advice to you. Do not allow pride, arrogance, conceit, fear, or negative thinking to consume you. Take heed to Philippians 4:8: "Think about things that are pure and lovely, and dwell on the fine, good things in others. Think about all you can praise God for and be glad about." Depression is something that one must subvert with joy, laughter, and peace. Understand that God is in control. We can plan and work toward goals, but ultimately, God has the final say. His plans are always bigger, better, and beyond our comprehension. "Our God is able to do exceedingly abundantly above all we ask or think." (Ephesians 3:30). Trust Him to guide your life. Seek first a meaningful relationship with the Lord by praying daily, praising Him, and asking for strength, good health, and wisdom. Your health is your wealth, so take care of your body and mind. All that is required is a mustard seed of faith. I have crazy faith, childlike faith. I believe dreams really do come true, and you really can live happily ever after.

Chapter 12
My Unconventional Path to Success

I wanted to include a chapter that covers my work and career history to give an overview of my professional experience and what has worked for me in life. I do not have an extensive education. Truth be told, school has never been a strong point for me. I struggled in school, although I was never identified as having any learning deficits. I was an energetic child and easily distracted at times. I was not good at testing, not an avid reader, and not particularly strong in math or science. These major subjects are essential and require the best grades to excel academically and to become a professional, like a doctor, lawyer, or CEO. Knowing this, I decided that I wanted to learn just enough to help me support myself well. That would be the best I could do. My only notable skills as a high school student were typing over 80 words per minute, telling interesting stories, disco dancing, and socializing. By graduation, I was trying to figure out where I could apply my natural talents to earn a decent living. I felt like I had missed the education bandwagon. It was too late to learn good study skills and become an avid reader. Television was my source of information and of escape to another life. I was a big dreamer both day and night. Deep down, I knew I was going to be somebody. I just did not know who I would become.

L. Renae Spann

The US Army National Guard proved to be the right direction for me. I thought I joined because I would look fabulous and important in the army uniform. I had no idea how much I would really gain from the experience. Through my Army training, I acquired the discipline I desperately needed and developed an appreciation for education. Eventually, I became a Radio Teletype Operator (O5C). That designation strengthened my resume and provided marketable skills with which I would begin a career.

The following are some of the many companies for which I have worked and the positions I have held. By using my gift of administration, each of these jobs helped to sharpen my skills and ultimately shaped me into a professional, one who was ready when God said it was time for me to become CEO and President of Symtech Corporation. All these jobs built a patchwork of experiences necessary for success in my final chosen profession.

Macy's Department Store (Various Locations)

Sales Associate

For more than 10 years, I worked on and off with Macy's as a part-time Sales Associate. This was my second job in addition to full-time office work with various companies. The part-time sales associate position never paid what I was worth. I was number one in opening new customer credit accounts as well as add-on sales. This is where my social skills came in handy. Customers would ask me exclusively to help them shop

Impossible Things

and get great bargains. I met many of my friends and acquaintances at Macy's. I worked so much that I did not have time to go to the Disco and have a fun single life. Earning money was my primary concern. So, working at Macy's was also my social outlet. I would have worked for Macy's full-time if the position paid enough to support my daughter and me. My wages started at $5.50 an hour, and after giving them my best work over the years, they only went up to $12.00 an hour. I would earn additional money when I opened charges. Each new account I opened paid me $3.00. I opened 3 to 5 credit card accounts during every shift I worked. Another advantage for me was being able to purchase all of the latest business attire on clearance with the addition of my employee discount. This allowed me to always dress nicely for my many office jobs over the years without spending a lot of money. I enjoyed working at different locations of Macy's, as whenever I relocated, I would transfer to the nearest Macy's store. Over the years, I worked at Macy's locations in Plainfield, NJ (then named Bamberger's), Short Hills, NJ, North Lake-Tucker, GA, Norcross, GA, and Pentagon City Mall in Arlington, VA.

I recall a time when I worked at the Macy's in Tucker, GA, and a co-worker came in for her shift. She opened up the register in the dress department when she fell dead from an aneurysm. Her bodily fluids were all over the floor near the register with the cashier drawer open. She was an older Jamaican woman who was raising her grandchildren while working several jobs. Within a short period, they had her body removed, cleaned the area, and called for me to come in early to work in that department that day. This incident showed me that these jobs don't give a damn about the employee, it was business as usual. I came in early that day and worked the extra hours because I needed the money. But I could not stop thinking about the women who died at the register as I was ringing up sales. I never looked at Macy's the same after that. Even though I did not move up with Macy's, it served its purpose to supplement my income as a single parent who received no public assistance or child support.

Rickel Home Centers (South Plainfield, NJ)

Security Officer & Sign Coordinator

I worked as a security officer for Rickel's when I returned from Army basic training and Advanced Individual Training (AIT). As a security officer, I logged in all trucks coming and going at the security shack in back of the warehouse. I also performed nightly security monitoring. After 6 months, I took a new position as a sign coordinator in the advertising department. Due to my new position, the company paid for me to go to Middlesex County College and study for a certificate in graphic arts. Nowadays, everything is done on Macintosh computers with no need for manual artwork. But back then, learning about fonts, photography, paste-up, printing, and using T-squares was fun for me. My job felt like being in art class every day as I made all the signage for monthly sales and promotions for the various stores. Thanks to my experience at Rickel's, I realized that I could enjoy going to school and learning. Rickel

Home Center no longer exists as it was a forerunner for Home Depot in the early 90s.

Merrill Lynch (Allentown, PA)

Mail Room & Wire Operator

I began my career in the mailroom at Merrill Lynch and was promoted to wire operator, where I would manually enter trade orders in a fast-paced, high-pressure environment. I admired a rare female broker in the male-dominated office, which had a very different, more relaxed corporate culture at the time. After becoming pregnant, I left the job to have a child and did not return, marking the end of my professional independence until a later divorce in 1985.

Law Office (Baltimore, MD)

Administrative Assistant

I worked in a law office for six months. There, I sharpened my reading skills and learned to type legal documents like bankruptcies, wills, and divorce decrees. With the new skills I learned there, I later started my own business typing documents for people. This was before the advent of the Internet and common access to personal computers everywhere. Through my business, which I named Rapid Typing Service, I typed term papers for students at Towson State and Morgan State Universities with a quick turnaround. I would go to the campuses, pick up the handwritten papers from students, type them up at home, and then return the typed papers to students in a day or two. I also typed bankruptcy forms for people for whom I charged only $100.00. I operated my business part-time while still working a full-time job. It provided a second income that allowed me to be independent and to provide for my daughter and myself. Necessity is truly the mother of invention. Working in the law office showed me that I could learn to apply my excellent typing skills to other tasks that I never considered before.

National Aquarium (Baltimore, MD)

Exhibit Assistant

As an exhibit assistant and the National Aquarium, I was an assistant to the director of exhibits. My job was to type up wording that is placed under exhibits. At the time, they were preparing a new section of the Aquarium, so my job had been newly created. This was the most enjoyable job I've ever had, even to this day. I, of course, dressed in business attire. After doing my administrative work on the Macintosh computer, I would walk around the aquarium talking with visitors, which I loved doing. I also received free passes to invite friends and family to visit the aquarium. My job did not feel like working at all. It was like a vacation every day. The pay was decent, but like all my clerical jobs, it was not enough to get me to the top of Maslow's Hierarchy of Needs. Meaning "Money is the answer to everything" (Ecclesiastes 10:19), I had to keep reaching for the higher dollar or the next promotion to give my daughter and me a better, more enjoyable life, not just surviving day to day. At the aquarium, I got to do some of my favorite things: dressing nicely, socializing with people, and having fun outings with friends and family. I also learned the meaning of the old saying, "Do what you love and you will never work a day in your life." There are jobs out there that don't feel at all like work.

Towson State University (Towson, MD)

Administrative Assistant

I was an administrative assistant in the Registrar's Office. I helped students register for their classes in Business Administration. This job paid just a little more than my dream job at the National Aquarium. It also allowed me to enroll my daughter, Michelle, in the private elementary school on Towson's campus, as it was a teacher's school. Michelle received a scholarship to attend, and I believe it helped her build a strong educational foundation, a love of learning, and excellent study skills. Although the aquarium was a dream job for me, at Towson State, I learned that other kinds of fringe benefits can come with a job. The additional pay was great, but the opportunity for Michelle to attend a private school was a deciding factor for me to leave the aquarium and to work at Towson State.

Johns Hopkins University (Baltimore, MD)

Secretarial Pool

This was a temporary position in a secretary pool where I transcribed documents. The office where I worked happened to be located on the same wing as Dr. Ben Carson's office. He would walk the halls and treat everyone with respect, and he was the only doctor there who did. Most of the physicians there would not speak to a lower-level employee or engage in conversation with us, but Dr. Carson did. My short time there was helpful and interesting. I was among the upper crust of higher education, and I only had an associate's degree. It was one more situation that boosted my self-esteem. Working in that prestigious environment made me feel important and that I, too, could somehow make a difference.

Black and Decker (Towson, MD)

Secretary

This was my second job in Maryland when I first moved there. I worked in the executive wing at Black and Decker Headquarters in Towson. I was the only black person who worked in that area in 1986. I came aboard initially as a temporary employee and was hired permanently to work in another department several months later. I remember talking with the president of the company, Mr. Nolan Archibald, in the executive parking lot. I was able to park my car there because I worked in the executive wing. He asked me how I liked the new car I had, the Yugo. For those who are not familiar with the Yugo, it was considered the worst car in history in 1986. It cost only $3,999.00 brand new and had major mechanical flaws. You get what you pay for. The Yugo was like a disposable car, not safe at all, but there had been a lot of hype in the advertising. It lasted on the automobile market for a short time and then was gone. Never to be heard of again. Just before the Yugo, I owned an old 1979 brown box style Volvo that was much safer but expensive to maintain. I shared with Mr. Archibald that the Yugo served the purpose of getting me around, but I did not feel safe driving it. I hoped to get back in a Volvo one day soon. I had no idea that I was conversing with the CEO of the company and that our paths crossed for a reason. The purpose was for me to get even more comfortable with folks in high places. God planned to later move me in those circles as a CEO.

All those years ago, I was moved to purchase high-end cars. Over the years I bought two newer Volvos, an Acura, an Infiniti QX4 SUV, a Range Rover, and a 2019 Porsche Cayenne before going back to the Volvo. God moved me from Glory to Glory. When thinking about my time at Black and Decker and my work experience there, I remember that moment I had with the CEO and how far I have come since then.

PHH Fleet America (Hunt Valley, MD)

Executive Secretary, Leasing Department

This job entailed many different administrative details. The leasing department processed leased cars for large companies. I did whatever was needed to help the group as it related to the paperwork. I had no direct customer contact as I remember it. The job was repetitive and somewhat monotonous, but it was steady work, and I made a good salary. The upside of this job was that we had great working conditions as the office buildings were luxurious, and my co-workers there were awesome. You have read earlier in this book what transpired at this workplace just days after I left. I know that this job too was part of my faith walk and work experience to get me to my final work destination years later. Through my experience there, I learned not to take any day for granted and to continue to praise the Lord for protection and guidance. I was enriched by my affiliation with this company and its employees, and I am forever humbled by God's grace to spare me. May God bless all those former co-workers who experienced the horrific incident that took place there on September 16, 1996, and may they all be healed and recovered.

Hoechst Marion Roussel Inc. (Bridgewater, NJ)

Clinical Trial Database Assistant

I worked at a company later named Aventis after a 1999 merger, where my hard work was first truly recognized. After just four months as a temp Clinical Trial Database Assistant, I was hired permanently and chosen to attend advanced training in Frankfurt, Germany—an opportunity that boosted my confidence and marked my first major professional responsibility. The success I experienced in that job inspired me to continue to work hard and to be more self-confident. It helped me realize that I was capable of accomplishing more than I knew. From my work at Hoechst, I gained a new perspective and became more willing to try new things.

Prudential Insurance Company (Newark, NJ)

Secretary in Securities

Impossible Things

This was a fast-paced, high-stress job with lots of running from building to building. As a secretary in securities, I was requested to pick up documents and type numerous memos and letters. My boss was always shouting at other executives whenever he was frustrated. I have mostly unpleasant memories of working there. I had a long commute every day in "dirty Jersey" downtown Newark, which was not appealing to me. I was looking for my next job within 6 months. Being back in the financial industry reminded me too much of when I worked at Merrill Lynch as a wire operator. At this job, we were paid every two weeks, which was hard for me to budget. I did not realize that they held two weeks in the hole and paid it out when you leave. Since I had moved to Baltimore and they did not have my forwarding address, it took over a year before they finally sent my final pay to my sister's address. Then she informed me that she had received a $5,100.00 check for me in the mail. I was amazed, and it came at the perfect time to purchase my old brown box-style Volvo. Michelle and I had been riding the bus for over a year in Baltimore. Well, that was also part of God's plan for me. The money came when I needed it the most.

AT&T Morristown (Piscataway, NJ & Bridgewater, NJ)

Administrative Assistant

I worked as a temporary administrative assistant on and off for 3 years. I was a floater for different departments throughout AT&T. I never transitioned to a permanent employee because I could not pass the test for employment. I received an hourly rate through a temporary employment agency of $15.00 to $19.00 per hour, depending on the assignment. This job helped to keep my administrative skills sharp, as they always had the latest computer software packages. I became proficient in all word processing systems as well as Lotus 123, Project Pro, QuickBooks, and Excel. I felt then that there would come a time when the traditional secretary would no longer exist. So, I learned as many software packages as possible to stay marketable. The value of working for AT&T was the access to all of the latest software, where I could always teach myself new skills.

Coca-Cola Company Headquarters (Atlanta, GA)

Legal Secretary

I worked as a temporary employee in the legal department in hopes of becoming a permanent employee. It was exciting to be in Coca-Cola's plush offices and have all the Coke products you can drink at any time. The cafeteria was awesome and served every dish you could think of for breakfast and lunch. Working for Coke was a big deal in Atlanta, especially for a black person. The work was not stressful, but the office environment was lily-white and super polished. Back in 1996, when I worked there, it still had that rigid, buttoned-up corporate culture with an air of implicit racism. All the pictures on the walls were of vintage Coke ads from the past, which depicted only white people. Everyone wore dark suits, pretending to be important, and ID badges that indicated their status within the company. Company badges were color-coded to indicate employee rank. People were highly professional to the point of being stuffy, though I do think that folks were generally genuine. Though I was a temp hoping to make the grade to become a permanent employee, I knew it was a long shot. So, I never banked on a permanent position in the legal department. I kept my resume floating in the downtown Atlanta area. When I received an offer for a permanent position with the Georgia Lottery, the lawyer I was working with was surprised. She complained to my agency because she was planning to hire me permanently. It just took too long, and truth be told, I didn't like the feel of Coke headquarters. It was not for me. I heard from a friend at Coke about 10 years later. Coke had changed its ways by placing more black employees in higher positions and allowing people to dress business casual. Black employees could also wear their natural hair without being considered unprofessional, and some black pictures went up on the walls.

Georgia Lottery (Atlanta, GA)

Executive Assistant

I applied for a position with The Georgia Lottery several weeks before starting with Coke as a temp. Georgia Lottery's Marketing and Credit Departments were a better fit for me since I was around fun and action. Working for one of the executives there, I typed letters and memos, assisted with customer winner functions, and whatever else was needed in the department. I had a good time there with great co-workers. After a year, I was promoted to Credit Representative in the Credit department. There we qualified convenience store owners and others wanting a Georgia Lottery Terminal in their stores. If there were issues with background checks, the store could put up a bond, and we aided with that process, too. I could not believe that someone like me, with two bankruptcies on record, was allowed to process and approve someone else's credit. This job also showed me how all things are possible with God. He will have his way and let you know His greatness and power. I never thought years later I would obtain and maintain an outstanding credit rating to this day of over 810.

Capital One (McLean, VA)

Administrative Assistant

I worked as an administrative assistant with Capital One for a year and a half. This job was also enjoyable in a beautiful headquarters building in McLean, VA. I also had to pass a test before working in the administrative field, and that test dictated my salary as well. I somehow passed the test, but not by much. So, the salary they offered was lower than I expected it to be. However, I did not mind because my life was different then. I had recently married Seymour Metters III and was no longer pressed for a salary that would cover my bills. The job was not stressful. At Capital One, we had a department outing scheduled every three months to keep up company morale. We went white water rafting in the Shenandoah River, visited a museum in Richmond, VA, and took other trips. The company also had a large training compound and other offices located in Henrico, VA.

Symtech Corporation LLC (Sarasota, FL)

CEO & President

I served as CEO and President of Symtech Corporation for 15 years alongside my husband, Seymour Metters III. Together, we ran a successful company until our retirement in 2020. The following is my professional biography used when I was leading at Symtech:

Mrs. L. Renae Spann has over 28 years of experience in Administrative Services and previously operated another company (Rapid Typing Services) in Baltimore, MD. She executed support efforts in task management, personnel management, and human resources. She became Chief Executive Officer of SYMTECH in 2005. Through her leadership, Mrs. Metters has been influential in facilitating SYMTECH's growth from 60 employees to over 320 employees by implementing a 2-year Strategic Plan and meticulous financial management practices.

With her direction and guidance, SYMTECH is able to contribute over 2 million dollars to the local economy, 3.5 million in the state of Florida to include four cities employing roughly 50 people statewide. Nationally, SYMTECH's economical contributions are nearly 10 million, operating in more than fourteen states, several diverse locations and employ some 300 people in over seven diverse industry fields.

SYMTECH donates every year, and the corporate employees take an afternoon during the holiday season to volunteer at the Food Bank, sorting donations and packaging them for delivery to needy families in the area.

On September 24, 2011, Ms. Metters was awarded the Col. Eileen Collins Professional Achievement Award from Corning Community College. The award recognizes the lifetime achievements of a seasoned career professional that made great strides in his/her career. It was presented by retired NASA Astronaut and United States Air Force Colonel, Eileen Collins, at their alma mater, Corning Community College.

On October 20, 2011, SYMTECH was one of 45 businesses from 17 states to graduate from the National Center for the Veteran Institute for Procurement (VIP) at the Bolger Center, a government-owned conference facility located in Potomac, MD. VIP is a comprehensive training and certification program that helps veteran-owned businesses strengthen their ability to win government contracts and do business with both military and civilian agencies they once served in uniform. During the program's graduation, Ms. Metters was presented with a congressional citation.

Ms. Metters was also a 2015 nominee for the SBA Woman Business Owner of the Year.

Metters-Spann Investments, LLC

My last major position as CEO and co-owner was with Metters-Spann Investments, a company that bought, renovated, and rented modest single-family homes in East Point, GA, for 8 years. We acquired over 20 homes in the Atlanta metro area, with a concentration in the East Point Area.

Impossible Things

My daughter had just divorced around 2004 and was leaving her home in Jonesboro, GA, and needed a place to stay in Atlanta. I started looking for homes that were inexpensive to purchase so that I could rent them out to her for a low rate. Rents were high, and she needed to get a fresh start and save her money. The first rental we bought was in East Point, GA, which we paid $22,000 for. It needed minor repairs, but was a large three-bedroom home in a small subdivision near the old Fort McPherson Army Base. It was perfect for Michelle to rent from us for only $600.00 a month.

After that purchase, we noticed other homes in the same subdivision that were fixer-uppers and ranging from $30,000 to $60,000. That is when I got the idea of starting to buy up the homes and rent them out for profit. Seymour was more than agreeable about this business endeavor, so within the next 4 years, we would purchase 15 homes in East Point, 2 in Atlanta, 2 in Decatur, GA, and 1 in Hapeville, GA.

It was my daughter who managed these homes for us and came up with the idea of renting to Section 8 tenants. She screened each candidate who would rent from us and was successful in keeping us from going through evictions in court and losing money with bad tenants. As a team, Seymour handled all the finances, I managed purchasing and worked with contractors to fix up and maintain homes, and Michelle was the upfront person to get the homes rented in record time. We were also doing a service to help single moms and other disadvantaged people with housing.

After 6 years with the homes, Tyler Perry bought Fort McPherson and put his studio there, causing our homes to increase in value greatly. Just before COVID-19, we sold all the homes and purchased our dream home in Sarasota, FL, for cash for $1,100,000, which is about how much we made after selling the homes in Georgia. God is great and greatly to be praised.

About the Author

Lucerchia Renae Spann-Metters is a U.S. Army Disabled Veteran, former CEO & President of Symtech Corporation, Former co-owner of Metters-Spann Investments, LLC, Ex-wife to Dr. Thomas O. Mensah, who is known as the father of fiber Optics, wife to Seymour Metters, III, founder of Symtech Corporation, and a son of a preacher, Mother to Helena Michelle Mensah, a successful business woman and a woman of enormous faith in God.

L. Renae Spann served 10 years in both the Army National Guard & Army Reserve. Having worked many jobs after her divorce from Dr. Mensah to support her daughter, she learned the hardships of life and was able to be an overcomer. Experiencing both physical and mental abuse and the loss of a set of twins, she was not discouraged from having all her dreams come true. Homelessness was temporary as she saw herself someday in a beautiful house with a handsome, loving prince. Her career achievements are no less than a miracle, only indicating that with perseverance, tenancy and faith you can have great joy and happiness ever after.

Mrs. Renae Spann has been married to Seymour Metters, III, for 25 years and now resides in Sarasota, Florida, in her dream home on over 5 ½ acres and has a downtown high-rise condo as well. They travel extensively internationally in retirement. She has two stepsons who both have two children, each making them proud grandparents of two boys and two girls. One of the grandsons has 3 children, which makes them great-grandparents.

You can contact or connect with L. Renae Spann-Metters at:

Email: Harmony4242@icloud.com

LinkedIn : L. Renae Spann

Impossible Things

Gallery

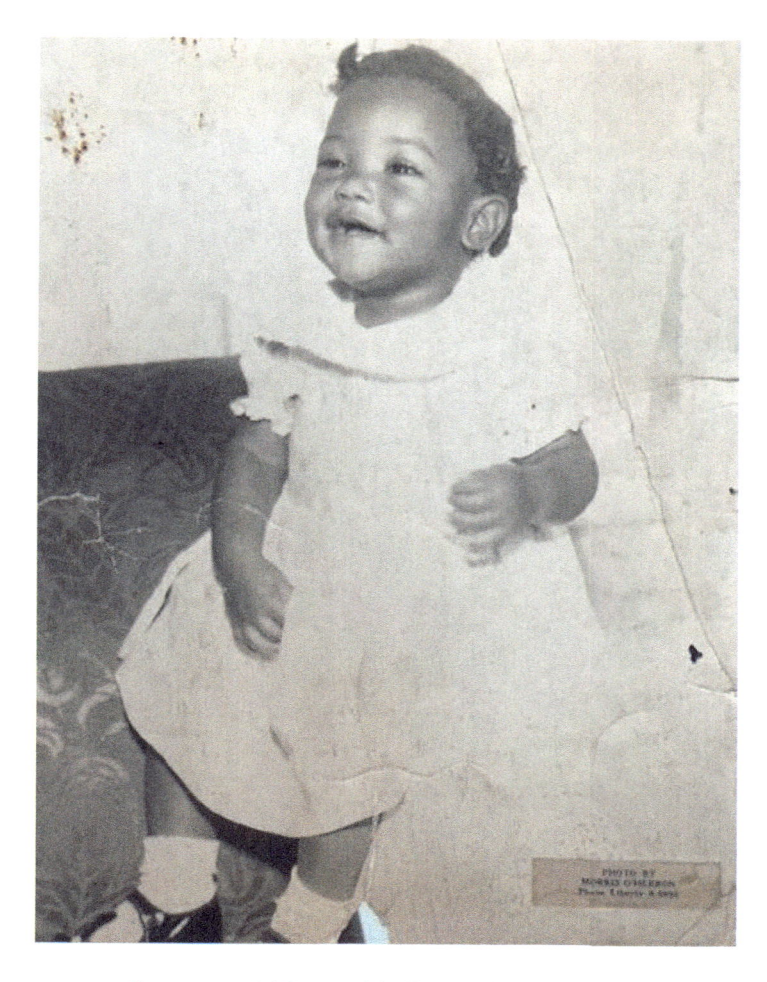

One year old Lucerchia Renae Spann (1959)

L. Renae Spann

Renae and Santa (1965)

Impossible Things

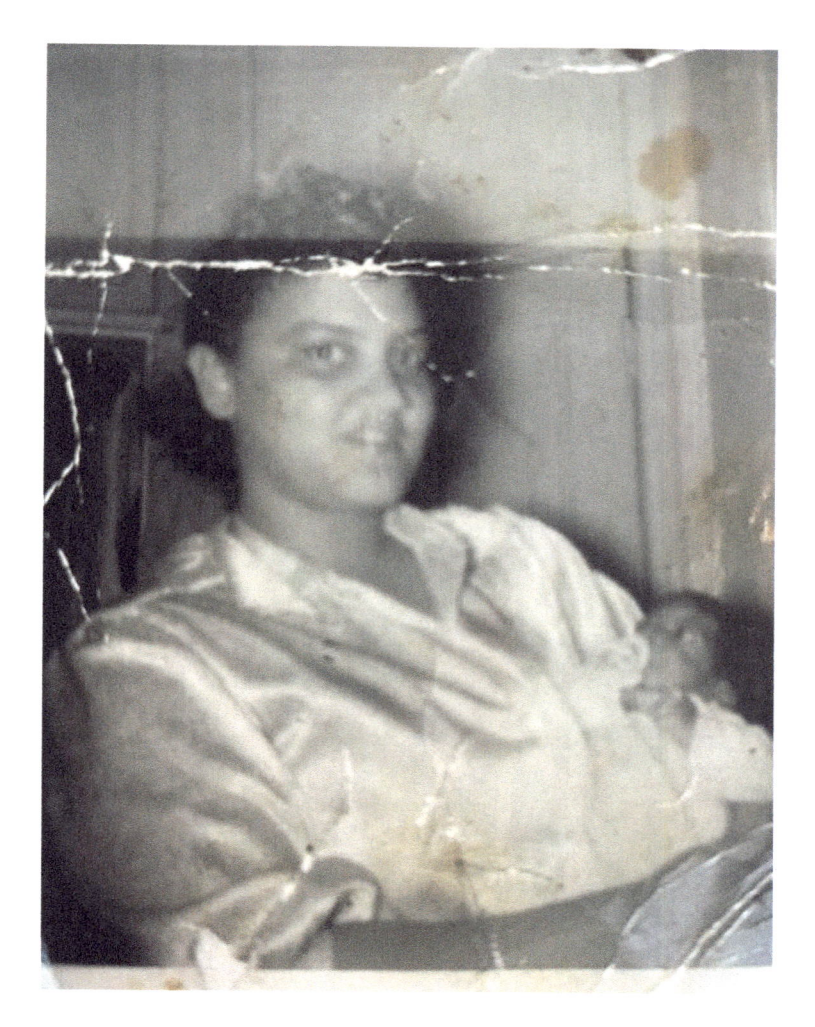

My mother Helena holding my cousin Robert Francis in 1950.

L. Renae Spann

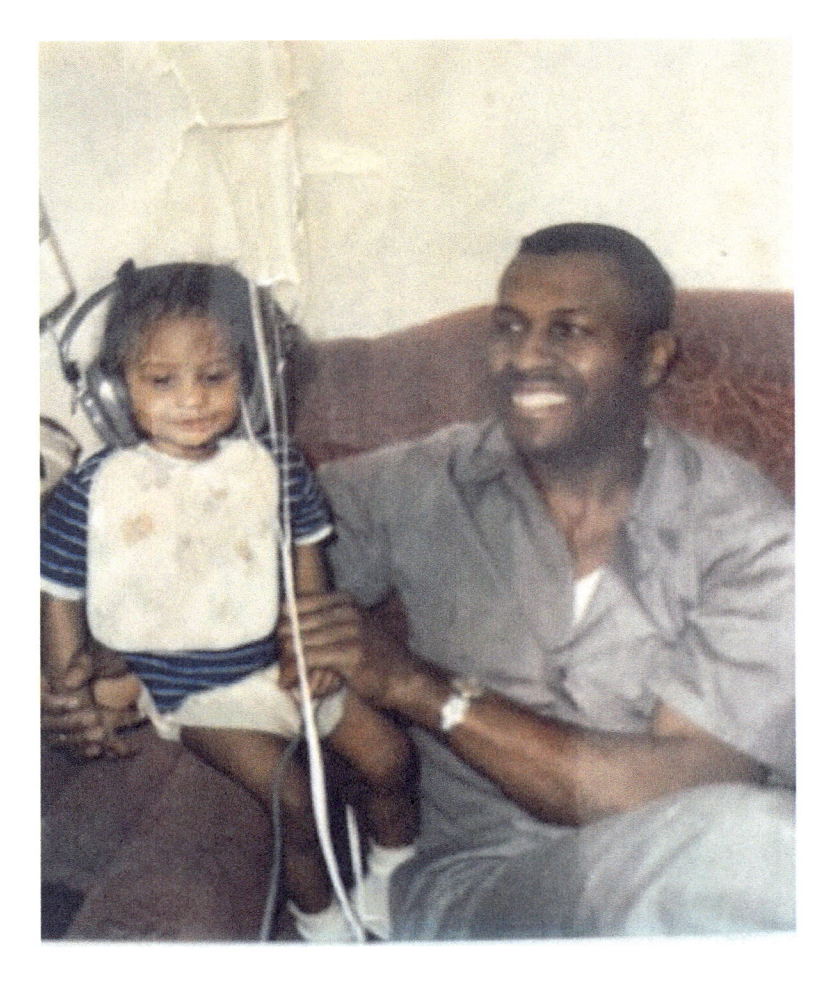

My Father Harmon and baby sister Marlene

959 West 3rd Street Plainfield NJ

L. Renae Spann

My father Harmon Spann late 70's

Impossible Things

My maternal grandfather Pat Garret Fulton

L. Renae Spann

Mother Helena and her sister Nettie Hodge

Impossible Things

My brother Harmon Jr and little sister Marlene

L. Renae Spann

My mother's younger sister Minerva

Impossible Things

HARMON SPANN   RENEE SPANN

L. Renae Spann

JASPER MILLER

Impossible Things

My childhood home at 959 West 3rd St Plainfield NJ

L. Renae Spann

The Plainfield Riot (1967)

Impossible Things

L. Renae Spann

Newspaper photos from the Plainfield riot and West Third Street (1967

Impossible Things

Going to my senior prom with Nate Brown (1977)

L. Renae Spann

My senior prom with Nate and friend (1977)

Impossible Things

Me with my sisters Marlene, Darlene, and Cousin Jean

L. Renae Spann

My sister Darlene in her mink coat

Impossible Things

My graduation from US Army National Guard (1978)

L. Renae Spann

My brother Harmon Jr's graduation from US Army (1977)

Impossible Things

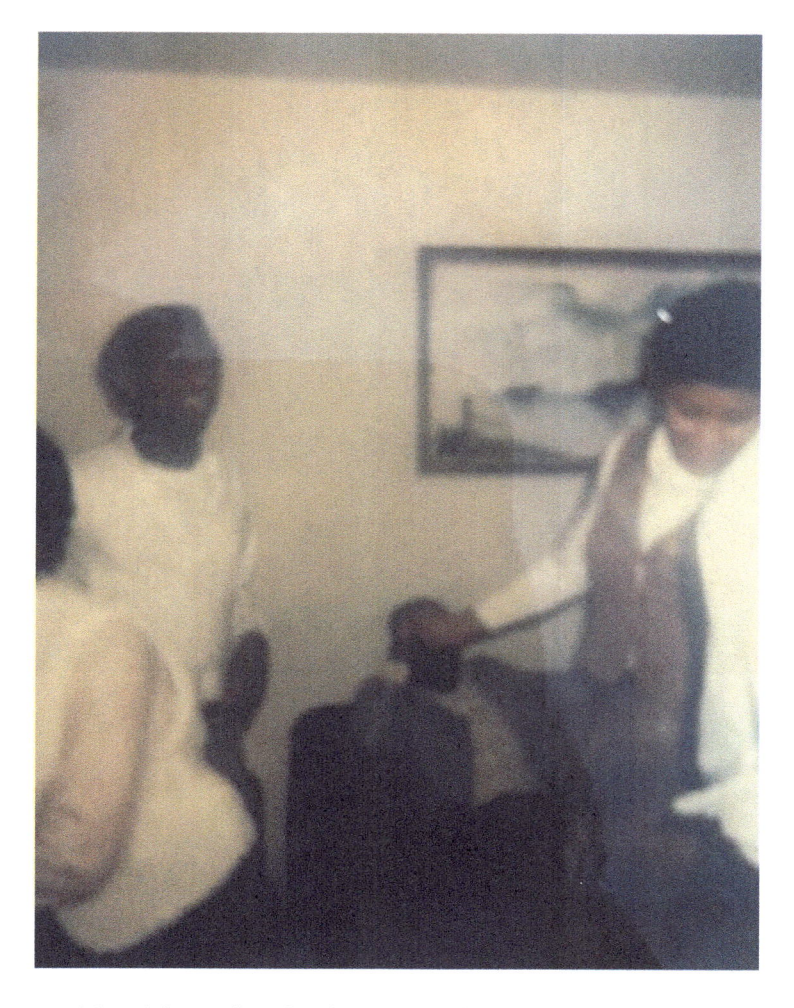

Me with my first husband Dr. Thomas Mensah (1980)

Me with my first husband Dr. Thomas Mensah (1980)

Impossible Things

Me with my first husband Dr. Thomas Mensah at our wedding (1980)

Me with my beautiful baby Helena Michelle (1983)

Impossible Things

Second husband Kenneth Johnson (1991)

A more current picture of second husband Kenneth Johnson

Impossible Things

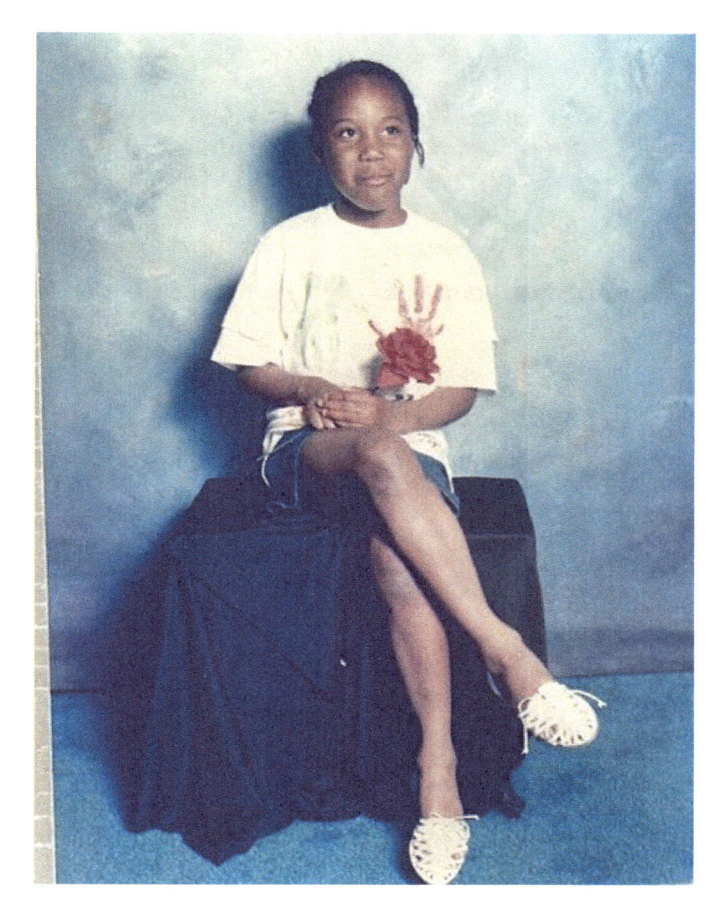

My beautiful daughter Helena Michelle Mensah at 9 years old

My lake house in the "Promised Land" Lithonia, GA

Impossible Things

Marriage to Seymour Metters III, my Prince Charming (2000)

L. Renae Spann

A visit to our favorite casino Mohegan Sun in Connecticut

Seymour and his adult sons Marlon and Seaton

My adult daughter Michelle

Impossible Things

Our grandsons Samaji and Isaiah

L. Renae Spann

Our granddaughters Eliana & Jahida

Impossible Things

Our great-grandchildren Valor, Anastasia, and Roman - Samaji's children

L. Renae Spann

Receiving the Col. Eileen Collins Professional Achievement Award from Corning Community College (2011)

Impossible Things

Meeting Cicely Tyson

L. Renae Spann

Meeting Cicely Tyson

Impossible Things

Seymour and I meeting Hillary Clinton (2015)

L. Renae Spann

Seymour and I meeting Ohio Governor John Kasich (2015)

Impossible Things

My Muhammad Ali memorabilia

L. Renae Spann

Our cabin in Naples, ME

Impossible Things

Christian sister Annette Pullen

Our good friends Jim and Lega Medcalf from Maine

My Christian friend, earthly angel, Cathy Tolbert

My Jersey girl sister Debbie Vaughn

Ruth Wilson and her daughters

My Christian sister Dr. Gladys Dark

L. Renae Spann

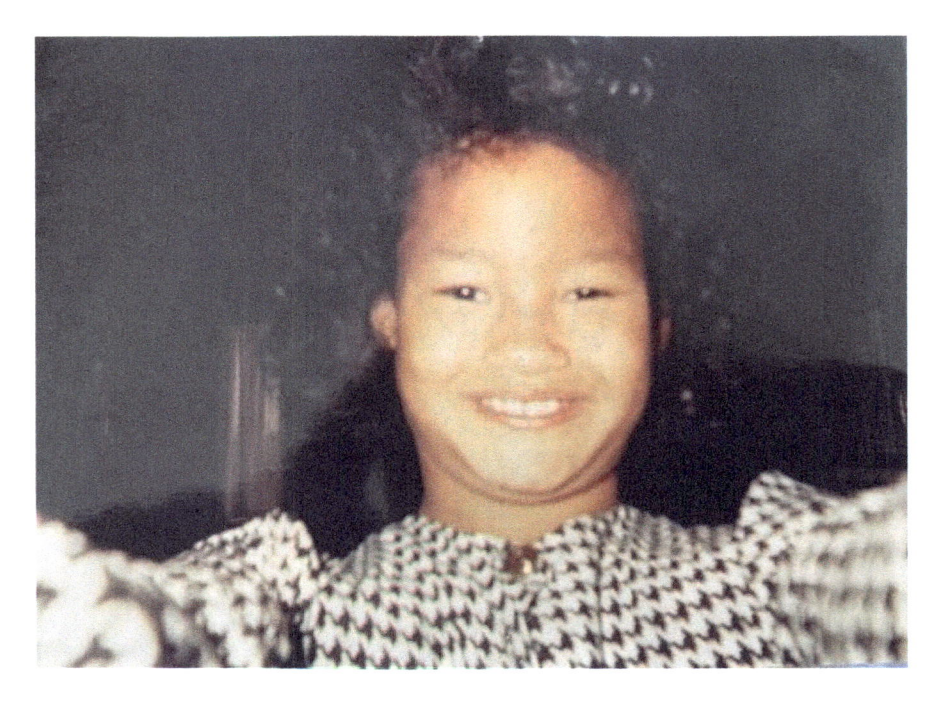

My niece Raina, Harmon Jr's daughter

Impossible Things

My nieces Rachel and Mya Darlene's daughters

L. Renae Spann

House crushed by fallen tree in GA

Impossible Things

Niece Rachel and daughter Michelle

L. Renae Spann

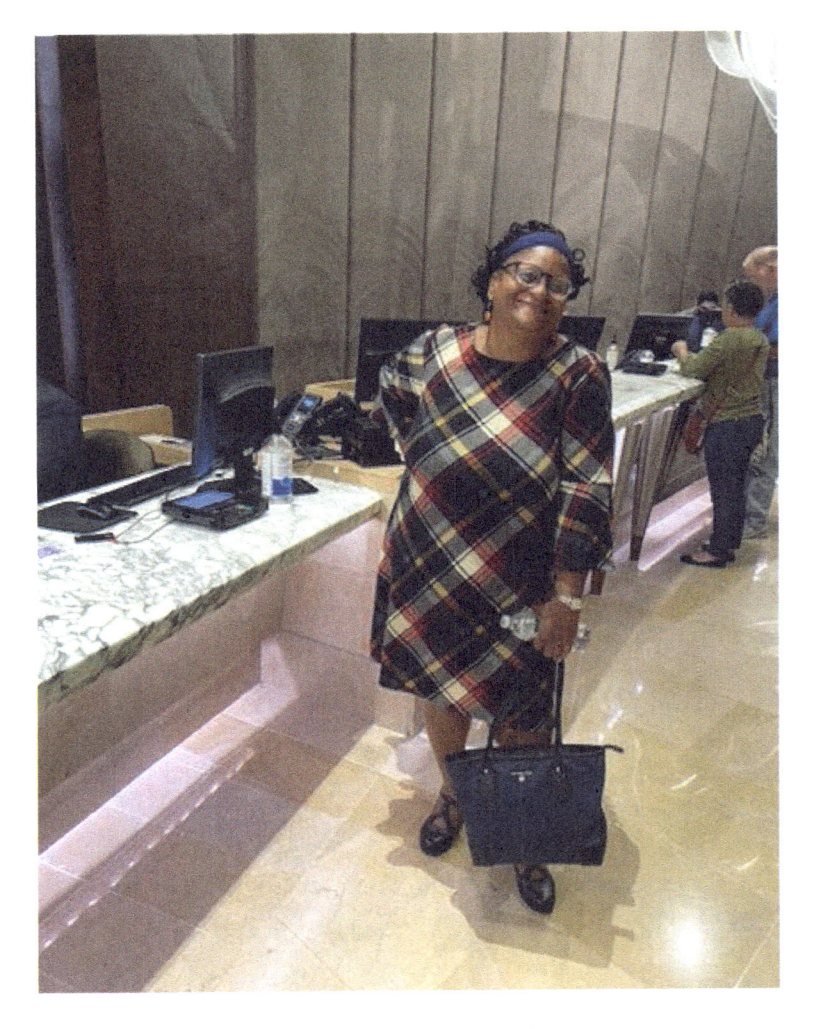

My younger sister Marlene

Impossible Things

L. Renae Spann

Impossible Things

Made in United States
Orlando, FL
15 June 2025